City University
Library Information Services
Law Innovation Centre

WITHDRAWN

AF805048

CITY LAW SCHOOL LIBRARY
Innovation Centre, Whiskin Street, London
EC1R 0JD
Tel: 020 7040 8191
Web: http://library.city.ac.uk

This book must be returned or renewed on or before the last date stamped below

HEAVY FINES ARE CHARGED ON OVERDUE BOOKS

SEVEN DAY LOAN

Democratic Sustainability in a New Era of Localism

Change and development are going on all around us. On an international platform, as well as at the local governmental and community level, governments and decision- and policy-makers constantly strive to improve the world in which we live, seeking to make it better and to improve quality of life.

This book focuses on such development in the context of localism in the UK. It strips the principle of local sustainability down to its constituent parts and considers the extent to which it can be said to be central to local life. As part of this, it presents the case for the importance of accountability and citizen participation in achieving objectives aligned with sustainability, and illustrates the relationships that these principles share. On this foundation, it evaluates local government in the UK, as well as examples of community-led regeneration initiatives and bodies, and seeks to determine both the nature of their pursuit of sustainability and the degree to which accountability and citizen participation play a part in that pursuit.

It shows that local sustainability is enhanced by accountability and citizen participation, those principles ensuring that local people can be central to the process. Whilst its evaluations of local democratic systems in the UK reveal certain issues as regards the extent to which this is reflected in practice, it at least demonstrates an enthusiasm for and an awareness of the important role that accountability and citizen participation can play in the process of local sustainability.

The book is aimed at legal academics, with relevance also to students in law, environmental politics and sustainable development, as well as those working in government policy and political practice.

John Stanton is Lecturer in Law, The City Law School, City University London, UK.

Routledge Studies in Sustainability

Critiquing Sustainability, Changing Philosophy
Jenneth Parker

Transdisciplinary Sustainability Studies
A Heuristic Approach
Katri Huutoniemi and Petri Tapio

Challenging Consumption
Pathways to a More Sustainable Future
Edited by Anna R. Davies, Frances Fahy and Henrike Rau

Democratic Sustainability in a New Era of Localism
John Stanton

Democratic Sustainability in a New Era of Localism

John Stanton

Routledge
Taylor & Francis Group
LONDON AND NEW YORK

earthscan
from Routledge

First published 2014
by Routledge
2 Park Square, Milton Park, Abingdon, Oxon, OX14 4RN

and by Routledge
711 Third Avenue, New York, NY 10017

Routledge is an imprint of the Taylor & Francis Group, an informa business

© 2014 John Stanton

The right of John Stanton to be identified as author of this work has been asserted by him/her in accordance with sections 77 and 78 of the Copyright, Designs and Patents Act 1988.

All rights reserved. No part of this book may be reprinted or reproduced or utilised in any form or by any electronic, mechanical, or other means, now known or hereafter invented, including photocopying and recording, or in any information storage or retrieval system, without permission in writing from the publishers.

British Library Cataloguing in Publication Data
A catalogue record for this book is available from the British Library

Library of Congress Cataloging-in-Publication Data
A catalog record has been requested for this book

ISBN13: 978-0-415-72483-8 (hbk)
ISBN13: 978-1-315-85698-8 (ebk)

Typeset in Times by
Keystroke, Station Road, Codsall, Wolverhampton

MIX
Paper from responsible sources
FSC® C013056
FSC www.fsc.org

Printed and bound in Great Britain by
TJ International Ltd, Padstow, Cornwall

To Theresa
Also to Mum, Dad, Anna, Graeme
and the rest of my loving family

Contents

Cases and legislation

Cases

Legislation

European Union legislation

United Kingdom legislation

Acknowledgements

This book started life in 2007 as a PhD project at Kingston Law School, Kingston University London. It was written and researched as part of a studentship funded by the EC1 New Deal for Communities partnership, of which my Director of Studies, Professor Matthew Humphreys MBE, was Chair. The EC1 partnership provided valuable support throughout the project, over and above the financial assistance and doctoral supervision, and I owe a huge debt of thanks to all involved for making the project possible.

I am grateful also to all those at Kingston Law School for the guidance and support that they gave. In particular, thanks to Professor Matthew Humphreys MBE for his constant direction and advice during the PhD as well as the more recent writing process, and thanks also to Professor Gwyneth Pitt, Professor Julia Fionda and Dr Philip Harris for their expert assistance along the way.

My colleagues at The City Law School, City University London, have also been hugely supportive and for this I am very grateful. Indeed, Head of Academic Programmes, Professor Jason Chuah, was especially instrumental in encouraging me to take the step towards publishing the PhD thesis.

More widely, I am grateful to many others who assisted with various aspects of the project, providing valuable assistance and support. In particular, thanks to Muna Sabbagh for her sterling research efforts in helping to bring the project up to date, to Rob Sugden for his assistance on the Big Society and the Coalition's regeneration projects and policies and to Mary Bigwood for her expert and diligent proof reading, her patience and her votes of confidence.

Both Khanam Virjee and Charlotte Russell at Routledge-Earthscan have been a constant source of guidance and assistance and I thank them for their own dedication to the project, their efforts in bringing the book to fruition and for accommodating my constant stream of emails. I really couldn't have done it without them.

I am eternally grateful to all my friends who, though far too many to name individually, have provided intellectual assistance, support and motivation along the way, as well as much-needed social relief from book writing. In particular, thanks to my dear friends in The Bach Choir for musical and social respite throughout the writing process and for the constant joy of music-making.

Theresa has been an absolute rock and has provided unwavering love, support and understanding at every step of the way. For always knowing what to say to encourage, for putting up with so much and for always being so wonderful, I thank her from the very bottom of my heart.

And finally, my parents, sister and wider family have always been a constant source of love, guidance, understanding and inspiration over the years, particularly during the PhD and throughout the recent writing process. This book could not have been written without them and words fail sufficiently to reflect the depth of my gratitude to them.

John Stanton
City University London
November 2013

Abbreviations

CRESR	Centre for Regional Economic and Social Research
DBIS	Department for Business, Innovation and Skills
DCLG	Department for Communities and Local Government
DEFRA	Department for the Environment, Food and Rural Affairs
DETR	Department for the Environment, Transport and the Regions
DoE	Department of the Environment
DTLGR	Department for Transport, Local Government and the Regions
GLA	Greater London Authority
ICLEI	International Council for Local Environmental Initiatives
LAA	Local Area Agreement
LDEDCA	Local Democracy, Economic Development and Construction Act 2009
LGPIHA	Local Government and Public Involvement in Health Act 2007
NDC	New Deal for Communities
NRU	Neighbourhood Renewal Unit
UN	United Nations
UNECE	United Nations Economic Commission for Europe
UNEP	United Nations Environment Programme
UNGA	United Nations General Assembly

1 Introduction

The importance of sustainability in today's changing world cannot be overestimated. It is vital for ensuring that future generations inherit 'a world free of the indignity and indecency occasioned by poverty, environmental degradation and patterns of unsustainable development', and it guides the creation of 'a humane, equitable and caring global society, cognizant of the need for human dignity for all'.[1] It is a principle with huge global relevance and one that has provided the basis for much international discussion, with states seeking to determine not only how their own environments might best be developed but also endeavouring to work together to reach a wider consensus with regard to the development and protection of environments across the world. Indeed, as Tony Blair stated in 2005:

> [M]ake the wrong choices now and future generations will live with a changed climate, depleted resources and without the green space and biodiversity that contribute both to our standard of living and our quality of life. Each of us needs to make the right choices to secure a future that is fairer, where we can all live within our environmental limits. That means sustainable development.[2]

On this basis, the principle has application across all levels of governance.[3] From the aforementioned international level and the need to work towards global environmental development, right down to the community level, and the need to tackle local deprivation, it is important not to take for granted or undervalue the

1 UN, *Johannesburg Declaration on Sustainable Development*, Annex to Resolution 1 of the *World Summit on Sustainable Development*, Johannesburg, 26 August–4 September 2002, A/CONF. 199/20, New York: UN, paras. 2 and 3 ('*Johannesburg Declaration*').

2 DEFRA, *Securing the Future: The UK Strategy for Sustainable Development*, Cm 6467 (London: HMSO, 2005) 3, © Crown Copyright, contains public sector information licensed under the Open Government Licence v2.0 <http://www.nationalarchives.gov.uk/doc/open-government-licence/version/2/> ('2005 Strategy').

3 UN, *Johannesburg Plan of Implementation*, Annex to Resolution 2 of the *World Summit on Sustainable Development*, Johannesburg, 26 August–4 September 2002, A/CONF.199/20, New York: UN, para. 4.

objectives that must be met if sustainable improvements are to be made for the benefit and ongoing appreciation of present and future generations. It is a key objective for all.

Despite its broad relevance, however, it is the purpose of this book to focus on sustainability in the context of localism in the UK. At this level, there have been, over recent years and decades, numerous attempts sustainably to regenerate deprived communities, both in terms of legislation and government policy aimed at ensuring sustainability and also in terms of programmes and initiatives which aim to concentrate energies and resources on the regeneration of certain areas.[4] This book considers such attempts in detail and explores the nature of their pursuit of local sustainability. In particular, it focuses on recent local governmental reform and community regeneration initiatives set up by the 1997–2010 Labour government and the succeeding Conservative–Liberal Democrat Coalition government.

The book's broad thesis is to consider the way in which local sustainability can best be achieved. Within this, the hypothesis it sets out to test is the extent to which principles of democracy and decision-making – namely, in this case, accountability and citizen participation – enhance the achievement of objectives aligned with local sustainability. It is predicated on the belief, to be tested, that accountability and citizen participation are fundamental aspects of local decision-making as they ensure that those most affected by decisions and policies relating to sustainability are borne in mind, consulted and even involved in the process itself, and it finds, consequently, that these principles, both together and in isolation, are essential aspects of local sustainability and, as a result, enhance and inform its achievement. This is justified on the basis that local sustainability is reliant on the decentralisation of power to a level best placed to deal with the issues concerning local sustainability and, once there, on the empowerment and engagement of local people in a decision-making process that is conducive to participation and that exists within a framework of accountability. It is these local people themselves who experience, at first hand, local deprivation, and who are best placed to advise and input into the process designed to tackle it, as they know best the needs and concerns of local people and the wider community. With this in mind, the hypothesis is tested through consideration of recent local governmental reform and the impact that it has had on local authorities' pursuit of sustainability, and also through a focus on recent and present community regeneration initiatives and policies. Through their evaluation in the context of the sustainability principle, this book will demonstrate the extent to which accountability and citizen participation can be said to enhance the achievement of local sustainability in practice.

4 See, for outline of initiatives over recent decades, P Foley and S Martin, 'A New Deal for the Community? Public Participation in Regeneration and Local Service Delivery' (2000) 28(4) *Policy & Politics* 479 at 480.

Much has been written on sustainability, particularly in terms of its global application and definition as well as the manner in which it has become established as a key principle of UK environmental law and policy.[5] Indeed, consideration from a legal perspective is something that has also increased since the government's response to the Brundtland Report, the principle thereafter assuming an increasing prominence in national policy.[6] The significance of and rationale for this book, however, rest on its specific focus. Exploration of sustainability at the local governmental and community level, from a legal perspective, is a relatively untrodden path, with constantly changing laws, policies and approaches increasing the opportunity for unique study. Within the context of the legal frameworks setting out the way in which local governmental and local community bodies operate and make decisions, this book considers the relevance of sustainability at the local level and explores government strategies and policies that set out the way in which it has become a central feature of local activity. Through such evaluation, it draws from the most recent local governmental policies and reforms as well as the work of the recently expired NDC programme and the Coalition's Big Society policy.

The most significant way in which this book fills a gap in the field, however, is through its juxtaposition of local sustainability with accountability and citizen participation, two key legal principles supervising democratic and effective decision-making. It draws from but also goes beyond the existing literature in defining and exploring accountability and citizen participation (the latter as both a model of democracy and a principle of environmental law and decision-making), considering in particular Arnstein's 'ladder of citizen participation'[7] and the relationship between the two principles. It then considers, on the basis of conceptual arguments, the way in which accountability and citizen participation can be said to enhance the achievement of objectives aligned with local sustainability.

The rationale for this study, therefore, lies in its significant exploration of issues and initiatives relating to local sustainability, alongside a consideration of the principles of accountability and citizen participation. As its chapters illustrate, there is constant development in this area, particularly in terms of policies setting out local democratic invigoration and community development, so its evaluations and conclusions serve to provide a topical study of key and relevant issues.

The book's methodology is very much principle-based, setting out as it does conceptual arguments and conclusions relating to accountability, citizen participation and local sustainability, and evaluating the way in which these are

5 See, in particular, A Ross, *Sustainable Development Law in the UK: From Rhetoric to Reality?* (London: Routledge-Earthscan, 2011) 10–34.

6 See DoE, *A Perspective by the United Kingdom on the Report of the World Commission on Environment and Development* (London: DoE, 1988) and, also, UK Government, *Sustainable Development: The UK Strategy*, Cm 2426 (London: HMSO, 1994).

7 S Arnstein, 'A Ladder of Citizen Participation' (1969) 35(4) *Journal of American Institute of Planners* 216.

reflected and demonstrated in practice. It is intended to be retrospective in its analyses and prospective in its conclusions, outlining, in the final chapter, lessons that might be learned from the evaluations in terms of future efforts to regenerate local areas, and also briefly assessing the relevance of the conclusions in terms of pursuits of local sustainability across the world.

Within this methodological framework, there are certain limitations that are necessary to explain here in order that the focus and purpose might best be understood. First, with respect to the treatment of sustainability, it does not seek to explore all the substantive details of the principle, these being the endless range of environmental, social and economic objectives that might be pursued in the name of sustainable development. The book considers the principle on the basis of established definitions and instead places emphasis on exploring its relationship with accountability and citizen participation on the basis of these definitions. Second, as regards geographical and jurisdictional scope, this book is founded on law and policy of the UK government and Parliament. That said, much of the legislation discussed applies only in England and Wales, whilst the NDC programme – discussed in Chapter 5 – was only set up in communities across England. The conclusions and evaluations, therefore, are based on specific foundations, limited both by the jurisdiction of the relevant laws and policies as well as the need to ensure particular examples that provide the most suitable illustrations.

Thus far, this chapter has introduced the issues that lie at the heart of the book, set out the significance and rationale for the project, and explained both its methodology and limitations. It is necessary now to outline the book's structure so as to provide an overview of the way in which it tackles the issues previously identified.

The book consists of two halves – first, a conceptual exploration of the principles, and then a practical evaluation of their relationship. Chapter 2 will introduce and define sustainability, setting out the way in which it has developed at the international level from the Brundtland Commission in the late 1980s to the *Rio Declaration* in 1992 and the *Johannesburg Declaration* in 2002. It will cite the Brundtland Report's widely accepted definition of sustainability and, alongside the three-pillar approach that emerged in the late 1990s, outline a clear understanding of the sustainability principle. On this foundation, it then explores the way in which it has developed in UK government policy, most notably through Strategies published in 1999 and 2005, and how it has emerged as a key objective at the local governmental and community level through various reforms and policies as well as through a number of community-led initiatives. With all this in mind, the chapter ends by setting out a 'model of local sustainability'. Identifying key aspects of the principle (meeting the needs of local people, sustainability and the three pillars of environmental, social and economic development), this model enables later chapters to explore the nature of local governmental and community pursuits of sustainability, and ensures structured evaluation of the extent to which their decision-making processes impact on its achievement.

Following this, Chapter 3 will then explore the principles of accountability and citizen participation. Drawing from a range of academic and political sources, it will define accountability and set out the way in which it relates to wider aspects of decision-making, such as responsibility, responsiveness and control.[8] On this foundation, the chapter will then evaluate accountability in the context of both representative and more participatory systems of democracy. It will cite a number of examples in explaining why accountability struggles to be achieved effectively in the UK's representative system, arguing that participation naturally gives rise to accountability as citizens who become involved in decision-making are more easily informed as to the way in which the system operates because they themselves play a part in that process.[9] On this basis and in light of the discussions in Chapter 2, Chapter 3 will move to consider the way in which accountability and citizen participation relate to and can be said to enhance the achievement of local sustainability. It will discuss, in particular, the degree of participation that is most appropriate,[10] highlighting the importance of maintaining a balance between citizen participation and a basic level of representation so as to ensure organised decision-making in line with citizens' input and their needs and interests.

The second half of the book will set out to provide a practical evaluation of the relationship shared by these principles. Chapters 4 and 5 will test the book's hypothesis and illustrate the manner in which it can be said to work in practice, both in terms of local government's work towards and responsibility for sustainability as well as the community-led initiatives set up as part of Labour's neighbourhood renewal strategy and the Coalition's Big Society.

Chapter 4 will introduce UK local government, briefly providing an outline of its historical development. Building on Chapter 2's identification of local government's role in respect of sustainability, it will explore, in detail, recent reforms introduced by the 1997–2010 Labour government and the current Coalition government. In this regard, the chapter will focus on three key themes – the strength of local leadership, the decentralisation of power and the empowerment of local citizens. It will consider the extent to which these provide a basis for the achievement of accountability and encouragement of citizen participation, before then applying the 'model of local sustainability' to evaluate the way in which local government's achievement of sustainability can be said to be enhanced as a result. Whilst it identifies a number of issues and concerns with regard to local governmental arrangements, the decentralisation of power and the wider participation of local citizens, it notes the extent to which local authorities have the potential to enhance the achievement of local sustainability on the basis of accountability and citizen participation.

8 See R Mulgan, 'Accountability: An Ever-Expanding Concept' (2000) 78(3) *Public Administration* 555.

9 See J Onyx and B Dalton, 'Accountability and Advocacy' (2006) 12(1) *Third Sector Review* 7.

10 See Arnstein (n 7).

Chapter 5 then moves on to explore the nature of community-led sustainability, focusing on the policies and initiatives of the 1997–2010 Labour government as well as those of the Coalition government through the Big Society policy. It will use the NDC programme as an example of Labour's commitment to community-led regeneration and, through application of the 'model of local sustainability', will explore both the nature of its pursuit of sustainability and the way in which accountability and citizen participation can be said to have enhanced the work that it did. As in Chapter 4, whilst it highlights a number of issues that hinder the full realisation of the NDC's potential, it nonetheless will demonstrate that, through accountability and citizen participation, the programme's achievement of sustainability can be enhanced. Chapter 5 also sets out the relevant aspects of the Big Society policy introduced by the current Coalition government, focusing in particular on the community rights and neighbourhood planning measures introduced through the Localism Act 2011. Though it stresses that the passage of time will provide more suitable opportunities for evaluation, it will highlight the potential for the reforms to achieve sustainability on the basis of accountability and citizen participation.

Chapter 6 will seek to consolidate the book's evaluations and conclusions and set out the essence of its findings. In particular, it will reflect on the lessons that can be taken from recent efforts to achieve local sustainability, focusing on ways of overcoming the issues identified in Chapters 4 and 5. It will then draw the book to a close by considering the *Local Sustainability 2012* report, published on the occasion of the Rio + 20 conference,[11] and highlight the way in which the conclusions and evaluations reached in the book can be said to be relevant and applicable to the pursuit of local sustainability across the world.

Local sustainability, therefore, is a topical and relevant area of environmental law and policy. It has featured with increasing prominence in UK government policy, with various reforms and initiatives setting out the manner in which it can and might be achieved. On this foundation, the discussion and evaluation on which this book now embarks is significant and fills a notable gap in the field by exploring, from a legal perspective, the way in which the achievement of local sustainability might be enhanced through adherence to accountability and the encouragement of citizen participation.

Bibliography

Arnstein, S, 'A Ladder of Citizen Participation' (1969) 35(4) *Journal of American Institute of Planners* 216.

DEFRA, *Securing the Future: The UK Strategy for Sustainable Development*, Cm 6467 (London: HMSO, 2005).

11 ICLEI, *Local Sustainability 2012: Taking Stock and Moving Forward. Global Review* (Bonn: ICLEI, 2012).

DoE, *A Perspective by the United Kingdom on the Report of the World Commission on Environment and Development* (London: DoE, 1988).

Foley, P and Martin, S, 'A New Deal for the Community? Public Participation in Regeneration and Local Service Delivery' (2000) 28(4) *Policy & Politics* 479.

ICLEI, *Local Sustainability 2012: Taking Stock and Moving Forward. Global Review* (Bonn: ICLEI, 2012).

Mulgan, R, 'Accountability: An Ever-Expanding Concept' (2000) 78(3) *Public Administration* 555.

Onyx, J and Dalton, B, 'Accountability and Advocacy' (2006) 12(1) *Third Sector Review* 7.

Ross, A, *Sustainable Development Law in the UK: From Rhetoric to Reality?* (London: Routledge-Earthscan, 2011).

UK Government, *Sustainable Development: The UK Strategy*, Cm 2426 (London: HMSO, 1994) © Crown Copyright, contains public sector information licensed under the Open Government Licence v2.0 <http://www.nationalarchives.gov.uk/doc/open-government-licence/version/2/>.

UN, *Johannesburg Declaration on Sustainable Development*, Annex to Resolution 1 of the *World Summit on Sustainable Development*, Johannesburg, 26 August–4 September 2002, A/CONF.199/20, New York: UN.

UN, *Johannesburg Plan of Implementation*, Annex to Resolution 2 of the *World Summit on Sustainable Development*, Johannesburg, 26 August–4 September 2002, A/CONF. 199/20, New York: UN.

2 Sustainable development in the UK

Sustainability defined

Sustainable development is a fundamental principle of environmental law and policy, originating 'from attempts to reconcile the environmental protection and human development agendas'.[1] Whilst it is a concept that is difficult to pin down in terms of any concrete definition, it is the purpose of this chapter to explore the sustainability principle and to consider the way in which it has developed in UK government policy. From this, the chapter will identify the importance and relevance of the concept at the local level and set out a 'model of local sustainability' which reflects the key aspects of the principle at that level. Application of this model, in later chapters, will enable consideration of efforts to achieve local sustainability.

Recalling its roots at an international level, the concept is defined in the Brundtland Commission's Report (1987) as 'development that meets the needs of the present without compromising the ability of future generations to meet their own needs'.[2] Development in this context 'involves a progressive transformation of economy and society'[3] and, as will be explored throughout the course of this chapter, a focus on environmental, social and economic development too. Whilst others have considered, at greater length, the historical development of the sustainability principle, it is necessary here briefly to identify the way in which it has emerged as a key objective of environmental law and policy at the international level and for governments the world over.[4]

1 A Ross, *Sustainable Development Law in the UK: From Rhetoric to Reality?* (London: Routledge-Earthscan, 2011) 3.

2 World Commission on Environment and Development, *Our Common Future* (Oxford: OUP, 1987) 43 ('Brundtland Report').

3 Ibid. 43.

4 Ross provides a more comprehensive consideration of the development of sustainability in international law, though also cites A Boyle and D Freestone, *International Law and Sustainable Development: Past Achievements and Future Challenges* (Oxford: OUP, 1999), P Sands, *Principles of International Law* (Cambridge: CUP, 2003) and D French, *International Law and Policy of Sustainable Development* (Manchester: Manchester University Press, 2005) as being 'significant literature' (Ross (n 1) 11 and 12).

Ross notes that the 1972 United Nations Stockholm Declaration[5] was the first major landmark in the global emergence of the principle, serving as a key 'turning point in the development of international environmental politics'.[6] This proclaimed that:

> Man is both creature and moulder of his environment, which gives him physical sustenance and affords him the opportunity for intellectual, moral, social and spiritual growth. In the long and tortuous evolution of the human race on this planet a stage has been reached when, through the rapid acceleration of science and technology, man has acquired the power to transform his environment in countless ways and on an unprecedented scale. Both aspects of man's environment, the natural and the man-made, are essential to his well-being and to the enjoyment of basic human rights – even the right to life itself.[7]

The Declaration set out a number of important principles which were broad in application and that 'sought to emphasise links between human development and environmental protection'.[8] Most notably, the Declaration underlined the importance of 'improving the environment for present and future generations' and affording everyone an equal right to freedom of adequate conditions of life, in an environment of a quality permitting dignity and well-being.[9]

Following Stockholm, however, it is the aforementioned Brundtland Commission that is most significant. Holder and Lee comment that this 'explored the possibility of reconciling demands for development from developing countries with demands for environmental protection, primarily from rich industrialised countries'.[10] Such reconciliation is one of the challenges of the international application of sustainable development, particularly bearing in mind the widely differing environmental priorities prevalent across the globe.[11] Working towards such reconciliation meant that the Brundtland Commission was committed to developing widespread agreement in respect of common objectives for sustainability between those with differing environmental priorities, something that is reflected in the report's title – *Our Common Future*.

5 UN, *Report of the United Nations Conference on the Human Environment*, Stockholm, 5–16 June 1972, A/CONF.48/14/Rev.1, New York: UN ('Stockholm Declaration').

6 Ross (n 1) 12.

7 Stockholm Declaration (n 5) 3.

8 J Holder and M Lee, *Environmental Protection, Law and Policy: Text and Materials* (2nd edn, Cambridge: CUP, 2007) 219.

9 Stockholm Declaration (n 5) Principle 1.

10 Holder and Lee (n 8) 219. They there cite: L Rajamani, 'From Stockholm to Johannesburg: The Anatomy of Dissonance in the International Environmental Dialogue' (2003) 12 *Review of European Community and International Environmental Law* 23.

11 See Ross (n 1) 11.

Post-Brundtland, the next legal landmark is the declaration made following the United Nations Conference on Environment and Development at Rio de Janeiro in 1992. This is widely regarded as one of the most significant statements of the global importance of sustainability, formulating the principle in strong legal terms.[12] As Barral notes, 'it is . . . undeniably a Declaration of legal principles *about* sustainable development, as the expression appears in no fewer than 12 different principles. Consequently, it is viewed as the keystone of the conceptual articulation of sustainable development'.[13] Indeed, if Brundtland's legacy was the bringing together of those with differing environmental priorities and establishing sustainable development as an important common objective, then Rio's was to make '"sustainable development" the centrepiece of international and domestic environmental policy'.[14]

Building upon that which had been agreed at Stockholm, the *Rio Declaration* laid out a number of principles that were introduced to 'establish a new and equitable global partnership through the creation of new levels of cooperation among States, key sectors of societies and people working towards international agreements which respect the interests of all and protect the integrity of the global environmental and developmental system'.[15] One of its most notable features, particularly with reference to later considerations as to how citizens and communities can work to achieve local sustainability, is the emphasis on the individual. Indeed, the first principle provides that '[h]uman beings are at the centre of concerns for sustainable development. They are entitled to a healthy and productive life in harmony with nature'.[16] Further highlighting the role that such individuals can play in the achievement of sustainability, Principle 10 adds that:

> Environmental issues are best handled with [the] participation of all concerned citizens, at the relevant level. At the national level, each individual shall have appropriate access to information concerning the environment that is held by public authorities, including information on hazardous materials and activities in their communities, and the opportunity to participate in decision-making processes. States shall facilitate and encourage public awareness and participation by making information widely available.[17]

12 See V Barral, 'Sustainable Development in International Law: Nature and Operation of an Evaluative Legal Norm' (2012) 23(2) *Environmental Journal of International Law* 377 at 379.

13 Ibid. 379 (emphasis added).

14 BJ Richardson and S Wood, 'Environmental Law for Sustainability' in BJ Richardson and S Wood (eds), *Environmental Law for Sustainability* (Oxford: Hart Publishing, 2006) 1.

15 UN, *Rio Declaration on Environment and Development*, Annex 1 to the *Report of the United Nations Conference on Environment and Development*, Rio de Janeiro, 3–14 June 1992, A/CONF.151/26 Vol. I, New York: UN ('*Rio Declaration*').

16 Ibid. Principle 1; also see Ross (n 1) 16.

17 Ibid. Principle 10.

This provision will be considered in greater detail below, in the context of discussions relating to the way in which accountability and citizen participation affect local sustainability; for now, however, it serves to demonstrate Rio's emphasis on the role that individuals can play in achieving sustainable development – the principle is not all about governments and policy groups, but also rests on a foundation of subsidiarity and citizen participation.[18]

The Rio Conference, however, did not just produce the *Declaration on Environment and Development*. In addition, there was a range of more specific outputs focusing on climate change, biological diversity and forest principles.[19] Of particular note, in relation to the focus on localism and sustainability, is that the conference also set out *Agenda 21*. This was notable for its support for the role that local bodies could play in achieving sustainability, outlining, as it did, 'a detailed . . . action plan for achieving sustainable development'[20] that emphasised the importance of tackling problems on as local a level as possible, as will be seen below.[21] The Rio Conference, therefore, played a vital role in developing sustainability as an important global principle of environmental law and policy, helping to 'lay out the core conceptual content of' the principle,[22] and mapping out the way in which its objectives could be achieved internationally as well as at a more local level.

The implementation process following the *Rio Declaration* and *Agenda 21*, however, was not widely regarded as being wholly successful. 'In 1997 a special session of the UN General Assembly [held in New York], known as "Rio+5" . . . review[ed] progress in the five years since [Rio]',[23] and concluded that whilst a number of positive results had been achieved, there remained deep concern that overall trends with respect to sustainable development were worse than they had been in 1992.[24] Bosselmann echoes this and, discussing issues underlying the lack of progress since Rio, argues that agreement at the 1992 conference itself was purely rhetorical, with concerns for sustainability remaining abstract and unrelated to pressing environmental crises.[25] He goes on to describe the 'Rio + 5' conference

18 Subsidiarity is a principle commonly at home within the realms of European Union law. At that level, it ensures that 'the Union shall act only if and in so far as the objectives of the proposed action cannot be sufficiently achieved by the Member States, either at central level or at regional and local level, but can rather, by reason of the scale or effects of the proposed action, be better achieved at Union level' (Consolidated Version of the Treaty on European Union [2012] OJ C326/15, Article 5(3)). The principle is applied here along similar lines and on the basis that it represents the making of decisions and taking of actions at the most appropriate level.

19 See Holder and Lee (n 8) 220.

20 J Ellis and S Wood, 'International Environmental Law' in BJ Richardson and S Wood (eds), *Environmental Law for Sustainability* (Oxford: Hart Publishing, 2006) 343 at 374.

21 See 'Local sustainability in the UK' section, p. 17 below.

22 Barral (n 12) 380.

23 Ross (n 1) 16.

24 See Ross (n 1) 16 and 17, who there cites: UNGA, *Programme for the Further Implementation of Agenda 21*, 1997, A/RES/S-19/2, New York: UN.

25 K Bosselmann, 'Rio + 10: Any Closer to Sustainable Development?' (2002) 6 *New Zealand Journal of Environmental Law* 297.

as sobering, noting that it ended without a political declaration or any consensus as to the best way forward, with 'government delegations and NGOs [merely agreeing] . . . that the trend of environmental degradation and decline of living standards had remained unbroken'.[26]

A further five years down the line, ahead of the 2002 World Summit on Sustainable Development in Johannesburg, it was further noted that 'progress since the 1992 Earth Summit has clearly been uneven within and amongst industry sectors and countries . . . we are still confronted with worrying, global trends related to biodiversity, air pollution, land degradation, chemical emissions and waste, [and] freshwater and the regional seas'.[27] The story at Johannesburg, therefore, was much the same as it had been at 'Rio + 5' in 1997.[28] Amid heightened concerns for global security in the aftermath of the terrorist attacks in 2001,[29] there remained a deep divide between developed states and developing countries,[30] suggesting that the reconciliation of global environmental objectives continued to pose a real challenge to the progress of sustainability.

Taking into account the struggles that had been encountered during the intervening years, however, the Johannesburg conference itself set out 'to provide for the implementation of the goals agreed at Rio'.[31] It was intended to be forward looking, and through its two most significant outputs – the *Johannesburg Declaration* and the *Johannesburg Plan of Implementation* – it served to progress further the understanding of the sustainability principle.[32] Indeed, it sought to 'promote the integration of the three components of sustainable development – economic development, social development and environmental protection – as interdependent and mutually reinforcing pillars'.[33] This identification of the 'three pillars of sustainable development' was perhaps the most significant clarification of the principle since Brundtland,[34] and though Stanton notes that the *Plan of Implementation* was 'not the first to develop . . . the . . . approach',[35] Holder and

26 Ibid. 301.

27 UNEP, *Industry as a Partner for Sustainable Development. 10 Years after Rio: The UNEP Assessment* (Paris: UNEP, 2002) 11.

28 See Bosselmann (n 25) 301.

29 See Ross (n 1) 17.

30 Ibid. 17. Ross cites the *Johannesburg Declaration*: UN, *Johannesburg Declaration on Sustainable Development*, Annex to Resolution 1 of the *World Summit on Sustainable Development*, Johannesburg, 26 August–4 September 2002, A/CONF.199/20, New York: UN, para. 12 ('*Johannesburg Declaration*').

31 Holder and Lee (n 8) 225.

32 Ross (n 1) 17.

33 UN, *Johannesburg Plan of Implementation*, Annex to Resolution 2 of the *World Summit on Sustainable Development*, Johannesburg, 26 August–4 September 2002, A/CONF.199/20, New York: UN, para. 2.

34 See J Stanton, 'Local Sustainable Development: Lessons Learned from the New Deal for Communities' (2012) 14(1) *Environmental Law Review* 26.

35 Ibid. 28. Stanton cites Holder and Lee as noting that 'the three-limbed approach appears in UK and EU documents, in some cases predating the Johannesburg Summit' (Holder and Lee (n 8) 237).

Lee go so far as to suggest that 'it seems to be emerging as a new international definition'.[36] Indeed, the 2012 'Rio + 20' conference supported this by acknowledging 'the need to ... mainstream sustainable development at all levels, integrating economic, social and environmental aspects and recognizing their interlinkages, so as to achieve sustainable development in all its dimensions'.[37]

Over and above its furtherance of the conceptual sustainability principle, however, the Johannesburg conference seemed hardly to break with the tradition established at Rio and New York in terms of its efforts to achieve widespread consensus and commitment to sustainability. Whilst, as Ross acknowledges, there was some small-scale agreement,[38] French considers that, on the basis of the *Johannesburg Plan of Implementation*, full implementation of *Agenda 21* seems unlikely.[39] Indeed, at the 'Rio + 20' conference itself, it was evident that progress during the 20 years since 1992 had been insufficient, with Martella and Smaczniak noting that, during the intervening time, the Earth Summit had failed to have any real global impact.[40] The passage of time itself will reveal whether further consensus and implementation can be realised in the future, though Ross stresses that the effect of various global events means that there is a 'need for more ambitious action'.[41]

The sustainability principle, therefore, has developed rapidly over the past 40 years and has quickly assumed its position as a fundamental objective of environmental law and policy. Whilst internationally common objectives and priorities have carefully been established, their process of implementation and agreement has not been so easy. Despite this, as Martella and Smaczniak state, it is worth noting that whilst:

> the measures of progress toward[s] certain goals set in the Earth Summit are disappointing or even alarming, Agenda 21 and the Rio Declaration are sound victories with more than symbolic importance. Since the Earth Summit, international attention to sustainable development and sound environmental governance has persisted. In turn, the language of sustainable development has gained greater currency in the two decades since the Earth Summit.[42]

36 Holder and Lee (n 8) 237.

37 UN, *The Future We Want*, Annex to Resolution 1 of the *Report of the United Nations Conference on Sustainable Development*, Rio de Janeiro, 20–22 June 2012, A/CONF.216/16 (Annex from A/66/L.56), New York: UN, para. 3.

38 Ross (n 1) 17.

39 D French, *International Law and Policy of Sustainable Development* (Manchester: Manchester University Press, 2005) 20, cited in ibid. 17.

40 See R Martella and K Smaczniak, 'Introduction to Rio + 20: A Reflection on Progress since the First Earth Summit and the Opportunities That Lie Ahead' (2012) 3 *Sustainable Development Law & Policy* 4 at 4–6.

41 Ross (n 1) 18. Ross there notes such events as including recent natural disasters: the tsunami across Southern Asia (2004), Hurricane Katrina in the USA (2005) and the earthquakes that occurred in Haiti and Chile (2010).

42 Martella and Smaczniak (n 40) 5.

We owe much, therefore, to the 1992 *Rio Declaration* and, of course, the Brundtland Commission before that. They served to build on what had gone before and to propel the sustainability principle on to the world stage, underlining the importance with which it should be regarded at all levels of society. Consequently, since the late 1980s and early 1990s the sustainability principle has also come to feature with increasing prominence at the national level, as this chapter now moves on to explore in considering the emergence of sustainability in UK law and policy.[43]

Sustainable development in the UK

This section sets out the UK government's interpretation and understanding of sustainability, considering the way in which it has developed through various Strategies published since the early 1990s, and identifying the approach that lies at their heart. Ross notes that the UK's commitment to sustainable development goes back to the mid-1980s, with acceptance at an early stage of the Brundtland Report's definition of the principle.[44] Whilst the *Sustaining Our Common Future* report (1989) and *Sustainable Development: The UK Strategy* (1994) outlined initial steps towards sustainability in the UK,[45] it was in the late 1990s that the achievement of the principle really gathered momentum, with the foundations being laid for more substantial pursuit of its objectives.

Indeed, when New Labour came to power in 1997, they brought with them a relatively strong commitment to achieving sustainability. In the 1999 Strategy for Sustainable Development entitled *A Better Quality of Life*, Tony Blair emphasised that:

> [S]ustainable development is . . . an important part of this Government's programme . . . We . . . have a strategy for making [it] a reality. The whole of Government is committed to this, as are many businesses, groups and individuals up and down the country. Together, we can ensure that our economy, our society and our environment grow and develop in harmony.[46]

This is reflected in the wide range of government departmental policies that were adopted and aligned with the government's prioritisation of sustainability. The Department for Transport's drive to develop cleaner fuels and to lower emissions, for instance, was based on ambitious targets to improve the quality of the

43 The discussion here focuses on the UK broadly, with the relevant policies being UK wide. This is contrasted with later discussions which involve consideration of legislation that only applied in England and Wales and regeneration initiatives only set up in England.

44 DoE, *A Perspective by the United Kingdom on the Report of the World Commission on Environment and Development* (London: DoE, 1988). As Ross notes, this report used the same chapter headings as the Brundtland Report (Ross (n 1) 23).

45 DoE, *Sustaining Our Common Future* (London: DoE, 1989) and UK Government, *Sustainable Development: The UK Strategy*, Cm 2426 (London: HMSO, 1994).

46 DETR, *A Better Quality of Life – Strategy for Sustainable Development for the United Kingdom*, Cm 4345 (London: HMSO, 1999) foreword ('1999 Strategy').

environment and reduce pollution,[47] whilst DEFRA's focus on climate change, energy efficiency and the local environment showed a broader aspect to New Labour's commitment to sustainable development.[48]

The government's understanding of sustainability through the 1999 Strategy was built on both an acknowledgement of the internationally accepted definition from the Brundtland Report[49] as well as the three-pillar approach, stating that its guiding principles 'give full weight to economic, social and environmental aspects of sustainable development'.[50] Whilst, as Holder and Lee stress, there were challenges with regard to this approach,[51] particularly in view of suggestions that it placed insufficient emphasis on environmental protection,[52] it nonetheless provided the foundation for the Strategy's objectives. Indeed, on this basis, it set out a number of aims that focused on a range of related issues with respect to the achievement of sustainable development in the UK.[53]

Whilst comprehensively setting out the government's agenda for sustainability, however, wider constitutional developments in the UK meant that the 1999 Strategy soon became outdated. Indeed, as Ross notes, 'the old 1999 strategy did not reflect the new political reality of a devolved UK with divided competences, and it was not clear which policies, actions and targets applied to all or only part of the UK'.[54] As a result, in 2005 the government – still Labour – introduced a new Strategy for Sustainable Development entitled *Securing the Future: The UK Strategy for Sustainable Development.*[55] This sought to clarify the levels at which various issues were relevant, taking into consideration changes to the law in terms of devolution,[56] and it brought the government agenda in line with the World Summit on Sustainable Development at Johannesburg.[57] In addition, though, and

47 Sustainable Development Unit, DEFRA, *What Government Is Doing: Department for Transport* (4 April 2006) <http://collections.europarchive.org/tna/20080530153425/; http://www.sustainable-development.gov.uk/government/department/dft.htm> accessed 7 November 2013.

48 Sustainable Development Unit, DEFRA, *What Government Is Doing: Department for Environment, Food and Rural Affairs* (22 July 2005) <http://collections.europarchive.org/tna/20080530153425/; http://www.sustainable-development.gov.uk/government/department/defra.htm> accessed 7 November 2013.

49 The 1999 Strategy (n 46) para. 1.1.

50 Ibid. para. 4.2.

51 Holder and Lee (n 8) 244. Also see, cited there, A Ross-Robertson, 'Is the Environment Getting Squeezed out of Sustainable Development?' (2003) *Public Law* 249.

52 Ibid. 247.

53 Such objectives included: putting people at the centre; taking a long-term perspective; respecting environmental limits; and transparency, information, participation and access to justice. See the 1999 Strategy (n 46) para. 4.1.

54 Ross (n 1) 26.

55 DEFRA, *Securing the Future: The UK Strategy for Sustainable Development*, Cm 6467 (London: HMSO, 2005), © Crown Copyright, contains public sector information licensed under the Open Government Licence v2.0 <http://www.nationalarchives.gov.uk/doc/open-government-licence/version/2/> ('2005 Strategy').

56 Ibid. 3.

57 Ibid. 3.

most importantly, it set out to renew the government's commitment to sustainability. Indeed, Tony Blair stated in the Foreword:

> [M]ake the wrong choices now and future generations will live with a changed climate, depleted resources and without the green space and biodiversity that contribute both to our standard of living and our quality of life. Each of us needs to make the right choices to secure a future that is fairer, where we can all live within our environmental limits. That means sustainable development.[58]

On this foundation, the 2005 Strategy sought to build on what had gone before and to develop principles set out in the 1999 Strategy.[59] It restated the importance and relevance of the Brundtland Report's definition[60] and noted that 'the goal of sustainable development is to enable all people throughout the world to satisfy their basic needs and enjoy a better quality of life, without compromising the quality of life of future generations'.[61] In addition, it built on the three-pillar approach which had been the basis of the 1999 Strategy and, bearing in mind suggestions that it 'should have a primarily environmental focus',[62] the 2005 Strategy set out a number of shared principles. These were agreed with the devolved authorities and included 'goals of living within environmental limits and a just society, and . . . [doing this] by means of a sustainable economy, good governance, and sound science'.[63]

The UK government's 1999 and 2005 Strategies for Sustainable Development, therefore, were notable. Through their guiding principles and related objectives, they set out the government's interpretation of and vision for sustainable development. This acknowledged the continued relevance and importance of the internationally recognised definition provided in the Brundtland Report, as well as building upon the interdependent and mutually reinforcing three pillars of sustainability popularised at Johannesburg.[64] It ensured a firm governmental commitment to sustainability and provided a platform for its aims to be spread across a range of policy areas. Indeed, the impact that these strategies had in terms of the national focus on sustainability was reflected in the Coalition government's own vision for sustainable development in the UK, published in 2011.[65] This stated

58 Ibid. 3.
59 Ibid. 15.
60 Ibid. 15.
61 Ibid. 16.
62 House of Commons Environmental Audit Committee, *The Sustainable Development Strategy: Illusion or Reality?* (2003–4, HC 624 – I), foreword; cited in Holder and Lee (n 8) 247.
63 The 2005 Strategy (n 55) 17.
64 *Johannesburg Declaration* (n 30) para. 5.
65 DEFRA, *Mainstreaming Sustainable Development: The Government's Vision and What This Means in Practice* (February 2011) <http://sd.defra.gov.uk/documents/mainstreaming-sustainable-development.pdf> accessed 7 November 2013.

that 'good progress has been made in the last 16 years since the first UK SD strategy was published . . . our commitments build on the principles that underpinned the UK's 2005 SD strategy, by recognising the needs of the economy, society and the natural environment, alongside the use of good governance and sound science'.[66]

The Coalition's continuation of the governmental focus on sustainability seems, on paper at least, to be far less comprehensive than Labour's strategies, appearing, for the most part, to be a statement of commitment rather than a more detailed outline of policies and reforms. Nonetheless, at the vision's heart there remains recognition of the interconnecting 'pillars' of the economy, society and the environment,[67] and this runs through its emphasis on creating a green economy; tackling climate change; protecting and enhancing the natural environment; improving well-being; engaging in national and international discussion in respect of sustainable development; and building a Big Society.[68] Furthermore, in noting that 'the time has come to move SD beyond being considered as a separate, "green" issue . . . this Government wants to mainstream SD so that it is central to the way we make policy',[69] there are evidently good intentions to ensure, in part, that sustainability can become 'the central organising principle of government'.[70] The Coalition, therefore, has ensured, in part, the continuation of the governmental commitment towards sustainability in the UK. Through seeking to broaden the relevance and application of the principle, it promises to pursue sustainability across wide policy areas, seeking to improve the quality of life throughout society, with a firm focus on long-term objectives. As with the progression of the principle at the international level, the extent to which central government's vision for sustainability can be realised will become evident in the fullness of time.

Local sustainability in the UK

Having mapped out the nature of the UK's understanding and interpretation of sustainability, and the manner of successive governments' pursuit of its objectives, this chapter now explores the way in which the UK government's Strategies for Sustainable Development have provided a foundation for local sustainability in the UK, and considers the nature of the principle at that level. Whilst, in considering the relationship between accountability, citizen participation and local sustainability, later chapters draw a clear distinction between the local governmental level

66 Ibid. 2.

67 Ibid. 2.

68 Ibid. generally.

69 Ibid. 2.

70 Ross (n 1) 26. Ross there cites: Sustainable Development Commission, *Where Are We Now: A Review of Progress on Sustainable Development* (London: Sustainable Development Commission, 2009), 2, J Dernbach, *Agenda for Sustainable America* (Washington, DC: Environmental Law Institute, 2009), 27–39 and K Bosselmann, *The Principle of Sustainability: Transforming Law and Governance* (Aldershot: Ashgate, 2008), 175–208.

and the local community level, this section deals with the two levels simultaneously, bringing them together as part of a wider discussion exploring the nature of local sustainability in the UK.

The justification for sustainability at the local level is strong, founded on both the need to target development initiatives to the particular needs of certain areas and, also, the local expertise and experience that those within a particular locality can invariably bring to the process through citizen participation. As Layard states, 'local decision-makers should "shape the place" because they "know best"'.[71] This is also recognised, however, at the international level, where the principle has its roots. Indeed, whilst the *Johannesburg Declaration* considers the importance of the 'interdependent and mutually reinforcing pillars of sustainable development . . . at the local [and] national . . . levels',[72] *Agenda 21* notes further that:

> [B]ecause so many of the problems and solutions being addressed by Agenda 21 have their roots in local activities, the participation and cooperation of local authorities will be a determining factor in fulfilling its objectives . . . As the level of governance closest to the people, they play a vital role in educating, mobilizing and responding to the public to promote sustainable development.[73]

On this foundation, *Agenda 21* also set out to encourage local authorities to 'enter into a dialogue with its citizens, local organizations and private enterprises and adopt "a local Agenda 21"'.[74] Though early efforts to implement these 'local *Agenda 21s*' in the UK were supported by a great deal of motivation, their implementation was met by a number of challenges. Early on in New Labour's government, 'progress on the development of the ['local *Agenda 21*'] initiative was . . . overtaken by the publication of proposals for the reform of local government which . . . included a commitment to place sustainable development at the heart of government decision-making'.[75] Nonetheless, consistent with the principle of subsidiarity discussed above,[76] it is clear that local people and local bodies have a key role to play in the achievement of local sustainability.

In terms of setting out what this actually entails, it is the 2005 UK government Strategy that provides the most clarity. It states that:

71 A Layard, 'Law and Localism: The Case of Multiple Occupancy Housing' (2012) 32(4) *Legal Studies* 551 at 552.

72 *Johannesburg Declaration* (n 30) para. 5. Also see Stanton (n 34) 29.

73 UN, *Agenda 21*, 1992, A/CONF.151/26, Vol. III, New York: UN, para. 28.1. Made available by the UN Division for Sustainable Development at <http://sustainabledevelopment.un.org/content/documents/Agenda21.pdf> accessed 7 November 2013.

74 Ibid. para. 28.3.

75 V Jenkins, 'Learning from the Past: Achieving Sustainable Development in the Reform of Local Government' (2002) *Public Law* 130 at 137–8.

76 See n 18 above.

> [O]ur aim is to create sustainable communities in England that embody the principles of sustainable development at the local level: balancing and integrating the social, economic and environmental components of their community; meeting the needs of existing and future generations, and respecting the needs of other communities in the wider region or internationally to make their communities sustainable.[77]

This shows the extent to which understandings of sustainability, even at the most local level, are still inspired both by the 1987 Brundtland Report and the three-pillar approach. In addition, it serves to underline the role that local bodies play not only in terms of the development of local areas, but also in contributing to the global achievement of sustainability. Indeed, as Jenkins notes, '"sustainable development" is . . . firmly established as an important policy issue of global concern. Local government is considered to have a central role in efforts to achieve this objective – both in the provision of key services to citizens and in educating and engaging local agencies and the public'.[78]

The importance of this role is reflected further in the statutory duties that are imposed on both local authorities and the plethora of community bodies and initiatives that have been set up to achieve sustainability in particular areas. In keeping with the above accepted understandings of sustainability in the UK, these provisions demonstrate the extent to which the principle at this level remains inspired by the three-pillar approach. The Local Government Act 2000, for instance, states in section 4 that 'every local authority must prepare a strategy . . . for promoting or improving the economic, social and environmental well-being of their area and contributing to the achievement of sustainable development in the United Kingdom'.[79] In fulfilling this duty, local authorities must consult and seek the participation of appropriate persons and take note of any guidance provided by the Secretary of State.[80] At the time of enactment, this duty was accompanied by the since repealed *well-being power*, in section 2 of the Act, which gave local authorities the 'power to do anything which they consider[ed] . . . likely to achieve . . . the promotion or improvement of the economic . . . social [and] . . . environmental well-being of their area'.[81] This power, repealed by the Localism Act 2011, was replaced with a much needed 'general power of competence' that is discussed further in Chapter 4. For now, however, these provisions underline the

77 The 2005 Strategy (n 55) 121. The 1999 Strategy, whilst superseded by that of 2005, provides further detail in suggesting that creating sustainable communities involves improving local surroundings; reducing crime and the fear of crime; addressing problems relating to poverty and social exclusion in deprived communities; and creating greater opportunities for citizen involvement at the community level (The 1999 Strategy (n 46) Chapter 7).

78 V Jenkins, 'Local Government Reform and Sustainable Development in Wales and Ireland' (2009) 11(1) *Environmental Law Review* 21 at 21.

79 Local Government Act 2000, s 4.

80 Ibid. s 4(3).

81 Ibid. s 2.

role that local authorities in the UK are expected to play in terms of achieving sustainability, serving, also, to exemplify the importance of the three pillars to that approach.

These are not the only examples, however, and are supplemented further by duties in respect of overseeing and encouraging sustainability in local communities. The Sustainable Communities Act 2007, for instance, invites local authorities to promote the sustainability of communities, encouraging the improvement of the economic, social or environmental well-being of a particular area,[82] whilst guidance relating to the aforementioned provisions of the 2000 Act states that their aim is 'to enhance the quality of life of local communities' and 'contribute to the achievement of sustainable development' therein.[83] The guidance states that local authorities must allow local communities to articulate their aspirations, needs and priorities; that the actions of the various local organisations and the council must be coordinated; that there must be clear focus on shaping existing and future activity of such organisations to meet community needs; and that there must be a firm contribution to the achievement of sustainable development both within the local community and on a wider level too.[84]

These provisions, therefore, emphasise the importance of the community dimension of sustainability. They encourage local authorities to work with and respect local neighbourhood needs and desires, ensuring, at the same time, that these are aligned with broader objectives and built on the foundation provided by the Brundtland definition and the three-pillar approach. Over and above the role that local authorities can play in encouraging local community sustainability, however, there are also, and have been over the years,[85] a range of bodies and initiatives, separate from local government and founded in government policy, which work towards sustainability in particular areas. Chapter 5 will consider these in much greater detail, but it is worth noting now that initiatives such as Labour's recently expired NDC programme have worked with local authorities, local people and other community organisations to implement a community-led approach to sustainability that strived to set and meet objectives relevant to the challenges posed by local urban deprivation in a particular neighbourhood. As at the local governmental level, the important role that such initiatives can play in delivering local sustainability is founded on the application of the three-pillar approach. As Humphreys notes, these regeneration initiatives involve 'the

82 Sustainable Communities Act 2007, s 1(1) and 1(2).

83 Office of the Deputy Prime Minister, *Preparing Community Strategies: Government Guidance to Local Authorities* (London: HMSO, 8 December 1999) para. 9 <http://webarchive.nationalarchives.gov.uk/20120919132719/; http://www.communities.gov.uk/documents/localgovernment/pdf/156672.pdf> accessed 7 November 2013. Also see A Arden, C Baker and J Manning, *Local Government Constitutional and Administrative Law* (2nd edn, London: Sweet & Maxwell, 2008) para. 1.6.35.

84 See ibid. para. 10, and Arden *et al.* (n 83) para. 1.6.36.

85 P Foley and S Martin, 'A New Deal for the Community? Public Participation in Regeneration and Local Service Delivery' (2000) 28(4) *Policy & Politics* 479 at 480.

implementation of environmental, social and economic improvements to an area of deprivation while ensuring such improvements are sustainable'.[86]

Sustainability, therefore, has become firmly established as a fundamental policy objective within the UK, both in terms of national efforts to tackle deprivation as well as efforts at the local governmental and community level. Whilst the 1999 and 2005 Strategies for Sustainable Development provided the policy platform for local sustainability in the UK, further statutory provisions and local initiatives have elaborated on the role that local bodies can fulfil in meeting objectives aligned with sustainability. The principle at this level remains true to its international roots, with echoes of the Brundtland definition and the three-pillar approach evident across the range of policy documents and legislation relevant to local sustainability. In order that the book might go on to consider examples of local governmental and community efforts sustainably to develop local areas, however, it is necessary – in this next section – to consolidate the chapter's considerations of the principle and to break it down into its constituent elements, so as to ensure clearer and easier application of all that it entails.

A model of local sustainability

This final section sets out a 'model of local sustainability'. This is extracted from the various definitions and locally relevant statements of the principle, as discussed above, and comprises three key aspects. These are: the needs of the people, sustainability, and the three pillars of environmental, social and economic development. This model will be applied throughout the book's later chapters to local governmental and community examples of local sustainability to enable evaluation of the extent to which they achieve local sustainability and, on that basis, to facilitate easier examination of the way in which that achievement is enhanced by accountability and citizen participation.

Needs of the people

The first aspect of this model relates to the meeting of local needs. It has become clear from this chapter's exploration of the sustainability principle that it is still to a large extent based on the definition set out at Brundtland[87] and developed thereafter. Whilst the *Rio Declaration* alludes to similar objectives,[88] the 2005 UK government's Strategy opens by echoing its definition, noting that 'sustainable development aims to enable all people throughout the world to satisfy their basic

86 M Humphreys, 'Leaseholder Charges and Urban Regeneration' (2006) *Journal of Planning and Environmental Law* 1625 at 1626.

87 It is recalled that it was there defined as 'development that meets the needs of the present without compromising the ability of future generations to meet their own needs' (Brundtland Report (n 2) 43).

88 See *Rio Declaration* (n 15) Principle 3.

needs and enjoy a better quality of life without compromising the quality of life of future generations'.[89] The most defining aspect of the Brundtland Report's iteration of the principle, however, is its focus on individuals, 'the satisfaction of human needs and aspirations . . . [being a] major objective of development'.[90] Indeed, as Banerjee notes, 'sustainable development must be people orientated. It must . . . provide for the basic needs of the people.'[91]

This is particularly true of development at the local level. Recalling that the issues and problems of particular areas are highly subjective (thus justifying the need for the local focus), understanding the needs and desires of those who experience those issues through living and working within that locality is absolutely vital to achieving sustainability in that area. As Grekos and Purdue note, central to sustainable development is the creation of 'strong, vibrant and healthy communities . . . [that] meet the needs of present and future generations'.[92]

Sustainability

The second limb of the 'model of local sustainability' also goes right to the heart of the Brundtland Report's definition, noting as it does the importance of the needs of future generations.[93] Whilst it is not possible to predict what the needs of future generations might be, it is important, at least, to ensure that they can benefit from the best possible environment and have sufficient foundation in place later to pursue regeneration in line with future needs. This means that developing changes should improve and preserve the environment and be sustainable. As Goodland considers, 'we must save the remnants of the only environment we have and allow time for and invest in . . . regeneration'.[94]

The importance of sustainability is also very much at the heart of the UK's policies for sustainable development, as Tony Blair has already been quoted as noting. He states:

89 The 2005 Strategy (n 55) 6.

90 Brundtland Report (n 2) 43.

91 UC Banerjee, 'The Doctrine of Sustainable Development: A Discussion' in MC Cordonier Segger and CG Weeramantry (eds) *Sustainable Justice: Reconciling Economic, Social and Environmental Law* (Leiden: Koninklijke Brill NV, 2005) 46 at 54.

92 M Grekos and M Purdue, 'Presumption in Favour of Sustainable Development' (2011) *Journal of Planning and Environmental Law* 1175 at 1175. Whilst Chapters 4 and 5 will explore specific examples and demonstrate the importance of locally focused approaches to sustainability, as guidance, the Brundtland Report identifies livelihood, employment, health care, housing and various other environmentally important needs as being a few examples of 'essential human needs' (Brundtland Report (n 2) 54 and 55).

93 See Brundtland Report (n 2) 43.

94 R Goodland, 'The Concept of Environmental Sustainability' (1995) 26 *Annual Review of Ecology and Systematics* 1 at 5.

> [M]ake the wrong choices now and future generations will live with a changed climate, depleted resources and without the green space and biodiversity that contribute both to our standard of living and our quality of life. Each of us needs to make the right choices to secure a future that is fairer, where we can all live within our environmental limits.[95]

On this basis, therefore, it is important to ensure that development in the UK is sustainable and that it is capable of accommodating or being altered to accommodate the changing needs of future generations.

In terms of working to ensure that this is the case at the local level, governmental and community bodies must not only introduce changes that are durable in terms of quality and longevity, but also demonstrate an ongoing commitment to development that can continue beyond the life of a particular scheme or policy. As Kemp *et al.* acknowledge, the 'pursuit of sustainability is a long-term . . . never-ending process';[96] it cannot be achieved purely on the basis of short-term objectives, but requires an ongoing process of dedication towards environmental, social and economic improvement. Such commitment and dedication are exemplified by the succession strategies that were devised and adopted upon the expiration of the NDC programme in 2011,[97] as Chapter 5 will discuss in greater detail. Through these, local people have the opportunity to continue the work overseen by the initiative and play a part in the ongoing development of their local areas. Sustainability, therefore, is a fundamental aspect of the principle.

The three-pillar approach: environmental, social and economic development

The final aspect of the 'model of local sustainability' is based on the three pillars of the principle: environmental, social and economic development which, as discussions throughout this chapter have demonstrated, is at the very heart of local sustainability in the UK.[98] Satisfaction of these elements would require local governmental and community pursuits of sustainability to take into consideration each of the interlinking and interconnecting strands of the principle. In terms of how that might be done, it inevitably depends on the nature of a particular community's deprivation as regards the prevalent issues that are the focus of its regeneration. Despite this, this section draws from the 2005 UK Strategy on

95 The 2005 Strategy (n 55) 3.

96 R Kemp, S Parto and RB Gibson, 'Governance for Sustainable Development: Moving from Theory to Practice' (2005) 8(1–2) *International Journal of Sustainable Development* 12 at 16.

97 See, for example, EC1 New Deal for Communities, *EC1 Beyond 2011* <http://www.renaisi.com/2011/wp-content/uploads/2011/05/EC1_Beyond_2011.pdf> accessed 7 November 2013.

98 Recall the *Johannesburg Plan of Implementation* (n 33), which sought to 'promote the integration of the three components of sustainable development – economic development, social development and environmental protection – as interdependent and mutually reinforcing pillars' (para. 2).

Sustainable Development,[99] which provides guidance in respect of what might amount to environmental, social or economic development in a deprived community or locality.

In terms of environmental development, this would generally relate to the physical aspects of a local area and be concerned with issues such as the state of streets and parks, local infrastructure and local pollution.[100] Social development would focus on issues such as the tackling of anti-social behaviour, the health and safety of a local area,[101] as well as community cohesion.[102] Indeed, this notion of cohesion is central to sustainability as it represents the idea that local people should feel a part of and belong to a neighbourhood that is, at the same time, imbued with a sense of community spirit. As will be discussed in Chapter 5, this leads to wider benefits such as stronger commitments to sustainability and improved citizen and community-wide involvement. Finally, economic development at the community level could relate to the state of local businesses and employment as well as the strength of the local housing market.[103] Though these are merely examples of the way in which local areas can develop in line with the three-pillar approach, they serve to illustrate the specific nature of real-life community objectives aligned with sustainability. Chapters 4 and 5 will offer greater detail.

The 'model of local sustainability', therefore, seeks to break down the constituent aspects of the principle. It demands that developments meet the needs of the people; that such development is sustainable and potentially accommodating for future generations; and that it falls within the three pillars of sustainability.

Concluding remarks

This chapter has defined sustainability and considered its importance both at the international level, where the principle has its roots, and, in more detail, at the national and local levels in the UK. Founded in the government's Strategies, as well as wider legislation and policy, the strength of the focus on local sustainability is clear and its justification self-evident. With this in mind, therefore, the chapter's 'model of local sustainability' will come to play a key role in Chapters 4 and 5 in examining the success of local governmental and community efforts to achieve sustainability, providing a foundation for this book later to test the hypothesis that accountability and citizen participation can enhance such achievements.

Bibliography

Arden, A, Baker, C and Manning, J, *Local Government Constitutional and Administrative Law* (2nd edn, London: Sweet & Maxwell, 2008).

99 The 2005 Strategy (n 55). In particular, see Chapter 6.
100 Ibid. 122.
101 Ibid. 122.
102 Ibid. 16 provides evidence of this being central to sustainability.
103 Ibid. 122 and 123.

Banerjee, UC, 'The Doctrine of Sustainable Development – A Discussion' in Cordonier Segger, MC and Weeramantry, CG (eds) *Sustainable Justice: Reconciling Economic, Social and Environmental Law* (Leiden: Koninklijke Brill NV, 2005) 46.

Barral, V, 'Sustainable Development in International Law: Nature and Operation of an Evaluative Legal Norm' (2012) 23(2) *Environmental Journal of International Law* 377.

Bosselmann, K, 'Rio + 10: Any Closer to Sustainable Development?' (2002) 6 *New Zealand Journal of Environmental Law* 297.

Bosselmann, K, *The Principle of Sustainability: Transforming Law and Governance* (Aldershot: Ashgate, 2008).

Boyle, A and Freestone, D, *International Law and Sustainable Development: Past Achievements and Future Challenges* (Oxford: OUP, 1999).

DEFRA, *Securing the Future: The UK Strategy for Sustainable Development*, Cm 6467 (London: HMSO, 2005), © Crown Copyright, contains public sector information licensed under the Open Government Licence v2.0 <http://www.nationalarchives.gov.uk/doc/open-government-licence/version/2/>.

DEFRA, *Mainstreaming Sustainable Development: The Government's Vision and What This Means in Practice* (February 2011) <http://sd.defra.gov.uk/documents/mainstreaming-sustainable-development.pdf> accessed 7 November 2013.

Dernbach, J, *Agenda for Sustainable America* (Washington, DC: Environmental Law Institute, 2009).

DETR, *A Better Quality of Life – Strategy for Sustainable Development for the United Kingdom*, Cm 4345 (London: HMSO, 1999).

DoE, *A Perspective by the United Kingdom on the Report of the World Commission on Environment and Development* (London: DoE, 1988).

DoE, *Sustaining Our Common Future* (London: DoE, 1989).

EC1 New Deal for Communities, *EC1 Beyond 2011* <http://www.renaisi.com/2011/wp-content/uploads/2011/05/EC1_Beyond_2011.pdf> accessed 7 November 2013.

Ellis, J and Wood, S, 'International Environmental Law' in Richardson, BJ and Wood, S (eds), *Environmental Law for Sustainability* (Oxford: Hart Publishing, 2006) 343.

Foley, P and Martin, S, 'A New Deal for the Community? Public Participation in Regeneration and Local Service Delivery' (2000) 28(4) *Policy & Politics* 479.

French, D, *International Law and Policy of Sustainable Development* (Manchester: Manchester University Press, 2005).

Goodland, R, 'The Concept of Environmental Sustainability' (1995) 26 *Annual Review of Ecology and Systematics* 1.

Grekos, M and Purdue, M, 'Presumption in Favour of Sustainable Development' (2011) *Journal of Planning and Environmental Law* 1175.

Holder, J and Lee, M, *Environmental Protection, Law and Policy: Text and Materials* (2nd edn, Cambridge: CUP, 2007).

House of Commons Environmental Audit Committee, *The Sustainable Development Strategy: Illusion or Reality?* (2003–4, HC 624 – I).

Humphreys, M, 'Leaseholder Charges and Urban Regeneration' (2006) *Journal of Planning and Environmental Law* 1625.

Jenkins, V, 'Learning from the Past: Achieving Sustainable Development in the Reform of Local Government' (2002) *Public Law* 130.

Jenkins, V, 'Local Government Reform and Sustainable Development in Wales and Ireland' (2009) 11(1) *Environmental Law Review* 21.

Kemp, R, Parto, S and Gibson, RB, 'Governance for Sustainable Development: Moving from Theory to Practice' (2005) 8(1–2) *International Journal of Sustainable Development* 12.

Layard, A, 'Law and Localism: The Case of Multiple Occupancy Housing' (2012) 32(4) *Legal Studies* 551.

Martella, R and Smaczniak, K, 'Introduction to Rio + 20: A Reflection on Progress since the First Earth Summit and the Opportunities That Lie Ahead' (2012) 3 *Sustainable Development Law & Policy* 4.

Office of the Deputy Prime Minister, *Preparing Community Strategies: Government Guidance to Local Authorities* (London: HMSO, 8 December 1999) <http://webarchive.nationalarchives.gov.uk/20120919132719/; http://www.communities.gov.uk/documents/localgovernment/pdf/156672.pdf> accessed 7 November 2013.

Rajamani, L, 'From Stockholm to Johannesburg: The Anatomy of Dissonance in the International Environmental Dialogue' (2003) 12 *Review of European Community and International Environmental Law* 23.

Richardson, BJ and Wood, S, 'Environmental Law for Sustainability' in Richardson, BJ and Wood, S (eds), *Environmental Law for Sustainability* (Oxford: Hart Publishing, 2006) 1.

Ross, A, *Sustainable Development Law in the UK: From Rhetoric to Reality?* (London: Routledge-Earthscan, 2011).

Ross-Robertson, A, 'Is the Environment Getting Squeezed out of Sustainable Development?' (2003) *Public Law* 249.

Sands, P, *Principles of International Law* (Cambridge: CUP, 2003).

Stanton, J, 'Local Sustainable Development: Lessons Learned from the New Deal for Communities' (2012) 14(1) *Environmental Law Review* 26.

Sustainable Development Commission, *Where Are We Now: A Review of Progress on Sustainable Development* (London: Sustainable Development Commission, 2009).

Sustainable Development Unit, DEFRA, *What Government Is Doing: Department for Environment, Food and Rural Affairs* (22 July 2005) <http://collections.europarchive.org/tna/20080530153425/; http://www.sustainable-development.gov.uk/government/department/defra.htm> accessed 7 November 2013.

Sustainable Development Unit, DEFRA, *What Government Is Doing: Department for Transport* (4 April 2006) <http://collections.europarchive.org/tna/20080530153425/; http://www.sustainable-development.gov.uk/government/department/dft.htm> accessed 7 November 2013.

UK Government, *Sustainable Development: The UK Strategy*, Cm 2426 (London: HMSO, 1994) © Crown Copyright, contains public sector information licensed under the Open Government Licence v2.0 <http://www.nationalarchives.gov.uk/doc/open-government-licence/version/2/>.

UN, *Report of the United Nations Conference on the Human Environment*, Stockholm, 5–16 June 1972, A/CONF.48/14/Rev.1, New York: UN.

UN, *Agenda 21*, 1992, A/CONF.151/26, Vol. III, New York: UN. Made available by the UN Division for Sustainable Development at <http://sustainabledevelopment.un.org/content/documents/Agenda21.pdf> accessed 7 November 2013.

UN, *Rio Declaration on Environment and Development*, Annex 1 to the *Report of the United Nations Conference on Environment and Development*, Rio de Janeiro, 3–14 June 1992, A/CONF.151/26, Vol. I, New York: UN.

UN, *Johannesburg Declaration on Sustainable Development*, Annex to Resolution 1 of the *World Summit on Sustainable Development*, Johannesburg, 26 August–4 September 2002, A/CONF.199/20, New York: UN.

UN, *Johannesburg Plan of Implementation*, Annex to Resolution 2 of the *World Summit on Sustainable Development*, Johannesburg, 26 August–4 September 2002, A/CONF.199/20, New York: UN.

UN, *The Future We Want*, Annex to Resolution 1 of the *Report of the United Nations Conference on Sustainable Development*, Rio de Janeiro, 20–22 June 2012, A/CONF.216/16 (Annex from A/66/L.56), New York: UN.

UNEP, *Industry as a Partner for Sustainable Development. 10 Years after Rio: The UNEP Assessment* (Paris: UNEP, 2002).

UNGA, *Programme for the Further Implementation of Agenda 21*, 1997, A/RES/S-19/2, New York: UN.

World Commission on Environment and Development, *Our Common Future* (Oxford: OUP, 1987).

3 Local democracy and decision-making

Accountability and participation

Introduction to local democracy

Chapter 2 has demonstrated the importance of local sustainability in the UK and has outlined the valuable role that local governmental and community bodies and initiatives can play in pursuing its objectives. It is the focus of this chapter, however, to consider the way in which such bodies make decisions affecting the achievement of local sustainability and to identify and explore the principles that enable such decision-making to operate effectively. Underlying this, therefore, is the need for some form of leadership and democracy. There must be some person or body that is tasked with the decision-making role, and that role must both derive its legitimacy from and be relevant to those affected by the decisions. Local sustainability is no different in this regard, with the leadership of local governmental and community bodies having a crucial role to play in its achievement at that level, and with democracy ensuring both the legitimacy and relevance of that leadership. On this basis, it is the purpose of this chapter to consider – on a conceptual level – the extent to which democracy can be said to enhance the leadership and decision-making relating to the achievement of local sustainability.

Democracy, however, is a difficult concept to define. Its uses and meanings differ greatly between states and at different levels, meaning that it is not easy to establish a general form of the concept. That said, it is invariably dependent on a number of key principles and mechanisms, which enable it to operate effectively and to ensure that there can be widespread consensus for the process of government, law-making and decision-making. In the UK, for instance, as explored in greater detail below, democracy manifests itself in the form of periodic elections, occasional referenda and representatives working in government on our behalf. Representation, as a mechanism here, ensures that periodic elections legitimise a parliament's five-year term[1] and a political party's position in government. With this in mind, it is on the basis of this representative system that this chapter determines the extent to which democracy enhances local sustainability, and it

1 Prior to the Fixed Term Parliaments Act 2011, a General Election could be called at any point within a five-year period, the power lying with a prime minister as to when that might be. The 2011 Act serves to ensure that the elections are now set by legislation.

does this by focusing on two key mechanisms – accountability and citizen participation. Accountable leadership and the encouragement of some form of citizen participation are important in a democratic system as they ensure a means through which people can communicate with and input into a decision-making process, scrutinising that process where necessary and ensuring that resultant decisions are desirable and appropriate. These principles potentially have a key role to play, therefore, in ensuring effective and democratic sustainability at the local level, as this chapter will go on to illustrate.

The chapter is structured so as to define accountability and the way in which it operates in relation to other principles of decision-making and democracy, considering, in particular, the way in which the principle operates in terms of basic representation as well as more active citizen participation. In this regard, it considers that accountability flows naturally from citizen participation.[2] The second half of the chapter will then set out the manner in which accountability and citizen participation relate to local sustainability, evaluating the extent to which the principles can be said to enhance its achievement. This provides the foundation for Chapters 4 and 5 later to test this hypothesis, exploring the way in which examples of local governmental and community bodies and initiatives demonstrate this in practice.

Accountability explored

First, then, let us consider the principle of accountability; this 'has a long, distinguished, and fascinating genesis in English law'[3] and in its broadest sense has always represented the need to give reasons and explanations for actions or decisions taken.[4] Oliver, who explores the principle across a range of levels and institutions, defines it as entailing 'being liable to be required to give an account or explanation of actions and, where appropriate, to suffer the consequences, take the blame or undertake to put matters right if it should appear that errors have been made'.[5]

The historical importance of the principle is reflected in the social contract theories first considered back in the seventeenth century by, *inter alia*, Grotius, Hobbes, Locke and Rousseau.[6] In simple terms, the theory is represented by the notion that citizens exist in 'a state of society, by means of a contract in which they undertake to respect each other and live in peace'.[7] This is balanced by a simultaneous undertaking under which citizens promise 'to obey a government

2 See J Onyx and B Dalton, 'Accountability and Advocacy' (2006) 12(1) *Third Sector Review* 7 at 15.

3 See, further, GI Seidman, 'The Origins of Accountability: Everything I Know about the Sovereign's Immunity, I Learned from King Henry III' (2004–2005) 49 *St Louis U.L.J.* 393 at 396 and generally.

4 See Public Service Select Committee, 1st report, *Ministerial Accountability and Responsibility* (1996–7, HC 234).

5 D Oliver, *Constitutional Reform in the UK* (Oxford: OUP, 2003) 48.

6 See, for further detail, MDA Freeman, *Lloyd's Introduction to Jurisprudence* (8th edn, London: Sweet & Maxwell, 2008) 105–12.

7 W Friedmann, *Legal Theory* (5th edn, London: Stevens & Sons, 1967) 118.

which they themselves have chosen'.[8] In terms of accountability, this translates into the concept that government is accountable to those who undertake to obey them in this way and who should be governed in a just manner, within the scope of the powers accorded and on the basis of the desires and wishes of citizens. It is, in essence, a safeguard against bad government, bad governance and corruption and is there for when things go wrong, so that some identifiable body, making the relevant decisions, is blameworthy or praiseworthy for the results.[9]

Since the early days of government, however, 'the scope and meaning of "accountability" has been extended in a number of directions well beyond its core sense of being called to account for one's actions'.[10] It is necessary, therefore, to go beyond this common understanding and to consider the principle more widely. In doing so, this section explores the manner in which accountability not only affords the opportunity for scrutiny and explanation, but also ensures that decision-makers take into account those affected by their decisions before they are actually taken. It highlights the extent to which accountability involves a dialectical activity and illustrates the manner in which it can be said to be a mechanism for control and responsiveness. It then finishes by considering the principle's close association with the wider notion of responsibility. All this ensures a more thorough consideration of and provides a strong foundation for the chapter's later analyses of the way in which accountability relates to representation and participation.

Ex-post facto *and* ex-ante *accountability*

Oliver's definition of accountability, above, reflects the notion of holding public officials accountable through law, other monitoring and sanctioning mechanisms and elections.[11] Moncrieffe describes this as *ex-post facto* accountability. As its name suggests, this imposes obligations after a particular event or decision, following which, explanations can be provided, rectifying actions taken and consequences faced. In addition, however, accountability can also exist *before* such events or decisions, as Moncrieffe demonstrates through her explanation of *ex-ante* accountability. She states that:

> [I]n order to act effectively in the citizen's interests, representatives must . . . know what these interests are; allow for deliberation and consultation so that policies may be corrected where appropriate; keep the public apprised of policy choices and provide explanations and opportunities for public response . . . and provide the appropriate mechanisms and act in such a way that citizens are able to assess the quality of their representation.[12]

8 Ibid. 118.
9 Oliver (n 5) 48.
10 R Mulgan, 'Accountability: An Ever-Expanding Concept' (2000) 78(3) *Public Administration* 555 at 556.
11 JM Moncrieffe, 'Accountability: Idea, Ideals, Constraints' (2001) 8(3) *Democratization* 26 at 27.
12 Ibid. 27.

This strikes a chord with the notion of local sustainability and the meeting of community needs, emphasising, as it does, the importance of citizens' interests in a process of decision-making as well as the opportunities that they should have to input into that process, as the chapter goes on later to explore.

Accountability as a dialogue

Above and beyond the instances where accountability might exist, however, and delving more deeply into the nature of the principle itself, accountability encourages interaction and conversation between decision-makers and those who are affected by their decisions. As Mulgan suggests, the principle 'involves social interaction and exchange, in that one side, that calling for the account, seeks answers and rectification while the other side, that being held accountable, responds and accepts sanctions'.[13] Whilst important in terms of ensuring democratic consultation with citizens, a flow of communication between those who are being held to account and those who are holding them to account is also a fundamental part of accountability, without which the principle would fail to operate effectively. Accountability is, as Mulgan suggests, a dialectical activity, requiring officials to answer, explain and justify their decisions and actions, whilst those holding them to account engage in questioning, assessing and criticising.[14] Indeed, this is echoed further by Day and Klein, who note that the principle is 'a social activity requiring a shared set of expectations and a common currency of justifications . . . political deliberation is at the heart of accountability'.[15]

In terms of considering how this might apply to a decision-making process, this key aspect of accountability is reflected in the voices of citizens who write letters of complaint and speak out and criticise decisions, policies and actions, and in the responding explanations and justificatory statements given in reply. It is fundamental to the principle because if those people to whom a body is accountable are not given an appropriate medium of dialogue and conversation through which to complain, assess or criticise the actions and decisions of the governing body, then the result would be a total failure of accountability. This notion of dialogue and communication is the essence of the principle.

A right to accountability

With this dialectical activity in mind and on its basis, it is clear that accountability can be said to give rise to a relationship between those making decisions, on the one hand, and those holding decision-making bodies to account on the other. The legitimacy for this relationship is rooted in the notion that those holding decision-makers to account have a *right* to accountability. They have a right to seek answers

13 Mulgan (n 10) 555.

14 Ibid. 569.

15 P Day and R Klein, *Accountabilities: Five Public Services* (London: Tavistock, 1987) 5 and 244.

and justifications in respect of those decisions, policies and actions by which they are affected, and to be offered redress where bad decisions, policies and actions have resulted in consequences. Indeed, this is substantiated by Mulgan, who states that accountability 'implies rights of authority, in that those calling for an account are asserting rights of superior authority over those who are accountable, including the rights to demand answers and impose sanctions'.[16]

This right to accountability is founded and dependent upon what Davies terms a 'legitimate interest',[17] which requires individuals to be directly affected by a particular decision at issue or to have a legitimate interest in that issue before they can be said to have the opportunity to hold decision-makers to account in its regard. This is important for two reasons. First, it limits the number of persons who are able to exercise a right to accountability. The justification here is that it would be unjust for those unaffected by particular decisions or actions to demand answers and explanations for them, both in terms of the heavy burden which that would place on decision-makers to satisfy a large and unforeseeable public and also in terms of devaluing the accountability that those affected by the decisions rightly hold. For example, if a local authority made a decision to increase the cost of its resident parking permits, only those living within that authority's jurisdiction and requiring such permits could be said to have a legitimate interest in the decision. Residents elsewhere or those not having a car would not have such an interest and could not be said to be affected by the increased cost. Consequently, only those affected by the decision would be entitled to exercise a 'right of accountability' in its regard.

The second rationale for limiting the scope of accountability relates to the protection of decision-makers from being held to account in respect of matters that are not of wider public concern. The justification here is, as Davies notes, that it is not legitimate to hold a decision-maker to account where that 'person . . . [is] acting on his or her own behalf',[18] and where other persons and the wider public are not affected by the consequences of that decision. A further example – local councillors can be called to account for decisions, policies and actions affecting their local ward and the local authority more widely, but they cannot be called to account for personal, private and individual decisions that they make which only affect themselves and those around them in a personal capacity.

This notion of having a right to accountability, therefore, is fundamental to the principle's scope and lies at the very heart of its dialectical activity. It not only ensures that individuals have access to a process of accountability, but it also serves to restrict that access to those who do not have a claim to it.

16 Mulgan (n 10) 555.

17 ACL Davies, *Accountability: A Public Law Analysis of Government by Contract* (Oxford: OUP, 2001) 75–6.

18 Ibid. 75–6.

Mechanisms for accountability

Once this 'right of accountability' has been determined, however, it is important to ensure that there are avenues and mechanisms for accountability available to those in need of them. Whilst such mechanisms can vary greatly across government levels and institutions, as Chapters 4 and 5 will demonstrate further through consideration of specific local examples, it is important here to consider some examples to understand better the way in which the principle operates in practice. This section does not seek to analyse these mechanisms and consider in any detail the way in which they achieve accountability – that is for later. It is merely intended to identify such examples, illustrating briefly the way in which they work.

Recalling Moncrieffe's distinction between *ex-post facto* and *ex-ante* accountability, discussed above,[19] either mechanisms of accountability serve to provide a process of accountability in those instances where citizens are in need of answers and explanations after a particular decision has been made, or they operate in advance of decisions being made, ensuring that representatives act in the best interests of those who may be affected by such decisions.

In respect of *ex-post facto* accountability, where errors in decision-making have perhaps been made, then individuals, having a 'right of accountability' as a result of their being affected by that decision, might wish to seek explanations and answers to enable them better to understand what has happened and to address any grievances which have perhaps occurred as a result. Complaints procedures, for example, provide such a mechanism and ensure that citizens have a platform to question, scrutinise and seek answers and explanations. As Kerrison and Pollock note, writing in the context of the NHS and in this instance citing Lloyd-Bostock and Mulcahy, 'complaints are a mechanism through which patients directly attempt to call health providers to account for conduct which has violated the complainant's normative expectations'.[20] They provide an important mechanism for accountability, therefore, available in the event of errors having been made or expectations unfulfilled.

As regards *ex-ante* accountability, an example would be referenda. In order that decision-makers can make what they believe to be the right decisions and take the best form of action, it is vital, as Moncrieffe notes, that representatives 'act effectively in the citizen's interests . . . [and] know what these interests are; allow for deliberation and consultation so that policies may be corrected where appropriate'.[21] Referenda satisfy this and involve putting to either a local or a national public a particular question relating to a certain matter or issue, enabling

19 See n 11 and n 12 above.

20 S Kerrison and A Pollock, 'Complaints as Accountability? The Case of Health Care in the United Kingdom' (2001) *Public Law* 115 at 116. See also S Lloyd-Bostock and L Mulcahy, 'The Social Psychology of Making and Responding to Hospital Complaints: An Account Model of Complaint Processes' (1994) 16 *Law & Policy* 123.

21 Moncrieffe (n 11) 27.

decision-makers to gauge public opinion and understand wider needs and interests. In this instance, those having a 'right of accountability' would be determined by the scope of the referendum and would include all those to whom it might have been addressed. Indeed, Moncrieffe herself goes on to note that it is embedded within the criteria for *ex-ante* accountability that referenda be sought in respect of certain decisions.[22] They exemplify, therefore, a further mechanism for accountability, ensuring as they do that citizens' interests are understood and acknowledged by decision-makers.

An example of a mechanism for accountability that falls under both of Moncrieffe's distinct heads of accountability is the widespread voting in periodic elections. In the UK, everybody over the age of 18 has the democratic right to cast a vote in local, national and European elections.[23] Through these elections, citizens satisfying this minimum-age requirement, and consequently having a 'right of accountability', have available to them the tools to choose whom they wish to form a government. Such a choice may be made on the basis of publicised mandates, previous governments' performances whilst in power as well as the need to ensure that their respective desires are met. Where a previous government has perhaps made errors or failed to meet public expectations, the process of election enables citizens to end their term in office and select a new form of power, thus exemplifying *ex-post facto* accountability. Similarly, in line with *ex-ante* accountability, citizens have the option to choose a candidate who best suits their particular needs and desires and who will, if in power, best serve to meet their collective interests. Both of these manifestations of the accountability principle in the context of elections are discussed by Manin *et al.*, who note that:

> [I]n one – the 'mandate' – view, elections serve to select good policies or policy-bearing politicians. Parties or candidates make policy proposals during campaigns and explain how these policies would affect citizens' welfare; citizens decide which of these proposals they want implemented and which politicians to charge with their implementation . . . In a second – 'accountability' – view, elections serve to hold governments responsible for the results of their past actions.[24]

Elections, therefore, exemplify a key mechanism for accountability, ensuring that citizens have an opportunity not only to call the elected to account in the event of errors being made, but also to determine how those elected might best meet the needs and concerns of the electorate.

22 Ibid. 30. Moncrieffe there highlights, in particular, the importance of having referenda for those decisions that have constitutional implications.

23 Pursuant to the Representation of the People Act 2000, s 1(1).

24 B Manin, A Przeworski and SC Stokes, 'Elections and Representation' in A Przeworski, SC Stokes and B Manin (eds), *Democracy, Accountability and Representation* (Cambridge: CUP, 1999) 29.

Whilst there are a wide range of other mechanisms through which accountability can be exercised, complaints procedures, referenda and elections have, in this section, served as examples of the way in which citizens might seek to exercise their 'right of accountability' in respect of decisions and policies affecting them. Whilst complaints procedures offer straightforward means through which individuals can seek explanations and answers, referenda and elections offer more substantial ways by which citizens can get their views across and determine the consequences of those views.

Over and above affording affected individuals opportunities to seek explanations, answers and actions in respect of their views, however, the principle of accountability also serves to bring wider consequences for citizens affected by a decision-making process, as this chapter now moves on to explain.

Accountability as a mechanism for control and responsiveness

One consequence of accountability is that it can be said to be a mechanism for control – that is, control exercised by citizens over a decision-making process.[25] Essentially, where individuals hold decision-makers to account for their decisions by questioning and demanding answers and explanations, they are able to exert a form of control over that process, influencing future decisions that affect them, on the basis of Moncrieffe's identification of *ex-ante* accountability.[26] Indeed, as Mulgan notes:

> [T]he core sense of accountability is . . . grounded in the general purpose of making agents or subordinates act in accordance with the wishes of their superiors. Subordinates are called to account and, if necessary, penalized as means of bringing them under control. In a democracy, it is because the people wish to control the actions of public officials that they (or their representatives) make these officials answer, explain and accept sanctions.[27]

Control in the sense discussed here manifests itself in the form of democratic mechanisms and through citizens' roles in the democratic process, holding decision-makers to account and controlling resultant decisions and actions.[28] For example, if citizens vote in elections or referenda, and input their wishes and desires into the system in this manner, they are holding decision-makers and governing leaders to account. Consequently, they are able to control the decision-making process, perhaps through deciding who the decision-makers will be on the basis of their political allegiance, or by making clear their own views on a particular issue. Accountability, therefore, has a key role to play in according citizens a mechanism for control over a decision-making process affecting them.

25 See J Uhr, 'Redesigning Accountability' (1993) 65 *Australian Quarterly* 1 at 6, cited by Mulgan (n 10) who considers at length the relationship between control and accountability (563–6).

26 Moncrieffe (n 11) 27; also see n 12 above.

27 Mulgan (n 10) 563.

28 Ibid. 563.

A further consequence of accountability, and, indeed, of the control that individuals can exercise over decision-makers as a result, is that the principle can also be said to be a mechanism for responsiveness. The idea here is that, through exercising their 'right of accountability' and controlling, in part, the decisions which are made, citizens can ensure that the process is responsive to their needs and desires.[29]

Whilst democratically elected leaders and politicians should always be responsive to the needs, opinions and desires of those who have elected them,[30] accountability in this context provides citizens with the necessary tools to enforce these and to ensure that the process is responsive and relevant to the needs of those whom it governs. Indeed, as Mulgan notes here too, 'accountability [is] . . . seen as . . . important in encouraging responsiveness',[31] adding that '"responsiveness" . . . refers to the aim of making governments accord with the preferences of the people . . . [It] points . . . to . . . public servants' general compliance with popular demands.'[32]

As an example, in a representative democracy, referenda are a valuable mechanism for accountability, used to gauge public opinion on a particular matter or issue – as considered above.[33] Whilst their results are not legally binding on a government, the process provides a valuable way in which citizens' needs and desires can influence the system, showing the extent to which accountability can encourage responsiveness. Indeed, as Oliver notes, 'the public accountability of government is supposed to secure . . . that it is responsive to, and therefore effective in meeting, the needs of those affected by its actions'.[34]

Accountability, therefore, is a valuable democratic principle. Over and above its basis as a dialectical activity, available to all those who legitimately have access to it, however, it also works on a broader level to provide citizens with the tools required to control a decision-making process, ensuring that it is, where possible, responsive to their needs and desires. A final point to consider, however, is accountability's relationship with responsibility.

Accountability and responsibility

Over the years, the manner in which these two principles can be said to relate has been the source of much academic discussion,[35] as the distinguishing lines

29 Mulgan also discusses this relationship at length (ibid. 566–9).

30 A King, *The British Constitution* (Oxford: OUP, 2007) 55.

31 Mulgan (n 10) 566.

32 Ibid. 566.

33 See 'Mechanisms for accountability' section, p. 33 above.

34 D Oliver, *Government in the United Kingdom: The Search for Accountability, Effectiveness and Citizenship* (Milton Keynes: Open University Press, 1991) 205.

35 Dunn, for example, explores the relationship between the two concepts in the context of the relationship between elected and administrative officials. See DD Dunn, 'Mixing Elected and Nonelected Officials in Democratic Policy Making: Fundamentals of Accountability and

between the principles are not entirely clear[36] and have frequently been blurred by the mistaken view that the two terms are interchangeable. Indeed, this confusion is summed up by Birch, who notes that 'usage of the term "responsibility" to signify the accountability of individual ministers or of the government as a whole to an elected assembly is more common in Britain than in most other countries'.[37] It is important to make clear, however, that accountability and responsibility are separate and distinct in the way in which they operate.[38] It is the purpose of this section, therefore, to make clear the boundary that lies between accountability and responsibility and to demonstrate the way in which the two principles relate more generally.

The distinction between accountability and responsibility is based on the scope of the two principles and the way in which they reflect differing decision-making duties. In essence, responsibility relates to a wider range of issues, whilst accountability requires a focus on specific duties within those issues. As Oliver states, '[a]cceptance of the importance of accountability . . . should not undermine the equal, even greater, importance of responsibility in the system'.[39] The effect which this has is that responsibility becomes a prerequisite for accountability in that decision-makers must be deemed responsible for a given role before they can be held to account for the consequences of carrying out that role. As Oliver explains, certain decisions are the responsibility of particular bodies and it is their job to make those decisions and to be held to account in their regard,[40] suggesting that where these decisions and acts fall within the responsibility of particular bodies, only then can they be held accountable. Indeed, this is supported further by Day and Klein, who state that 'one cannot be accountable to anyone, unless one also has responsibility for doing something'.[41] The foundation of this relationship, therefore, is based on two factors. First, responsibility covers wider issues, whilst accountability focuses on specific duties within those issues. Second, responsibility is a prerequisite for accountability in that, before any accountability can be said to exist, one must first be able to identify the responsibility.

The most obvious example of this in practice relates to accountability in respect of a government department. Consistent with the convention of ministerial responsibility,[42] ministers who lead a government department are responsible for all the various issues and policies with which it is concerned, whilst individual

Responsibility' in A Przeworski, SC Stokes and B Manin (eds), *Democracy, Accountability and Representation* (Cambridge: CUP, 1999) 297.

36 D Oliver and G Drewry, *Public Service Reforms: Issues of Accountability and Public Law* (London: Frances Pinter Publishers Ltd, 1996) 6.

37 AH Birch, *Representative and Responsible Government: An Essay on the British Constitution* (Toronto: University of Toronto Press, 1964) 20.

38 See Mulgan (n 10) 557–8.

39 Oliver (n 5) 48.

40 Ibid. 48.

41 Day and Klein (n 15) 5, as cited in Davies (n 17) 75.

42 See G Marshall, *Constitutional Conventions: The Rules and Forms of Political Accountability* (Oxford: OUP, 1984) Chapter IV.

ministers, at a lower level and within the department itself, focus on specific duties and are accountable for the particular aspects of their role. This shows that responsibility lies not only at a broader level than accountability, relating as it does to the full remit of a department's activities, but also at a higher level, focusing on senior ministers and the full scope of their role. At a lower level, accountability relates to the specific decisions, policies and duties within the remit of a department's activities, often overseen by an individual or team with duties relating to that particular policy area. Responsibility, therefore, is both a broader and higher concept and one that forms the foundation for accountability to exist.

This section has illustrated that, although often used interchangeably, the terms accountability and responsibility denote different levels of authority and reflect a focus on different roles within decision-making processes. Whilst responsibility is a broader concept, relating to the full scope of decision-making powers, accountability is narrower and relates to specific issues.

Accountability summarised

In bringing the discussion on accountability to a close, it is the purpose of this section to consolidate this chapter's consideration of the principle and to summarise it so as to make later explorations of the way in which it relates to representation and citizen participation more manageable.

Accountability, at its most basic level, is a relatively straightforward concept. Different from responsibility, it refers to the need for explanations and justifications in respect of decisions and actions, as well as the requirement to face the consequences and take rectifying actions where errors have been made.[43] Delving more deeply, however, the principle has a number of key features. As Moncrieffe observes, through her distinction between *ex-post facto* and *ex-ante* accountability, the principle can operate in different contexts – not only affording the opportunity for scrutiny and explanation in the aftermath of a decision, consistent with Oliver's consideration of the principle, but also ensuring that decision-makers take account of the needs and interests of those affected by their decisions before they are taken, allowing for deliberation and consultation and keeping the public apprised.[44] Within both of these contexts, however, the principle is reliant upon social interaction and communication. It is, as Mulgan notes, a dialectical activity, requiring officials to answer, explain and justify, whilst those holding them to account engage in questioning, assessing and criticising.[45] On this basis, the principle ensures that citizens with legitimate interests have a 'right of accountability' and, in exercising this right, they are entitled to question and demand answers from decision-makers in respect of decisions and policies that directly affect them.

43 Recall Oliver's definition (n 5) 48.
44 Moncrieffe (n 11) 27.
45 Mulgan (n 10) 569.

Consequently, and more widely, accountability serves as a mechanism to enable citizens both to control decision-making procedures and to ensure that they are responsive to their needs and concerns.

Accountability is a fundamental principle of democracy and, as both this section and the one that follows serve to demonstrate, it plays an important role alongside wider concepts in ensuring effective and democratic decision-making. Going beyond the nature of the principle itself, however, and the way in which it relates to control, responsiveness and responsibility, it is necessary now to consider the democratic base upon which it can be said to operate most effectively.

Accountability, representation and citizen participation

With this in mind, and recalling the book's later focus on citizen participation in the context of local sustainability, it is the purpose of this section to explore the way in which accountability and participation relate. In doing so, and bearing in mind the representative democratic foundation prevalent in the UK, it is structured first to explore the way in which accountability operates on the basis of representation before then analysing the effect of increased opportunity for participation. It notes that the UK's representative democracy struggles to ensure an effective working system of accountability and that, by contrast, where individuals have the opportunity to involve themselves in decision-making, accountability can be achieved more easily. Indeed, it draws from the observation of Onyx and Dalton that 'where there is a strong culture of participation, then accountability will occur naturally'.[46]

Accountability and representation

Britain's system of government can be described as a representative democracy because of the way in which the composition of the legislature and the nature of the executive are determined by a system of periodical democratic elections.[47] These give rise to single, clearly identifiable representatives in each constituency, who are potentially blameworthy and automatically answerable to their electorates. Indeed, as Oliver notes, 'ministers, Members of Parliament, councillors and other public officials are in practice under obligation to explain and justify their actions to the public, and may find themselves obliged through pressures of criticism and embarrassment to make amends where errors have been made. Elected bodies are publicly accountable through the ballot box.'[48] The potential for accountability here is obvious. Through voting for a particular representative in their area, electorates have a legitimate interest in the manner in which a

46 Onyx and Dalton (n 2) 15.

47 See H Barnett, *Britain Unwrapped: Government and Constitution Explained* (London: Penguin Books, 2002) 265.

48 Oliver (n 34) 25.

representative's duties are discharged and in the decisions and policies made that directly affect them. This means that they can exercise a degree of control, through the elections themselves, over the decisions that that representative makes, aiming to ensure that they are responsive to the needs and desires of citizens and the wider society.

On the face of it, therefore, and conceptually speaking, through the valuable medium of elections the UK's representative democracy can be said to be compatible with and conducive to effective accountability. As Manin *et al.* note: 'Governments are "accountable" if citizens can discern representative from unrepresentative governments and can sanction them appropriately, retaining in office those incumbents who perform well and ousting from office those who do not.'[49] Such sanctions are, as they imply, possible through the process of elections – a mechanism at the very heart of the UK governmental system. Indeed, the importance of accountability in the UK's democracy has been acknowledged more widely. King notes, for instance, that it was 'the value of accountability that lay at the very heart of Britain's traditional constitution',[50] whilst Beetham adds that the institution of representation has 'served not only as a necessary instrument of accountability, but also as a means of keeping the people at arm's length from the political process'.[51]

Despite this, however, these statements are reflective of a simpler constitutional era, before changes to the operation of the system sought to alter the way in which the decision-making process affects individuals. Indeed, consideration of the extent to which the principle has operated successfully in the UK's representative democracy in recent times reveals a number of issues.

The first such issue relates to accountability at the *local* level and in the context of the centralised nature of legislative and executive power in the UK. Whilst local authorities are blessed with certain powers, these are heavily regulated by central government and are easily susceptible to change and control by those at the central level. As Chandler notes, 'there is substantial evidence to suggest that, in Britain, local government is far more subject to central control than in the United States.'[52] This severely weakens any sense of accountability at the local level between citizens and government, as those representing the people work on a level that is far removed from the problems and issues that trouble local areas. Consequently, though having a legitimate interest in local matters affecting them, citizens are not able easily to assert any democratic control over the process, which means that the needs and desires of the people are not adequately reflected in governmental decisions, thus demonstrating a lack of responsiveness. The impact that centralisation can have on accountability is also noted by Farag, who comments that, 'in

49 Manin *et al.* (n 24) 10.

50 King (n 30) 58.

51 D Beetham, 'Liberal Democracy and the Limits of Democratization' in D Held (ed.), *Prospects for Democracy: North, South, East, West* (Stanford, CA: Stanford University Press, 1993) 55 at 60.

52 JA Chandler, *Local Government Today* (4th edn, Manchester: Manchester University Press, 2009) 178.

principle, decentralisation can increase . . . access to decision-making by otherwise excluded groups, as well as increasing accountability, through proximity of decision-makers to citizens'.[53] In a similar vein, therefore, the huge gap between those who are accountable and those at the local level who hold a 'right of accountability', which exists due to the centralised state of government in the UK, severely hinders the effective working of the principle in the representative system.

This is an issue that has been exacerbated by the UK's membership of the European Union, as a result of which domestic institutions have suffered a limitation of the scope of their powers in certain areas in favour of unified authority in Europe.[54] Indeed, as King observes, the effect of 'Britain's EU membership on accountability within the British system . . . [is that] . . . citizens may continue to hold their elected government to account for every government-related thing that happens in Britain, but, if they do continue to, one consequence of Britain's membership of the EU is that it is increasingly irrational for them to do so'.[55] Having power at a level far removed from citizens, therefore, whilst sensible and beneficial in many respects, means that it is harder for individuals at the more local level to ensure that decisions and policies are relevant and responsive to local issues.

A second issue concerning accountability in the UK's representative system relates to a deficiency of both transparency and any meaningful and widespread communication with citizens. Bearing in mind the dialectical activity that goes to the very heart of the principle, if it is not known who has made a particular decision or the way in which it was made, then upholding a system of accountability becomes increasingly difficult as citizens cannot know where to point the finger of blame or, indeed, whether or not it should be protruding from their collective fist at all. Conversely, if governments are able to provide adequate levels of disclosure and transparency in respect of the decision-making process, then accountability can more easily be achieved.

In the UK system, however, whilst individuals are occasionally given opportunities to vote in elections and referenda, take part in consultations and engage freely in protests, these opportunities are perhaps insufficient to provide adequate responsiveness to and satisfaction of citizens' needs and interests. Indeed, writing in respect of the way in which accountability traditionally operates at the national level in the UK, Liddle echoes this in noting that 'traditional forms of public accountability no longer provide a sufficient basis for explanation'.[56] Consequently,

53 AS Farag, 'Decentralization: Objectives, Forms and Implementation of Decentralized Governance' (2013) 11(1) *International Journal of Social Sciences* 138 at 139.

54 The European Union enjoys exclusive competence in certain areas, limiting the scope of powers that can be exercised by member states. See Consolidated Version of the Treaty on the Functioning of the European Union [2010] OJ C83/47 Article 2(1).

55 King (n 30) 113.

56 J Liddle, 'Challenges to Democratic Legitimacy, Scrutiny, Accountability in the UK National and Local State' (2007) 31(3/4) *Public Administration Quarterly* 397 at 406. She there cites: J Stewart, 'Accountability', speech delivered in 1992 at the 'Accountability to the Public Conference', Queen Elizabeth 2 Conference Centre, Westminster, London.

despite best efforts, as governmental decisions are generally made behind closed doors and with limited awareness on the part of individuals, accountability suffers. The lack of accountability to which such practice can give rise is supported by Onyx and Dalton, who state that 'where there is a form of representative democracy, accountability occurs [only] when there is adequate disclosure of the action taken',[57] as well as Moncrieffe: 'it is difficult to conceive how representatives can truly "perform" without knowledge of the interests they should serve.'[58] This can be contrasted with systems involving a greater degree of participation. In these, accountability is achieved more easily due to those individuals who exercise the 'right of accountability' playing a more active role in the decision-making process and forming an integral part of the system itself, resulting in greater and more natural transparency, communication and responsiveness.

The final issue affecting accountability in the UK's representative democracy follows on from this suggested lack of transparency and communication and relates to the limited mechanisms for accountability that are available to citizens. Whilst, as noted above, periodic elections and referenda, along with broader opportunities for consultation, provide a degree of accountability, there are generally limited ways through which citizens can influence the decisions and policies that affect them, something that is perhaps typical of a traditionally representative system. Following an election, for example, there is no method through which the public are able to direct or input into the decisions of those for whom they voted; as a result, decision-makers and representatives are effectively left to their own devices, without any binding influence from the wider public and, consequently, with limited opportunity for accountability. Indeed, as Müller and Meyer note in respect of representation more generally:

> [O]nce the votes are counted and the seats allocated elected representatives take over . . . they represent the citizens for the entire lifetime of the legislature . . . Save for rare moments of democratic choices, it is only through these representatives that citizens participate in the making of policy decisions. And the government remains only indirectly accountable to the voters through their elected representatives.[59]

A consequence of this is that there is a huge element of trust involved on the part of citizens. Indeed, with echoes of social contract theories, discussed above,[60] Moncrieffe notes that 'elected officials have a responsibility to perform in the

57 Onyx and Dalton (n 2) 15.

58 Moncrieffe (n 11) 28.

59 WC Müller and TM Meyer, 'Meeting the Challenges of Representation and Accountability in Multi-party Governments' (2010) 33(5) *West European Politics* 1065 at 1065. They there cite: M Laver and KA Shepsle, 'Government Accountability in Parliamentary Democracy' in A Przeworski, SC Stokes and B Manin (eds), *Democracy, Accountability and Representation* (Cambridge: CUP, 1999) 279.

60 See 'Accountability explored' section, p. 29 above.

public interest'; they are 'under a contract to serve' and have a duty to 'ensure the integrity of the democratic procedures'.[61] The fact that she also alludes to 'the intransigence of . . . political leaders and [a] . . . lack of political will to demand and insist on change'[62] serves to show the nature of the problem. Once elected, the responsiveness of a decision-making process depends largely on the decision-maker honouring their responsibility to make appropriate decisions; if, for whatever reason, this does not occur, then there are inadequate mechanisms of accountability available to the wider public to seek redress.

Whilst appearing conducive to effective accountability, therefore, the UK's representative democracy presents a number of issues as regards the way in which the principle operates in practice. The centralised nature of governmental power, exacerbated by the UK's membership of the European Union, alongside issues relating to transparency, communication and a lack of appropriate mechanisms, all conspire to encumber its effective application. Consequently, and with this in mind, the chapter now moves on to consider whether increased opportunity for citizen participation provides a more effective base for the principle of accountability.

Accountability and citizen participation

This section defines citizen participation and explores the way in which it relates to accountability, noting that – as Onyx and Dalton state – 'where there is a strong culture of participation, then accountability will occur naturally . . . in that those most affected by the decision have been a part of making it, and will be immediately aware of its implementation'.[63] On this basis, the chapter will later explore how this impacts on the achievement of local sustainability in the UK.

Citizen participation is founded on the idea that individuals move away from a passive state of being represented and play a more active role in a political or decision-making process.[64] Its value is suitably described by Arnstein, who states that 'participation of the governed in their government is the cornerstone of democracy – a revered idea that is vigorously applauded by virtually everyone'.[65]

There are many democratic benefits of citizen participation, though the knowledge and first-hand experience that citizens can bring to a decision-making process are the most significant. Indeed, recalling that a representative system can

61 Moncrieffe (n 11) 27 and 28.

62 Ibid. 26.

63 Onyx and Dalton (n 2) 15.

64 Such involvement can take a number of forms, as Chapters 4 and 5 will more suitably exemplify. As an example here, citizens can participate in local government and decision-making by sitting on boards and councils, volunteering for local projects and schemes and generally playing a more central role in the process through increased opportunities for consultation and discussion.

65 S Arnstein, 'A Ladder of Citizen Participation' (1967) 35(4) *Journal of American Institute of Planners* 216 at 216.

sometimes struggle to provide sufficient responsiveness to citizens' needs and interests, due to the way in which power is held within centralised authority far removed from citizens, where they can be more actively involved in decision-making processes and have opportunities to participate, they bring to those processes their knowledge and expertise of a local area and a first-hand understanding both of local issues and of the best ways in which they should be tackled. Consequently, recalling that *ex-ante* accountability is based on the idea that representatives should understand the interests of those affected by their decisions, where citizens have the opportunity to involve themselves in the process, their interests will directly inform the decisions in which it results, thus facilitating accountability. As Richardson and Razzaque note, writing in the context of sustainable development, public participation assists decision-makers in understanding and identifying public-interest concerns in the formulation of policies.[66] Gibson *et al.* add that 'direct democracy offers the opportunity not only for citizens to become more informed but also for leaders, planners and officials to ascertain what programs and decisions are important to citizens and to demonstrate and communicate performance and accountability in more meaningful ways'.[67] As a consequence and in line with discussions above, the accountability that is based on such an awareness of the knowledge, experience, needs and interests of local people acts to ensure that the resultant decisions are inherently more responsive to those who are affected. Indeed, the comparable benefit of participation over representation in this regard is echoed by King, who states that, in terms of being 'responsive to the opinions and desires' of the people, 'representative democracy . . . can never be more than second-best. The first-best would always be direct democracy, with the whole people acting directly on their own account.'[68] This suggests, as is explored in greater detail below, that a decision-making process can be driven less by political policies and more on the basis of citizens' needs and desires. In justifying the responsiveness that stems from this citizen participation, Craig notes that there is no reason to suppose that the inputs of those who contribute independently of political parties are any less valuable than the contributions that pass through the parties, adding that a strong participatory democracy 'rests on the idea of a self-governing community of citizens who are united less by homogeneous interests than by civic education'.[69] Where citizens have the opportunity to participate, therefore, accountability can be more effectively achieved with decisions potentially more responsive to local needs and

66 BJ Richardson and J Razzaque, 'Public Participation in Environmental Decision-Making' in BJ Richardson and S Wood (eds), *Environmental Law for Sustainability* (Oxford: Hart Publishing, 2006) 165.

67 PD Gibson, DP Lacy and MJ Dougherty, 'Improving Performance and Accountability in Local Government with Citizen Participation' (2005) 10(1) *Innovation Journal: The Public Sector Innovation Journal* 1 at 3.

68 King (n 30) 55.

69 PP Craig, *Public Law and Democracy in the United Kingdom and the United States of America* (Oxford: Clarendon Press, 1990) 360 and 367.

interests and consequently based less on political justifications and more on those needs and interests.

In addition to this and recalling the importance of transparency and communication in a decision-making process, having citizens involved means not only that they see more clearly the way in which the system works, but it also becomes easier to engage and communicate with them and for them to engage and communicate with those making decisions. Consequently, accountability can be more effectively achieved. Indeed, as quoted previously, Onyx and Dalton argue that 'where there is a strong culture of participation, then accountability will occur naturally . . . [as] those most affected by the decision have been a part of making it, and will be immediately aware of its implementation'.[70]

Finally, it was noted above in respect of the UK's representative democracy that, due to limited mechanisms for accountability and citizens having no effective influence over decisions and policies, a resultant emphasis on citizens' trust in politically motivated decision-makers forms the basis of the system, with the potential danger that decision-making might – in extreme cases – be founded on 'the intransigence of . . . political leaders and [a] . . . lack of political will to demand and insist on change'.[71] Where citizens are able to participate more actively in that system, however, there is a potential opportunity for a greater number of mechanisms for accountability. Consequently, there can be less of a dependency on trusting representatives and more of an emphasis on citizens playing a constantly participative role and having the power to rectify any breach of trust that might occur. Indeed, Parr and Gates note that 'many community and public leaders . . . are beginning to realize that public participation is important in an environment where the citizens have a diminished trust in government and are demanding more accountability from public officials'.[72] Whilst it is not necessarily being suggested that the UK *should* or *does* have a diminished trust in decision-makers, recalling that accountability is there, in part, for when things go wrong, participation provides a framework within which it can at least operate more effectively. Indeed, as Steffek and Ferretti state, 'public contestation is an integral part of a process of publicly holding governments and international organisations to account'.[73]

It is clear, therefore, that citizen participation can bring many benefits to a decision-making process. It means that resultant decisions can be based less on politically motivated policies and thinking and, due to the local knowledge and

70 Onyx and Dalton (n 2) 15.

71 Moncrieffe (n 11) 26.

72 See J Parr and CT Gates, 'Assessing Community Interest and Gathering Community Support' in International City Management Association (ed.), *Partnerships in Local Governance: Effective Council-Manager Relations* (Washington, DC: International City Management Association, 1989), as cited in Gibson *et al.* (n 67) 2.

73 J Steffek and MP Ferretti, 'Accountability or "Good Decisions"? The Competing Goals of Civil Society Participation in International Governance' (2009) 23(1) *Global Society* 37 at 41.

expertise that individuals can bring to the process, coupled with increased transparency and communication, decisions are more responsive to local needs and desires as a result.

Conclusion on accountability, representation and citizen participation

The first part of this chapter has explored the fundamental democratic principles of accountability and citizen participation. It has defined accountability and considered both its constituent elements and the way in which it operates more widely in respect of representation and citizen participation. Whilst there are elements of a representative system that are clearly conducive to successful accountability, the UK system provides inadequate opportunities for citizens to uphold the principle of accountability since the institutions are arranged and operate in such a way that power is not easily accessible to the people. It has been shown, as a consequence, that citizen participation accommodates, more effectively, the principle of accountability. Through an emphasis on citizens' knowledge and expertise, better communication and a more transparent system of decision-making, a more active role for citizens ensures that accountability can be more easily achieved. In simple terms, it occurs more naturally where a decision-making system involves citizen participation.[74]

These conclusions enable a conceptual consideration of the hypothesis that is at the heart of this book, namely whether accountability and citizen participation can be said to enhance the achievement of local sustainability. Whilst Chapters 4 and 5 will seek to test this in the context of local governmental and community examples of sustainability, this chapter now sets out – in light of the principles explored both here and in Chapter 2 – to consider the most effective, democratic and appropriate decision-making process for the achievement of local sustainability. In addressing this, the chapter focuses on accountability and citizen participation separately, although it does, at the relevant juncture, seek also to discuss the relationship that the principles share, in the context of sustainability.

Accountability and sustainability

Recalling that at the heart of local sustainability is the necessity to meet 'the needs of the present without compromising the ability of future generations to meet their own needs',[75] it is of fundamental importance that decision-makers are able to discover those needs, understand them and meet them. In terms of how this might best be done, Moncrieffe's notion of *ex-ante* accountability provides a foundation:

74 Onyx and Dalton (n 2) 15.

75 World Commission on Environment and Development, *Our Common Future* (Oxford: OUP, 1987) 43 ('Brundtland Report').

> [I]n order to act effectively in the citizen's interests, representatives must . . . know what these interests are; allow for deliberation and consultation so that policies may be corrected where appropriate; keep the public apprised of policy choices and provide explanations and opportunities for public response . . . and provide the appropriate mechanisms and act in such a way that citizens are able to assess the quality of their representation.[76]

In short, this means that, in order to meet and understand adequately the needs of individuals, in line with accepted definitions of local sustainability, it is essential that relevant decision-making be accountable to those whom it affects.

Indeed, international authorities underpinning the sustainability principle also reflect this. The *Johannesburg Plan of Implementation*, for instance, states in Chapter XI that:

> [A]ll countries should promote sustainable development at the national level by . . . enacting and enforcing clear and effective laws that support sustainable development. All countries should strengthen governmental institutions . . . by providing necessary infrastructure and by promoting transparency, accountability and fair administrative and judicial institutions.[77]

Similarly, the Committee on Legal Aspects of Sustainable Development notes that 'the new international law of sustainable development . . . embraces good governance, including democratic accountability'.[78]

Above and beyond merely stating the importance of accountability in sustainability, however, it is necessary to go further and to consider in greater depth the way in which the nature and constituent elements of the principle affect the achievement of local sustainability and the extent to which it can be said actually to enhance it.

On the basis that meeting the needs and interests of citizens is central to the sustainability principle and fundamental to the role that accountability can play here, it follows that some degree of communication with local people, for whom the regeneration is taking place, is necessary to ensure that citizens' needs and interests can be understood and relevant objectives set in their regard. Whilst also of importance in terms of citizen participation, discussed below, this brings to the fore the dialectical activity of accountability. It was earlier noted that, as Mulgan

76 Moncrieffe (n 11) 27.

77 UN, *Johannesburg Plan of Implementation*, Annex to Resolution 2 of the *World Summit on Sustainable Development*, Johannesburg, 26 August–4 September 2002, A/CONF.199/20, New York: UN, para. 163.

78 International Law Association, Committee on Legal Aspects of Sustainable Development, *Fifth and Final Report: Searching for the Contours of International Law in the Field of Sustainable Development* (New Delhi, India, 2002) 396.

suggests, the principle involves a process of dialogue, requiring officials to answer, explain and justify, with those holding them to account engaging through questions and criticisms.[79] Furthermore, Day and Klein were also quoted as stating that the principle is 'a social activity requiring a shared set of expectations and a common currency of justifications . . . political deliberation is at the heart of accountability'.[80] Simply, in providing avenues through which citizens can engage in dialogue with decision-makers, the needs and desires of those affected by the decisions can be taken into consideration and better understood. Consequently, it means that there is a democratic foundation on which decisions achieving sustainability can be made.

Accountability, therefore, can be said to enhance the achievement of local sustainability, ensuring as it does satisfaction of one of its key components – meeting the needs of affected citizens. Without that accountability and in the absence of any communication with affected citizens, efforts to achieve local sustainability would fail to take proper consideration of local needs and problems, and would potentially be insufficient in meeting them. Indeed, the 2005 UK government's Strategy on Sustainable Development echoes this through its emphasis on the need for leadership and awareness relating to sustainability at the local level.[81] It looks at the application of the principles of good governance to ensure that sustainable communities are well run and that citizens are able to have some degree of control over the decisions that affect them.[82] Furthermore, in Chapter 7 of the Strategy, accountability is identified as being a key principle underlying delivery of its objectives.[83] All of this indicates, therefore, an acknowledgement of the importance of accountability in achieving local sustainability, as Chapters 4 and 5 will further illustrate. Having considered the extent to which accountability can be said to enhance local sustainability, it is necessary now to assess the importance of citizen participation.

Citizen participation and sustainability

This section draws from the international foundations of the sustainability principle as well as wider academic discussions to demonstrate the extent to which citizen participation can be regarded as fundamental to sustainability, enhancing its achievement.

79 Mulgan (n 10) 569.

80 Day and Klein (n 15) 5 and 244.

81 DEFRA, *Securing the Future: The UK Strategy for Sustainable Development*, Cm 6467 (London: HMSO, 2005) © Crown Copyright, contains public sector information licensed under the Open Government Licence v2.0 <http://www.nationalarchives.gov.uk/doc/open-government-licence/version/2/> ('2005 Strategy') 119.

82 Ibid. 120 and 121.

83 See ibid. Chapter 7.

The importance of citizen participation in sustainability is supported, in the first instance, by its status as an important aspect of environmental law. Principle 10 of the *Rio Declaration* states that 'environmental issues are best handled with participation of all concerned citizens, at the relevant level',[84] whilst the Aarhus Convention, described as '. . . by far the most impressive elaboration of Principle 10 of the Rio Declaration',[85] further entrenches participation as a principle of environmental law. It states in Article 1 that, 'in order to contribute to the protection of the right of every person of present and future generations to live in an environment adequate to his or her health and well-being, each Party shall guarantee the rights of access to information, public participation in decision-making, and access to justice in environmental matters'.[86] Finally, in 2002, at the Johannesburg Summit, 'the principle of participation received significant support and was taken into account in many different aspects of the sustainable development agenda'.[87] Indeed, it was stated that 'sustainable development requires a long-term perspective and broad-based participation in policy formulation, decision-making and implementation at all levels'.[88]

These provisions, therefore, not only demonstrate that all citizens have a right to involve themselves and play a vital role in the development of their societies, but also that citizen participation is an entrenched principle of environmental decision-making and a key component of sustainability. Richardson and Razzaque suitably describe the way in which '[p]ublic participation in environmental decision-making has become an indelible feature of many environmental regulatory systems', adding that 'parliamentary democracy ratified through periodic electoral contests is widely viewed as insufficient to provide meaningful public input into day-to-day environmental decision-making'.[89] This emphasises the benefits of a participatory system over a more representative process.

Whilst noting that these sources exist and exemplify consideration of the principles of citizen participation and sustainability at an international level, it is stressed that this in no way means that they have any less significance at the local level. Indeed, 'participation within international law relating to sustainable development . . . embodies a framework in which critical decisions can be made at the level

84 UN, *Rio Declaration on Environment and Development*, Annex 1 to the *Report of the United Nations Conference on Environment and Development*, Rio de Janeiro, 3–14 June 1992, A/CONF.151/26, Vol. I, New York: UN, Principle 10 ('*Rio Declaration*').

85 K Annan, 'Foreword' in S Stec and S Casey-Leftkowitz, *The Aarhus Convention: An Implementation Guide* (New York: UNECE, 2000) v.

86 UNECE, *Convention on Access to Information, Public Participation in Decision-Making and Access to Justice in Environmental Matters*, 25 June 1998, Aarhus, Denmark, Article 1 ('Aarhus Convention').

87 MC Cordonier Segger and A Khalfan, *Sustainable Development Law: Principles, Practices and Prospects* (Oxford: OUP, 2004) 164.

88 UN, *Johannesburg Declaration on Sustainable Development*, Annex to Resolution 1 of the *World Summit on Sustainable Development*, Johannesburg, 26 August–4 September 2002, A/CONF. 199/20, New York: UN, para. 26 ('*Johannesburg Declaration*').

89 Richardson and Razzaque (n 66) 165.

most consistent with effectiveness.'[90] Sustainability must be tackled at 'the lowest level of public authority consistent with effective action',[91] in accordance with the subsidiarity principle,[92] meaning that the importance of citizen participation, as set out by the *Rio Declaration*, Aarhus Convention and at the Johannesburg Summit, can be equally probative at the local governmental and community level as within the spheres of international environmental law and policy.

Going beyond the declarations and statements supporting the importance of citizen participation, it is necessary now to examine more closely the way in which it affects sustainability and can be said to enhance its achievement. It has already been noted that participation is democratically valuable because it ensures that citizens' knowledge and expertise can directly inform the decision-making process and increase its responsiveness, and it is on this basis that the important encouragement of citizen participation in local sustainability can also be justified. Indeed, recalling sustainability's emphasis on individuals and the meeting of people's needs, both in terms of current issues and future generations,[93] it is submitted that it would not be possible to meet the needs of the present and achieve effectively the objectives of sustainability without some participative input from local citizens. These are the people who live and work in the areas, and who know and experience the issues affecting their community. Consequently, they will be most affected by the decisions and policies taken to achieve local sustainability. Participation is essential, therefore, in ascertaining what local people want, what issues they suffer and how they want their communities to develop. Indeed, as the Aarhus Convention observes, participation is important 'to the protection of the right of every person of present and future generations to live in an environment adequate to his or her health and well-being'.[94] As Holder and Lee also agree, whilst environmental decisions, such as those relating to the achievement of sustainability, 'rest on values as well as expertise, taking those decisions without democratic involvement is untenable in terms of either a good decision or a good process';[95] 'public values inherent in an environmental decision . . . mean that "experts" have no monopoly on judgment'.[96]

90 Cordonier Segger and Khalfan (n 87) 163.

91 UN, *Agenda 21*, 1992, A/CONF.151/26, Vol. III, New York: UN, para. 8.5 (g). Made available by the UN Division for Sustainable Development at <http://sustainabledevelopment.un.org/content/documents/Agenda21.pdf> accessed 7 November 2013.

92 Defined and highlighted in the previous chapter (see there n 18). Subsidiarity, it is recalled, relates to the notion of making decisions and taking action at the most appropriate level. See further Consolidated Version of the Treaty on European Union [2012] OJ C326/15, Article 5(3).

93 Recall the Brundtland Report (n 75), which notes that 'the satisfaction of human needs and aspirations is the major objective of development' (43) and that 'sustainable development requires meeting the basic needs of all and extending to all the opportunity to satisfy their aspirations for a better life' (44).

94 Aarhus Convention (n 86) Article 1.

95 J Holder and M Lee, *Environmental Protection, Law and Policy* (Cambridge: CUP, 2007) 87.

96 Ibid. 85.

The value that citizens' involvement can bring to decision-making processes relating to sustainability, therefore, is self-evident. Their participation ensures that local knowledge and expertise inform decisions and policies, which, in turn, more effectively meet the needs of local people. As Baker *et al.* note, citing Achterberg, 'participation in the decisions which affect one's own life is a central political value of democracy . . . the required changes of lifestyle connected with a shift to sustainable development can never be lasting if they are imposed in an authoritarian way'.[97] It is clear, therefore, that 'a commitment to participation is embedded in the rhetoric of sustainable development itself'.[98] It is not possible to meet the needs of citizens and communities, and achieve necessary environmental, social and economic changes in line with those needs, without some degree of involvement from affected people.

At this juncture and before embarking on consideration of the further benefits that citizen participation can bring to local sustainability, it seems prudent to acknowledge the discussion above relating to the importance of accountability in local sustainability. It has already been emphasised that Moncrieffe's notion of *ex-ante* accountability reflects the important role that the principle can play in enhancing decision-making relating to sustainability, ensuring that representatives communicate with citizens affected by their decisions and take account of their interests to ensure responsive decision-making.[99] Bearing in mind, then, that citizen participation is vital in terms of sustainability, providing as it does the means through which citizens can input their needs into the system, the meeting of the principle in this fashion serves to exemplify the conceptual discussion, earlier in the chapter, which concluded that accountability arises naturally as a result of participation.

In essence, application of accountability here shows, quite clearly, that decision-makers must take account of citizens' needs and interests in providing responsive decision-making, whilst citizen participation works to afford local people the opportunity to get those needs and interests recognised. In short, and in line with the statement by Onyx and Dalton quoted above, citizen participation in this way means that accountability can occur naturally, as citizens have been part of the decision-making process relating to local sustainability.[100]

In addition to the knowledge and expertise that citizens can bring to a decision-making process, there are also wider justifications for citizen participation in sustainability. Recalling that the need for greater citizen involvement can, in

97 S Baker, M Kousis, D Richardson and S Young (eds), *The Politics of Sustainable Development: Theory, Policy and Practice within the European Union* (London: Routledge, 1997) 23–24, who there cite: W Achterberg, 'Can Liberal Democracy Survive the Environmental Crisis? Sustainability, Liberal Neutrality and Overlapping Consensus' in A Dobson and P Lucardie (eds), *The Politics of Nature: Explorations in Green Political Theory* (London: Routledge, 1993) 81 at 82.

98 M Lee and C Abbot, 'The Usual Suspects? Public Participation under the Aarhus Convention' (2003) 66(1) *Modern Law Review* 80 at 83.

99 Moncrieffe (n 11) 27.

100 Onyx and Dalton (n 2) 15.

certain instances, stem from disenchantment with decision-makers and a lack of trust in a process, where there is a lack of trust in the decision-makers leading the regeneration and development of any given area, then it is vitally important that citizens have some input into the process to counter this. The achievement of sustainability involves a great many changes and sacrifices at the local level, especially by those who live and work there and who are likely to be most affected by such changes.[101] Citizens should not, consequently, leave the current and future well-being of their areas entirely in the hands of those whom they may, in some instances, distrust and with whom there could be general dissatisfaction. They themselves must have opportunities to participate in and have some input into the way in which their communities are changing. As Baker *et al.* argue, 'weaknesses in the legitimacy of the state and lack of trust in governments have fuelled popular demands for more . . . direct involvement in decisions',[102] which is echoed by Richardson and Razzaque: 'prevailing concerns . . . for "good governance" and the strengthening of civil societies have contributed to increasing interest in the use of participatory mechanisms'.[103] In those instances and in local areas where citizens are unsure of the process and perhaps disenchanted with decision-makers, citizen participation can serve to counter negative effects and ensure more appropriate and locally relevant sustainability.

The importance of citizen participation in local sustainability is further highlighted and supported by reference to the 'broken windows' theory, developed by criminologists Wilson and Kelling in the context of policing and neighbourhood safety.[104] They suggest that:

> [I]f a window in a building is broken and is left unrepaired, all the rest of the windows will soon be broken . . . [because] one unrepaired broken window is a signal that no one cares, and so breaking more windows costs nothing . . . Untended property becomes fair game for people out for fun or plunder . . . [and] . . . 'untended' behavior . . . leads to the breakdown of community controls. A stable neighborhood of families who care for their homes, mind each other's children, and confidently frown on unwanted intruders can change, in a few years or even a few months, to an inhospitable and frightening jungle. A piece of property is abandoned, weeds grow up, a window is smashed. Adults stop scolding rowdy children; the children, emboldened,

101 Sustainable development policies require changes to be made to the structure of the economy, industry, transport, agriculture and food production of a given area. See Baker *et al.* (n 97) 23.

102 Ibid. 24–5. Also see A Dobson, *Justice and the Environment* (Oxford: OUP, 1998), cited in Richardson and Razzaque (n 66) 167.

103 Richardson and Razzaque (n 66) 166, who there cite: M Pimbert and T Wakeford, 'Overview-Deliberative Democracy and Citizen Empowerment' (2001) 40 *PLA Notes* 24 <http://pubs.iied.org/pdfs/G01925.pdf> accessed 7 November 2013.

104 JQ Wilson and G Kelling, 'Broken Windows: The Police and Neighbourhood Safety' (1982) 249 *Atlantic Monthly* 29. Also see J Fionda, *Devils and Angels: Youth Policy and Crime* (Oxford: Hart Publishing, 2005) 236.

> become more rowdy . . . Fights occur. Litter accumulates . . . the neighborhood will cease to exist.[105]

Whilst not founded on issues relating to local sustainability in the context discussed here, there is at least scope to draw some parallels with this idea. Indeed, if a certain feature in a local community falls into disrepair, or there is a particular aspect of community life causing dissatisfaction and discontent amongst local people, then, without action being taken to rectify or address the situation, further disrepair and dissatisfaction will inevitably follow, leading to the community becoming deprived and lacking cohesion and development. If, however, repairs are initiated promptly and problems and issues addressed as soon as they arise, cohesion and development can grow from these actions and the community will continue to thrive, much in the same way that fixing that first broken window prevents further damage occurring. Citizen participation is crucial to this; just as 'a stable neighborhood [depends on] . . . families who care for their homes, mind each other's children, and confidently frown on unwanted intruders',[106] so a sustainable and well-developed community depends on a firm and ongoing commitment from citizens actively involved to ensure that their community is a pleasant and enjoyable place to live and work in, as Chapter 2 acknowledged.[107] In this way, therefore, citizen participation is crucial to ensuring local sustainability.

A final justification for citizen participation in the pursuit of sustainability derives from the growing importance with which people regard environmental issues and the resultant passionate desire to play a part in improving and sustaining the environment. Many members of the public have their own values and opinions on environmental issues. As Bosselmann notes, in respect of the 1992 Rio Conference:

> [T]he 'spirit of Rio' has motivated and activated people around the world. The idea of sustainability has inspired environmentalists, development experts, business people, unionists, church members and human rights activists as much as 'ordinary' citizens working within neighbourhoods, schools and community groups. The inspiration here has often been a practical desire for making a difference.[108]

Indeed, some members of the public view themselves as having a right to participate in decisions pertaining to environmental issues or, at the very least, a right to be consulted by those making decisions and policies affecting their environment. This is supported by Richardson and Razzaque who, citing Barton, suggest that 'the growth of human rights in legal and political systems has

105 Ibid. 32.
106 Ibid. 32.
107 See 'A model of local sustainability' section, p. 21 above.
108 K Bosselmann, 'Rio + 10: Any Closer to Sustainable Development?' (2002) 6 *New Zealand Journal of Environmental Law* 297 at 299.

heightened people's expectations of participation in policy-making'[109] and, therefore, has led to increased demands for involvement by the public in environmental decision-making, particularly in relation to sustainability.

As shown throughout this section, participation is not only an important principle of environmental decision-making; it is also an essential part of sustainable development. It ensures that local values, knowledge and expertise inform the decisions that give rise to development in local communities, and it serves to combat any lack of trust in the decision-making process that might, in some cases, have arisen. In addition, as consideration of 'broken windows' theory has demonstrated, citizen participation also helps to ensure the ongoing sustainability of changes and improvements, whilst an increasing public focus on environmental issues further justifies the role that individuals can play in guaranteeing a sustainable and environmentally sound future for their communities. Chapters 4 and 5 will demonstrate this over and above these conceptual considerations; for now, note that the 2005 Strategy for Sustainable Development states that 'people want to be able to have a say in, and make a . . . tangible contribution to the way their local area and services are managed'.[110] Consequently, at the heart of the Strategy's sustainable communities agenda is 'the drive to improve neighbourhood participation . . . and support delivery at the local level'.[111] In summary, therefore, and as Lee and Abbot note, 'a commitment to participation is embedded in the rhetoric of sustainable development itself'.[112]

Accountability and citizen participation, therefore, are fundamental to the achievement of local sustainability and can both be said, in their own way, to enhance the pursuit of its objectives. Whilst accountability is very much aligned with sustainability's focus on individual needs and desires, participation affords an opportunity not only to input these into a decision-making process but also to combat issues relating to any lack of trust that may exist in respect of decision-makers and to fuel an increasingly common desire for individual involvement in environmental development. In addition, and recalling discussions above, this section has set out to demonstrate in practice the manner in which accountability can be said to derive naturally from citizen participation.[113] Whilst accountability emphasises the need to take into account the interests of affected citizens, participation ensures that there are avenues through which these can be addressed responsively.

In demonstrating the importance of accountability and citizen participation to local sustainability, therefore, this chapter has laid the conceptual framework for Chapters 4 and 5 to evaluate examples of local governmental and community

109 B Barton, 'Underlying Concepts and Theoretical Issues in Public Participation in Resource Development' in DN Zillman, A Lucas and G Pring (eds), *Human Rights in Natural Resource Development: Public Participation in the Sustainable Development of Mining and Energy Resources* (Oxford: OUP, 2002) 77 at 81–3, cited in Richardson and Razzaque (n 66) 166.

110 The 2005 Strategy (n 81) 121.

111 Ibid. 120.

112 Lee and Abbot (n 98) 83.

113 Onyx and Dalton (n 2) 15.

efforts sustainably to develop local areas. Before this, however, there remains one outstanding consideration, as the final section now explores.

How much participation?

The chapter thus far has discussed at length the manner in which both accountability and local sustainability relate to the notion of citizen participation. Whilst this has been based on accepted definitions of accountability and sustainability, it is much more difficult to pin down one clear idea of what it means to participate in decision-making. To explain further, it has already been noted that representation involves the casting of votes in elections and the elected representatives governing and making decisions on the basis of the mandate given.[114] The model is fairly generic and variations are limited. The idea of citizen participation, however, is not so easily identifiable with one single process or method of practice. There are a number of ways in which people can participate in decision-making and varying degrees of involvement. This section seeks to consider these and does so on the basis of Arnstein's 'ladder of citizen participation'.[115] Figure 3.1 sets out the varying degrees of participation as a theoretical ladder, ranging from total manipulation at one end of the spectrum to total citizen control at the other.[116]

Arnstein states the theory as follows:

> The bottom rungs of the ladder are (1) Manipulation and (2) Therapy. These describe levels of 'non-participation' . . . Rungs 3 and 4 progress to levels of 'tokenism' that allow the 'have-nots' to hear and to have a voice: (3) Informing and (4) Consultation. . . . Rung (5) Placation is simply a higher level tokenism because the ground rules allow 'have-nots' to advise, but retain for the powerholders the continued right to decide . . . Further up the ladder are levels of citizen power . . . Citizens can enter into a (6) Partnership that enables them to negotiate and engage in trade-offs with traditional power holders. At the topmost rungs, (7) Delegated Power and (8) Citizen Control, 'have-not' citizens obtain the majority of decision-making seats, or full managerial power.[117]

114 See Barnett (n 47) 265.

115 Arnstein (n 65).

116 Ibid.

117 Ibid. 217. Morison provides something by way of an explanation of Arnstein's 'ladder of citizen participation', stating that: 'At the first stage there is cosmetic consultation where citizens may hear or be heard, although they lack the resources to ensure that their views will be taken into account. The ladder moves through various degrees of token consultation where the ground rules allow the consulted to advise but these rules retain, for those who hold the power, the right to decide. Further up the ladder citizen power begins to develop, with partnership at stage 6 encouraging negotiation and trade-offs between the consulted and decision takers. At stages 7 and 8 citizens have obtained full managerial control and participation is complete and real' (J Morison, 'Models of Democracy: From Representation to Participation?' in J Jowell and D Oliver (eds), *The Changing Constitution* (6th edn, Oxford: OUP, 2007) 134 at 154).

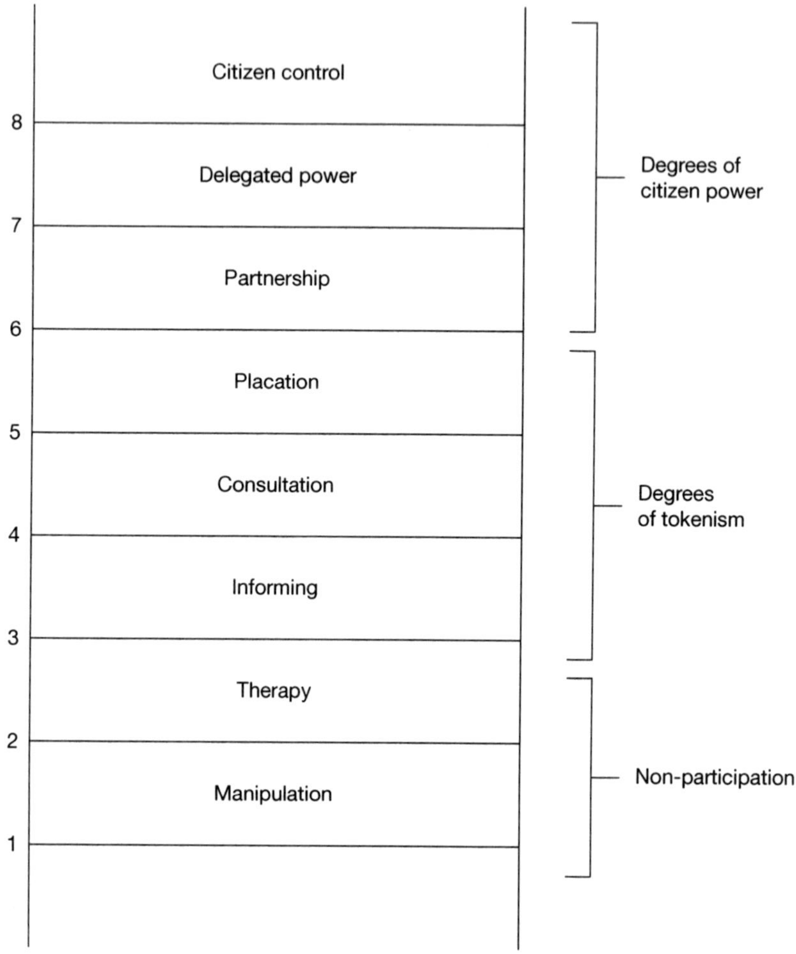

Figure 3.1 Arnstein's 'ladder of citizen participation'

Source: Reprinted by permission of the American Planning Association <http://www.planning.org>.

In terms of placing representation on the 'ladder of citizen participation', Arnstein's levels of informing and consultation most accurately reflect the extent to which citizens become involved in a decision-making process, ensuring that citizens have some form of a voice in the system, but not extending to them the authority to ensure that their views are heeded.[118] To explain, the periodic casting of votes and the occasional referendum enable the government to consult with citizens as to who should be in power and, at times, the way in which decisions and policies should be decided. In addition, wider mechanisms – such as the media and

118 Arnstein (n 65) 217.

public protests – ensure public opinion has suitable outlets. Aside from these opportunities, however, once a system of representation is in place following an election, it generally involves little more than informing citizens as to laws, policies and decisions. 'Informing' and 'consulting', therefore, best reflect the level of citizen involvement inherent within a basic representative system.

Using this as a starting point, then, it follows that where there is increased citizen participation in a decision-making system, this must exist at a level higher on the ladder – somewhere between placation and absolute citizen control. The top two rungs of the ladder, delegated power and citizen control, represent the highest possible degree of citizen participation and, essentially, give the people as much power as is democratically possible. Placation and partnership, however, ensure that decision-makers retain ultimate authority, whilst allowing active citizen involvement in the decision-making process, working alongside decision-makers and occasionally adopting certain roles and responsibilities within the process.

The argument here is that a hypothetical model based on total citizen control and 'maximum participation' would perhaps be a step too far. Leaving all power in the hands of citizens might, in extreme cases, render any system of organised government redundant because the people themselves would be making all the decisions and, essentially, running the process. Having so many personal views directing the course of decision-making could potentially lead to mass disorganisation, giving rise to a process that would be counter-productive in terms of democracy and successful decision-making. The number of people involved would mean that decision-making would be very difficult and resulting policies would fail to satisfy all the needs of all the people, leading to dissatisfaction and, in the absence of any organised and superior authority, a potential failure of the system. Indeed, when discussing more widely the advantages and disadvantages of citizen participation, Roberts echoes these concerns and notes that

> too much citizen participation heightens political conflict and is dysfunctional . . . Public sympathies are almost without exception incoherent, incompatible with one another, of variable consistency, and imprecise. The increased 'noise' in the system makes it hard for decision makers to respond . . . There is no guarantee that common interests and the welfare of the whole will be addressed or protected.[119]

On this basis, and recalling that citizen participation, as considered in this book, is built on the foundation of the UK's representative democracy, a democratic model, whilst encouraging citizen participation, should also maintain a 'minimal degree of representation'. This would mean that decision-makers could retain the

119 N Roberts, 'Public Deliberation in an Age of Direct Citizen Participation' (2004) 34(4) *American Review of Public Administration* 315 at 325. She there cites: JS Fishkin, *Democracy and Deliberation: New Directions for Democratic Reform* (New Haven, CT: Yale University Press, 1991) and MG Kweit and RW Kweit, *Implementing Citizen Participation in a Bureaucratic Society: A Contingency Approach* (New York: Praeger, 1981).

final say in the process, thus facilitating effective and organised decision-making at the same time as affording citizens an active and involving role in the system and providing a representative base on which the satisfaction of their needs and interests can be questioned and scrutinised. Indeed, as Harrison notes, 'creating a more participatory democracy requires a healthy representative democracy at [the] local level. If citizens can influence local decisions more effectively, and hold service providers to account, that can only be a good thing.'[120] Translating this onto Arnstein's 'ladder of citizen participation', the degree of participation most suitable for achieving accountability is placed on the rungs of placation and partnership. These ensure a minimal degree of representation, but also enable citizens to work alongside decision-makers and play an active part in the democratic process.

Placation and partnership can also be said to be the most suitable level of citizen participation on the basis of which to achieve local sustainability. Indeed, recalling the emphasis that sustainability places on meeting the needs of the people, relying on total citizen control could potentially lead not only to disorganised decision-making but also to difficulties in reconciling the views, needs and interests of all citizens with regard to the manner in which a local area should best be regenerated, potentially leading to dissatisfaction with the system and unsuccessful development of local areas. By contrast, and bearing in mind the words of Baker *et al.*, citing Achterberg, decisions relating to sustainability and the changes in lifestyle to which these give rise should not be imposed in an authoritarian way.[121] Consequently, it follows that a level of participation that facilitates negotiation, deliberation and the opportunity for active involvement is the most suitable with which to achieve objectives of local sustainability. Indeed, as Steele suggests, the 'most helpful models of participation for environmental law are those concerned . . . with . . . citizen deliberation'.[122]

This is reflected in Arnstein's notions of partnership and placation.[123] Indeed, recalling that placation suggests something of an advisory role for citizens whilst partnership represents the negotiation and trading-off of power,[124] these levels suggest that citizens' local knowledge and expertise can be valued in a decision-making process to the extent that they are advising and informing decision-makers through a process of deliberation and negotiation, and occasionally enjoying key roles or powers themselves. Translating this to a process pursuing sustainability, it would enable local people to voice their opinions, put forward their suggestions and desires to decision-makers and advise on local issues, perhaps through actively taking on a community or decision-making role themselves, as part of the wider process. It would, as Lee and Abbot suggest, ensure that, through the rational

120 A Harrison, 'Greater Scrutiny' *Solicitors Journal*, 22 January 2008, 12 at 13.

121 Baker *et al.* (n 97) 23–4.

122 J Steele, 'Participation and Deliberation in Environmental Law: Exploring a Problem-Solving Approach' (2001) 21(3) *Oxford Journal of Legal Studies* 415 at 417.

123 Arnstein (n 65) 217.

124 Ibid. 217.

debate of citizens, real democratic engagement and the curbing of selfish instincts, decisions could be made through reason and reflection rather than exogenous private preferences or interests.[125] As regards the achievement of local sustainability, therefore, placation and partnership, on Arnstein's ladder, best reflect the level of citizen participation that ensures citizens' needs and interests can be input into the system appropriately. At the same time, and in line with discussions above, placation and partnership would also ensure that decision-makers could retain the ultimate say, upholding, therefore, the 'minimal degree of representation' that would serve to maintain accountable, effective and organised decision-making.

This final section has provided a firmer understanding of what it means for citizens to participate in decision-making and the level of participation that is most conducive to accountability and effective sustainability. As will be explored in Chapters 4 and 5, it is important that such involvement takes place on a foundation of representation so as to ensure that citizens' views build upon an organised system. However, it is necessary at the same time to give individuals the appropriate means through which to voice their concerns and input their needs and interests into the process, and even actively to involve themselves in initiatives where such opportunities allow.

Concluding remarks

This chapter has explored the principles of accountability and citizen participation and has demonstrated the extent to which they relate to and enhance the achievement of local sustainability. It has explored the nature of the accountability principle and demonstrated the way in which it affords those citizens who can be said to have a legitimate right to accountability the opportunity to engage in dialogue with decision-makers, questioning and scrutinising their decisions and ensuring that they are in line with and responsive to the needs of citizens. Though it is a concept that has, in recent years, struggled to operate appropriately in the context of the UK's representative democracy, it is achieved with greater ease where there is increased citizen participation.[126] Indeed, not only does such participation afford individuals the opportunity actively to input their needs and interests into decision-making processes, thus ensuring appropriate and responsive decisions, but it also means that local knowledge and expertise can inform the process, giving local people valuable opportunities to play an active role in the regeneration of their community, rather than leaving it in the hands of those whom they elect periodically.

These two principles, therefore, complement the focus that local sustainability places on the needs of individuals and ensure opportunity not only for the scrutiny and examination of decisions, but also for the input of local needs and interests into the system. As a consequence, it can be said that local sustainability is enhanced

125 Lee and Abbot (n 98) at 85.
126 Onyx and Dalton (n 2) 15.

by adherence to accountability and the encouragement of citizen participation. They ensure that decision-makers can engage and work with local people to deliver the most suitable, relevant and appropriate improvements to local areas and to meet 'the needs of the present without compromising the ability of future generations to meet their own needs'.[127] Chapters 4 and 5 test and demonstrate the extent to which this has been the case in practice.

Bibliography

Achterberg, W, 'Can Liberal Democracy Survive the Environmental Crisis? Sustainability, Liberal Neutrality and Overlapping Consensus' in Dobson, A and Lucardie, P (eds), *The Politics of Nature: Explorations in Green Political Theory* (London: Routledge, 1993) 81.

Annan, K, 'Foreword' in S Stec and S Casey-Leftkowitz, *The Aarhus Convention: An Implementation Guide* (New York: UNECE, 2000).

Arnstein, S, 'A Ladder of Citizen Participation' (1967) 35(4) *Journal of American Institute of Planners* 216.

Baker, S, Kousis, M, Richardson, D and Young, S (eds), *The Politics of Sustainable Development: Theory, Policy and Practice within the European Union* (London: Routledge, 1997).

Barnett, H, *Britain Unwrapped: Government and Constitution Explained* (London: Penguin Books, 2002).

Barton, B, 'Underlying Concepts and Theoretical Issues in Public Participation in Resource Development' in Zillman, DN, Lucas, A and Pring, G (eds), *Human Rights in Natural Resource Development: Public Participation in the Sustainable Development of Mining and Energy Resources* (Oxford: OUP, 2002) 77.

Beetham, D, 'Liberal Democracy and the Limits of Democratization' in Held, D (ed.), *Prospects for Democracy: North, South, East, West* (Stanford, CA: Stanford University Press, 1993) 60.

Birch, AH, *Representative and Responsible Government: An Essay on the British Constitution* (Toronto: University of Toronto Press, 1964) 20.

Bosselmann, K, 'Rio + 10: Any Closer to Sustainable Development?' (2002) 6 *New Zealand Journal of Environmental Law* 297.

Chandler, JA, *Local Government Today* (4th edn, Manchester: Manchester University Press, 2009).

Cordonier Segger, MC and Khalfan, A, *Sustainable Development Law: Principles, Practices and Prospects* (Oxford: OUP, 2004).

Craig, PP, *Public Law and Democracy in the United Kingdom and the United States of America* (Oxford: Clarendon Press, 1990).

Davies, ACL, *Accountability: A Public Law Analysis of Government by Contract* (Oxford: OUP, 2001).

Day, P and Klein, R, *Accountabilities: Five Public Services* (London: Tavistock, 1987).

DEFRA, *Securing the Future: The UK Strategy for Sustainable Development*, Cm 6467 (London: HMSO, 2005), © Crown Copyright, contains public sector information licensed under the Open Government Licence v2.0 <http://www.nationalarchives.gov.uk/doc/open-government-licence/version/2/>.

127 Brundtland Report (n 75) 43.

Dobson, A, *Justice and the Environment* (Oxford: OUP, 1998).

Dunn, DD, 'Mixing Elected and Nonelected Officials in Democratic Policy Making: Fundamentals of Accountability and Responsibility' in Przeworski, A, Stokes, SC and Manin, B (eds), *Democracy, Accountability and Representation* (Cambridge: CUP, 1999) 297.

Farag, AS, 'Decentralization: Objectives, Forms and Implementation of Decentralized Governance' (2013) 11(1) *International Journal of Social Sciences* 138.

Fionda, J, *Devils and Angels: Youth Policy and Crime* (Oxford: Hart Publishing, 2005).

Fishkin, JS, *Democracy and Deliberation: New Directions for Democratic Reform* (New Haven, CT: Yale University Press, 1991).

Freeman, MDA, *Lloyd's Introduction to Jurisprudence* (8th edn, London: Sweet & Maxwell, 2008).

Friedmann, W, *Legal Theory* (5th edn, London: Stevens & Sons, 1967).

Gibson, PD, Lacy, DP and Dougherty, MJ, 'Improving Performance and Accountability in Local Government with Citizen Participation' (2005) 10(1) *Innovation Journal: The Public Sector Innovation Journal* 3.

Harrison, A, 'Greater Scrutiny' *Solicitors Journal*, 22 January 2008, 12.

Holder, J and Lee, M, *Environmental Protection, Law and Policy* (Cambridge: CUP, 2007).

International Law Association, Committee on Legal Aspects of Sustainable Development, *Fifth and Final Report: Searching for the Contours of International Law in the Field of Sustainable Development* (New Delhi, India, 2002).

Kerrison, S and Pollock, A, 'Complaints as Accountability? The Case of Health Care in the United Kingdom' (2001) *Public Law* 115.

King, A, *The British Constitution* (Oxford: OUP, 2007).

Kweit, MG and Kweit, RW, *Implementing Citizen Participation in a Bureaucratic Society: A Contingency Approach* (New York: Praeger, 1981).

Lee, M and Abbot, C, 'The Usual Suspects? Public Participation under the Aarhus Convention' (2003) 66(1) *Modern Law Review* 80.

Liddle, J, 'Challenges to Democratic Legitimacy, Scrutiny, Accountability in the UK National and Local State' (2007) 31(3/4) *Public Administration Quarterly* 397.

Lloyd-Bostock, S and Mulcahy, L, 'The Social Psychology of Making and Responding to Hospital Complaints: An Account Model of Complaint Processes' (1994) 16 *Law & Policy* 123.

Manin, B, Przeworski, A and Stokes, SC, 'Elections and Representation' in Przeworski, A, Stokes, SC and Manin, B (eds), *Democracy, Accountability and Representation* (Cambridge: CUP, 1999) 29.

Marshall, G, *Constitutional Conventions: The Rules and Forms of Political Accountability* (Oxford: OUP, 1984).

Moncrieffe, JM, 'Accountability: Idea, Ideals, Constraints' (2001) 8(3) *Democratization* 26.

Morison, J, 'Models of Democracy: From Representation to Participation?' in Jowell, J and Oliver, D (eds), *The Changing Constitution* (Oxford: OUP, 2007) 134.

Mulgan, R, 'Accountability: An Ever-Expanding Concept' (2000) 78(3) *Public Administration* 555.

Müller, WC and Meyer, TM, 'Meeting the Challenges of Representation and Accountability in Multi-party Governments' (2010) 33(5) *West European Politics* 1065.

Oliver, D, *Government in the United Kingdom: The Search for Accountability, Effectiveness and Citizenship* (Milton Keynes: Open University Press, 1991).

Oliver, D, *Constitutional Reform in the UK* (Oxford: OUP, 2003).

Oliver, D and Drewry, G, *Public Service Reforms: Issues of Accountability and Public Law* (London: Frances Pinter Publishers Ltd, 1996).

Onyx, J and Dalton, B, 'Accountability and Advocacy' (2006) 12(1) *Third Sector Review* 7.

Parr, J and Gates, CT, 'Assessing Community Interest and Gathering Community Support' in International City Management Association (ed.), *Partnerships in Local Governance: Effective Council-Manager Relations* (Washington, DC: International City Management Association, 1989).

Pimbert, M and Wakeford, T, 'Overview-Deliberative Democracy and Citizen Empowerment' (2001) 40 *PLA Notes* <http://pubs.iied.org/pdfs/G01925.pdf> accessed 7 November 2013.

Public Service Select Committee, 1st report, *Ministerial Accountability and Responsibility* (1996–7, HC 234).

Richardson, BJ and Razzaque, J, 'Public Participation in Environmental Decision-Making' in Richardson, BJ and Wood, S (eds), *Environmental Law for Sustainability* (Oxford: Hart Publishing, 2006) 165.

Roberts, N, 'Public Deliberation in an Age of Direct Citizen Participation' (2004) 34(4) *American Review of Public Administration* 315.

Seidman, GI, 'The Origins of Accountability: Everything I Know about the Sovereign's Immunity, I Learned from King Henry III' (2004–5) 49 *St Louis U.L.J.* 393.

Steele, J, 'Participation and Deliberation in Environmental Law: Exploring a Problem-Solving Approach' (2001) 21(3) *Oxford Journal of Legal Studies* 415.

Steffek, J and Ferretti, MP, 'Accountability or "Good Decisions"? The Competing Goals of Civil Society Participation in International Governance' (2009) 23(1) *Global Society* 37.

Stewart, J, 'Accountability', speech delivered at the 'Accountability to the Public Conference', Queen Elizabeth 2 Conference Centre, Westminster, London, 1992.

Uhr, J, 'Redesigning Accountability' (1993) 65 *Australian Quarterly* 1.

UN, *Agenda 21*, 1992, A/CONF.151/26, Vol. III, New York: UN. Made available by the UN Division for Sustainable Development at <http://sustainabledevelopment.un.org/content/documents/Agenda21.pdf> accessed 7 November 2013.

UN, *Rio Declaration on Environment and Development*, Annex 1 to the *Report of the United Nations Conference on Environment and Development*, Rio de Janeiro, 3–14 June 1992, A/CONF.151/26, Vol. I, New York: UN.

UN, *Johannesburg Declaration on Sustainable Development*, Annex to Resolution 1 of the *World Summit on Sustainable Development*, Johannesburg, 26 August–4 September 2002, A/CONF.199/20, New York: UN.

UN, *Johannesburg Plan of Implementation*, Annex to Resolution 2 of the *World Summit on Sustainable Development*, Johannesburg, 26 August–4 September 2002, A/CONF.199/20, New York: UN.

UNECE, *Convention on Access to Information, Public Participation in Decision-Making and Access to Justice in Environmental Matters*, 25 June 1998, Aarhus, Denmark.

Wilson, JQ and Kelling, G, 'Broken Windows: The Police and Neighbourhood Safety' (1982) 249 *Atlantic Monthly* 29.

World Commission on Environment and Development, *Our Common Future* (Oxford: OUP, 1987).

4 Local government democracy and sustainability

Introduction

'Local government is a unique and valuable institution. It is the only organisation subject to election . . . other than the national Parliament . . . [It] refers to the authorities . . . that . . . provide a range of specified services and represent the general interests of a specific area under the direction of a locally elected council.'[1] Through representing these interests, it is well placed to 'enable citizens to *participate* in [local] governance more readily and to a greater extent than would be possible if all governance occurred at a national level'.[2] Due to its unique position and potential capabilities, therefore, local government is well placed to tackle and deal with the challenges posed by urban deprivation in local areas. Indeed, as *Agenda 21* notes:

> [B]ecause so many of the problems and solutions being addressed by *Agenda 21* have their roots in local activities, the participation and cooperation of local authorities will be a determining factor in fulfilling its objectives . . . Through consultation and consensus-building, local authorities would learn from citizens . . . and acquire the information needed for formulating the best strategies.[3]

In view of this, it is the purpose of this chapter to explore the nature of local government in the UK and the role that it plays in achieving local sustainability. It seeks to test the hypothesis set out in Chapters 2 and 3 that accountability and citizen participation enhance the achievement of local sustainability. This is obviously dependent, however, on a strong democratic base defined by the decentralisation of power. This ensures that the appropriate accountability of decision-makers and the encouragement of citizen participation can be better

1 JA Chandler, *Local Government Today* (4th edn, Manchester: Manchester University Press, 2009) 1.

2 S Bailey and M Elliott, 'Taking Local Government Seriously: Democracy, Autonomy and the Constitution' (2009) 68(2) *Cambridge Law Journal* 436 at 438–9 (emphasis added).

3 UN, *Agenda 21*, 1992, A/CONF.151/26, Vol. III, New York: UN, para. 28.1. Made available by the UN Division for Sustainable Development at <http://sustainabledevelopment.un.org/content/documents/Agenda21.pdf> accessed 7 November 2013.

achieved. This chapter first explores the historical development of local government in the UK, looking back to its modern roots in the late nineteenth century, and then analyses more recent local governmental reform in greater detail, considering the extent to which it provides this strong democratic base for sustainability. In doing this, it identifies three prevalent themes in the reforms – strengthened local leadership, the decentralisation of power and the empowerment of citizens – and assesses the extent to which these accord with the principles of accountability and citizen participation as set out in Chapter 3. It argues that the reforms, on paper, promote local accountability and encourage citizen participation, but that challenges and issues have led to certain difficulties in realising their potential in practice. On this basis, and following application of the 'model of local sustainability' outlined in Chapter 2, the chapter concludes that recent local governmental reform shows the potential to enhance the achievement of sustainability at that level, but that, as Chapter 6 covers in greater detail, more needs to be done to realise the full potential of the reforms.

Modern local government and its development

The starting point is to explain the institution of local government and to set out its historical development. Being the only body, outside Parliament,[4] that is selected through a process of regular, democratic elections, 'local government is a vital part of our democracy. [Indeed], the vast majority of interactions between citizens and the state take place through local government.'[5] It represents an example of local autonomy and democracy, having the powers to make decisions that affect local people and the ability to consider and address issues that are prevalent within any given local society, such as sustainability.

The institution of local government refers to 'locally elected, non-legislative bodies which provide a range of local services and fulfil other local functions'[6] and, in its current form, can be said to derive from the Local Government Acts of 1888 and 1894.[7] These Acts secured the stability of local authorities and allowed central and local government to coexist happily, keeping their differences apart

4 Chandler (n 1) 1.

5 Tony Blair in the Foreword to DCLG, *Strong and Prosperous Communities: The Local Government White Paper* (White Paper, Cm 6939-I, 2006) 2, © Crown Copyright, contains public sector information licensed under the Open Government Licence v2.0 <http://www.nationalarchives.gov.uk/doc/open-government-licence/version/2/> ('2006 White Paper').

6 A Arden, C Baker and J Manning, *Local Government Constitutional and Administrative Law* (2nd edn, London: Sweet and Maxwell, 2008) para 1.2.1.

7 The constitutional position of local government in 1894 was made clear by Jenks, who stated that 'England is pre-eminently the country of local government'. E Jenks, *An Outline of English Local Government* (5th edn, London: Methuen, 1921) 9, cited in M Loughlin, 'The Demise of Local Government' in V Bogdanor (ed.), *The British Constitution in the 20th Century* (Oxford: OUP, 2004) 521 at 523. Loughlin also notes there that 'local institutions, reflecting historic communities and exercising a voice at the centre through the workings of the parliamentary system, were a central aspect of British constitutional arrangements' (523).

and ensuring that they kept well off each other's turf.[8] Indeed, as Wilson and Game note, from the 1890s there was 'a system of multi-functional, elected and genuinely local authorities . . . provid[ing] . . . major services to its citizens' and remaining 'substantially free from detailed central direction and intervention'.[9] Though a mere creature of statute, local government had numerous powers which it could exercise freely, within the boundaries drawn up by central government.[10] It enjoyed, as King notes, a relationship of collaborative coexistence with central government – 'by no means one of superordination and subordination . . . But, equally . . . not one that granted local authorities complete autonomy.'[11] The foundations of modern local government, therefore, are firmly rooted in its democratic and autonomous beginnings. Things soon changed, however, with this 'golden age' lasting only up until the mid-twentieth century,[12] as the next section seeks to illustrate.

Local government and the wave of centralisation

Since the mid-1960s, local government has been subjected to a great many changes and reforms which have resulted in it being stripped of many of the powers which it enjoyed in the aftermath of the 1888 and 1894 Acts. Proposals set out by the Herbert Commission in 1960[13] and the Redcliffe-Maud Commission in 1969,[14] some of which were enacted in the Local Government Act 1972,[15] instigated a rapid decline in local government autonomy, a huge reduction in local authority functions, a wave of widespread restructuring and a period of dynamic constitutional reform, giving rise to a huge centralisation of government power. Indeed, Loughlin states that 'the reforms . . . were not part of a programme of creating functionally effective units through which . . . centralisation could be

8 See A King, *The British Constitution* (Oxford: OUP, 2007) 155–6.

9 D Wilson and C Game, *Local Government in the United Kingdom* (5th edn, Basingstoke: Palgrave Macmillan, 2011) 59.

10 Despite being 'heavily constrained by national statute', local government enjoyed a fair amount of autonomy, and the leader of a council was 'the local man in charge' and could choose how to run the council and committees (King (n 8) 153).

11 Ibid. 155.

12 Wilson and Game (n 9) 59.

13 The Herbert Commission resulted in the enactment of the London Government Act 1963, which saw the abolition of the London County Council and the implementation of its replacement – the Greater London Council. This covered a wider area than its predecessor and included responsibilities in such matters as transport, main roads and fire protection. See further *Royal Commission on Local Government in Greater London*, Cmnd 1164 (London: HMSO, 1960) ('Herbert Report').

14 The Redcliffe-Maud Commission made proposals that were partly implemented by the Local Government Act 1972. It proposed the two-tier structure of county boroughs and district councils. See further *Royal Commission on Local Government in England*, Cmnd 4040 (London: HMSO, 1969) ('Redcliffe-Maud Report').

15 The 1972 Act's most notable reform was the widespread introduction of the two-tier system of local government (comprised of county and district councils), which was chosen in favour of the unitary authorities recommended in the Redcliffe-Maud Report. See further Loughlin (n 7) 534.

reversed . . . but part of the centralisation process itself'.[16] This continued into the 1980s, with the 'steady attrition of local authorities' powers'.[17] The Local Government Act 1985 abolished the Greater London Council and other metropolitan councils, which were labelled as 'a wasteful and unnecessary tier of government'.[18] The general attitude towards local government at that time was reflected in numerous ministerial statements. The then Secretary of State for the Environment, for example, noted that 'local government cannot be a fully independent power in the land. It traditionally derives its power from Parliament, and it must complement and not compete with central government and its activities.'[19] In addition, the Prime Minister herself was said not to have had much time for local councils,[20] whilst other ministers saw local government as 'wasteful, profligate, irresponsible, unaccountable, luxurious and out of control'.[21]

The early 1990s brought further change, with the enactment of the Local Government Act 1992. This established the Local Government Commission, which was given the unwelcome task[22] of reviewing possible alternatives to the two-tier structure of local government which, since its widespread introduction in 1972, had been heavily criticised and was deemed to be hugely unsatisfactory.[23] Though the Commission returned four years later with the proposal for a new unitary structure of local government,[24] in the end only 46 unitary authorities were created,[25] meaning that the two-tier structure remained in certain areas, alongside the unitary authorities elsewhere, giving rise to something of a hybrid system of local government.[26]

16 M Loughlin, *Local Government in the Modern State* (London: Sweet and Maxwell, 1986) 9.

17 S Jenkins, 'Accountable to None' (1996) 16(2) *Public Money & Management* 3 at 3.

18 See Conservative Party, *1983 Conservative Party General Election Manifesto* <http://www.conservative-party.net/manifestos/1983/1983-conservative-manifesto.shtml> accessed 9 November 2013.

19 See HC Deb 21 March 1991, vol 188, col 401.

20 Wilson and Game (n 9) 64. They there cite: K Baker, *The Turbulent Years: My Life in Politics* (London: Faber & Faber, 1993) 111.

21 K Newton and T Karran, *The Politics of Local Expenditure* (London: Macmillan, 1985) 116, cited in ibid. 64.

22 See DJ Wilson, 'The Local Government Commission: Examining the Consultative Process' (1996) 74 *Public Administration* 199. Wilson there notes the extent to which the review of English local government was 'heavily criticized by academics, practitioners and politicians' (199).

23 See DoE, *Local Government Review: The Structure of Local Government in England. A Consultation Paper* (London: DoE, 1993), cited in K Parry and J Roll, House of Commons Library, *Local Government and Public Involvement in Health Bill*, 10 January 2007, Research Paper 07/01 at 14. In relation to the Consultation Paper, Michael Heseltine stated that 'two tiers may lead to excessive bureaucracy and duplication of effort' (HC Deb 23 April 1991, vol 189, col 901, cited in Parry and Roll).

24 First recommended in the Redcliffe-Maud Report (n 14) but rejected in favour of the two-tier approach. See King (n 8) 158.

25 King (n 8) notes the extent to which the public were content with the status quo (158).

26 See ibid. 158–9. Also see Wilson (n 22) who uses the term 'hybrid' in respect of Leicestershire's proposed mixture of unitary and two-tier authorities (201).

The period from the 1960s until the late 1990s, therefore, was 'a period of great turbulence in local government'.[27] It brought huge restructuring of the system, a steady centralisation of power and a consequent reduction of local authority functions. As a result, whilst the reforms set out initially to improve the quality of local democracy in the UK, if anything the reverse happened.[28] Indeed, recalling the strong democratic base that has already been identified as being crucial to ensuring that accountable leadership and citizen participation can enhance the achievement of local sustainability, it is safe to assume that the state of local government thus explained would be insufficient. Change was needed not only to improve the health of local democracy, but also to ensure that local government could fulfil its potential roles and capabilities, as previously identified in respect of local sustainability.

Local government under New Labour: a turning tide?

Efforts to secure such change came aplenty during the 13 years of Labour's government, as this section now discusses. It identifies the key proposals and enactments that were introduced and analyses the underlying governmental attitude in which these changes were rooted. This lays the foundation for the chapter later to consider key themes within these reforms in more detail and to evaluate the extent to which they ensured the accountability and encouraged the citizen participation necessary for, *inter alia*, the achievement of local sustainability.

During their first term in government, starting in 1997, Labour showed good initial intentions to reform local government and to restore some of the democracy and autonomy that had typified its existence half a century previously. They published two White Papers within the first year – *A Mayor and Assembly for London*[29] and *Modern Local Government – In Touch with the People*.[30] The first of these proposed the creation of a Greater London Authority, filling the democratic deficit left by the abolition of the Greater London Council 15 years earlier, a proposal that was enacted by the Greater London Authority Act 1999.[31] The second White Paper, 'welcomed by the Local Government Association as a move away from "a centralised and over-prescriptive approach"',[32] proposed

27 Ibid. 160.

28 Ibid. 160.

29 DETR, *A Mayor and Assembly for London* (White Paper, Cm 3897, 1998).

30 DETR, *Modern Local Government – In Touch with the People* (White Paper, Cm 4014, 1998).

31 The Greater London Authority (GLA) is made up of a directly elected Mayor of London and a London Assembly. The 1999 Act also created four functional bodies, which are all answerable to the GLA, and which carry out a number of functions to help achieve the key aims and objectives of London's regional government. (These are: the London Development Agency; Transport for London; the Metropolitan Police Authority; and the London Fire and Emergency Planning Authority.) See further B Pimlott and N Rao, *Governing London* (Oxford: OUP, 2002).

32 JS Davies, 'Double-Devolution or Double-Dealing? The Local Government White Paper and the Lyons Review' (2008) 34(1) *Local Government Studies* 3 at 3, there citing: <http://www.local.gov.uk/blg/lgcommentary.htm> accessed 5 April 2007.

giving local authorities responsibility for the well-being and sustainable development of their areas.[33] The Local Government Act 2000 enacted this proposal and consequently provided that every local authority could have the power to do anything they considered likely to achieve the promotion or improvement of the environmental, economic and social well-being of a particular area,[34] language consistent with the principle of sustainable development and a provision underlining the vital role that local authorities could play in pursuing sustainability. In addition, the 2000 Act also required councils to move to an executive-based system, recommending one of three proposed models whereby the governing power is vested in either a council leader, with a cabinet as an executive authority, or a directly elected mayor with a cabinet made up of local councillors or a council manager.[35] From the early days of New Labour's government, therefore, there was evidently a changed attitude towards local authorities compared with that which had been prevalent 15 or so years previously.[36] Indeed, Lowndes notes that, 'in contrast to the Conservatives' attempted "managerialisation" of local politics, Labour sees local democracy as the normative *raison d'être* for local government',[37] which is evident in the reforms proposed and enacted during their first term. These demonstrate a motivation to organise local authorities more democratically and to empower them with greater autonomy.

On the face of it, the initial effects of this changed attitude gathered momentum in Labour's second term, with the then Secretary of State for Transport, Local Government and the Regions, Stephen Byers, promising to tackle 'excessive central prescription and interference', taking a 'pronounced step away from centralisation'.[38] It was suggested, however, that the White Paper which carried these promises was a mere reiteration of pledges made in 1997 and an acknowledgement that the centralising trends of the Conservative era had persisted.[39]

The government tried again, and in 2006 published the Local Government White Paper *Strong and Prosperous Communities*.[40] Seeking to take an altogether more significant step towards local democratic reinvigoration than its predecessors, this White Paper was 'proclaimed . . . [to be the] third new dawn for localism',[41] with the then Secretary of State for Communities and Local Government, Ruth Kelly, stating in the White Paper itself that 'we must have the courage at the centre to let go. The challenges we face are too complex, the needs often too local, for all

33 *Modern Local Government – In Touch with the People* (n 30) Chapter 8.

34 Local Government Act 2000, s 2 (recall, though, that this provision was repealed by the Localism Act 2011, s 1, and replaced with a 'general power of competence').

35 Ibid. s 31.

36 See n 19, n 20 and n 21 above.

37 V Lowndes, 'Rescuing Aunt Sally: Taking Institutional Theory Seriously in Urban Politics' (2001) 38(11) *Urban Studies* 1953 at 1966, cited in Davies (n 32) 4.

38 DTLGR, *Byers Sets out Vision for Stronger Local Government with New Freedoms to Deliver Better Quality Services*, 11 December 2001, News Release 2001/0535, cited in Davies (n 32) 4.

39 Davies (n 32) 4.

40 The 2006 White Paper (n 5).

41 Davies (n 32) 4.

solutions to be imposed from the centre . . . people no longer accept the "one size fits all" service models of old.'[42] Indeed, this was supported further by Gordon Brown, who noted in September 2006 that '[i]t is right that local councils, not Whitehall, should have more power over things that matter to their community and from economic regeneration to public transport, the empowerment and strengthening of local councils and local communities is what we must now do.'[43]

Labour's third attempt at local democratic reinvigoration, therefore, was published amidst a range of promises to decentralise and empower; it displayed a marked attempt to look forward rather than simply to acknowledge the transgressions of those who had gone before. Its provisions were far-reaching and focused, in particular, on the improvement of local leadership and community cohesion, proposing reforms to improve the responsiveness of local services, to empower local citizens and to strengthen local leadership – making it more accountable, effective and responsive to local issues.[44] It saw local authorities as 'place shapers' and strategic leaders and set out a performance framework within which it could partner other organisations to improve local public services.[45] As the White Paper itself concludes,

> [it] puts in place systemic reforms that will help . . . local areas to . . . meet the standards of the best . . . [giving] communities a bigger say in the things that matter to them. The reforms . . . empower citizens and communities; create stronger and more visible leadership; and put in place a new framework within which local authorities and their partners can work.[46]

Though notable in terms of length, and the breadth of its promise to reinvigorate the state of local democracy, it was not really felt that it had had the impact that was initially forecast. As Davies noted, in the White Paper's aftermath 'there has been no paradigm shift in central–local relations . . . this White Paper does not signify a political renaissance for local government or indeed for "localism"'.[47] That being true, it was undeniably significant not only in recognising an altered commitment to local democratic reinvigoration than that which had been evident 20 years previously, but also in bringing to issue forms of decentralisation that had perhaps been forgotten and bringing to light options to empower that had not previously been explored.[48]

42 The 2006 White Paper (n 5) 4.

43 See Local Government Association, 'Prosperous Communities: Beyond the White Paper', *Local Government Association*, 7 June 2006, 3 <http://www.local.gov.uk/publications/-/journal_content/56/10180/3367441/PUBLICATION> accessed 11 November 2013.

44 The 2006 White Paper (n 5) 7–13.

45 Ibid. 10.

46 Ibid. 13.

47 Davies (n 32) 7. He there cites: G Stoker, *Transforming Local Governance: From Thatcherism to New Labour* (Basingstoke: Palgrave, 2004) and G Stoker, *What Is Local Government For?* (London: New Local Government Network, 2005).

48 The White Paper proposed, for example, significant changes in respect of parish councils, a level of local government that had not seen such focus for many years.

The motivation underlying these promises to decentralise and empower bore fruit just a year later in the form of the Local Government and Public Involvement in Health Act 2007.[49] This saw the enactment of many reforms proposed and considered in 2006. In particular, it laid the foundations for the potential introduction of widespread unitary authorities across the UK. It also made changes to both the electoral process and the executive arrangements of local authorities and strengthened the role that parish councils could play at the local community level, providing for their wider introduction and extending to them the 'well-being power' introduced by the Local Government Act 2000. Though this chapter later goes on to address key aspects of these reforms and to consider the manner in which they were successful in practice in terms of their achievement of accountability and encouragement of citizen participation, it is worth noting here that the Act did much to facilitate the decentralisation of power to the local level and to encourage those there to use these powers.[50]

Simultaneously with the LGPIHA's journey through Parliament, Gordon Brown's new government was publishing the *Governance of Britain* Green Paper.[51] Though covering a range of issues besides local government, its provisions, *inter alia*, proposed fundamental improvements to the accountability and the democracy of local authorities. Indeed, in the foreword, Gordon Brown stated that '[w]e want . . . a new constitutional settlement – a settlement that entrusts . . . people with more power. The proposals published in this Green Paper seek to address two fundamental questions: how should we hold power accountable, and how should we uphold and enhance the rights and responsibilities of the citizen?'[52] In particular, the Green Paper looked at a number of ways in which direct democracy could be put to better use,[53] to re-invigorate UK democracy and ensure that decisions can be made as close as possible to the people they affect and are responsive to the needs of local communities.[54] Indeed, the Green Paper stated that 'the Government is committed to finding new ways for citizens and communities to influence decisions . . . [to] participate in the political process . . . and . . . influence the decisions that affect their lives'.[55] Though of little impact and significance now, the 2007 Green Paper further demonstrated the government's commitment to improving local accountability and to decentralising power to a more local level, empowering citizens to participate in local democracy.

A year later, in 2008, a White Paper entitled *Communities in Control: Real People, Real Power* was published.[56] Using the 2007 Green Paper as a foundation,

49 Hereinafter LGPIHA.

50 See J Stanton, 'Local Democracy, Economic Development and Construction Act 2009: A reinvigorated local democracy?' (2011) *Public Law* 1 at 2.

51 Ministry of Justice, *Governance of Britain*, Cm 7170 (London: HMSO, 2007).

52 Ibid. 5.

53 Ibid. 40–52.

54 Ibid. para. 128.

55 Ibid. para. 128.

56 DCLG, *Communities in Control: Real People, Real Power* (White Paper, Cm 7427, 2008), © Crown Copyright, contains public sector information licensed under the Open Government Licence

it proposed reforms that sought to further the powers of local government, increase decentralisation and create further opportunities for citizen participation. Indeed, it stated the intention 'to pass power . . . [to] local communities . . . to generate vibrant local democracy in every part of the country, and to give real control over local decisions and services to a wider pool of active citizens'.[57] In seeking to achieve this, it proposed the imposition of a duty on local councils to promote democracy through ensuring greater clarity and transparency and encouraging wider participation amongst citizens, and a broad duty to involve, enabling citizens to participate in local politics and have greater opportunities to influence the decision-making processes by which they are affected.[58] Like the 2006 White Paper before it, *Communities in Control* reflected a clear motivation to re-invigorate local democracy, proposing to decentralise power to the local level and empower those at the receiving end. As the then Prime Minister Gordon Brown emphasised at the time, 'there are many challenges that cannot be met by central government acting alone – and to address those challenges effectively, we need to harness the energy and innovation of . . . local government, citizens and communities'.[59] He went on to state that the White Paper built upon the aims and objectives of the *Governance of Britain* Green Paper and moved to the next stage in the process by 'enhancing the power of communities and helping people up and down the country set and meet their own priorities. In this way [it] strengthen[s] local democracy by increasing participation.'[60]

This commitment to local democracy and some of the proposals set out in the 2008 White Paper were evident in the Local Democracy, Economic Development and Construction Act 2009.[61] In particular, the Act introduced the imposition of duties relating to the promotion of democracy and the encouragement of citizen involvement, as set out in the White Paper, and introduced provisions for the holding of local petitions and changes to the governance and electoral arrangements of local authorities. Though, as with the 2007 Act, many of these reforms have since been repealed, their significance lies in the extent to which they demonstrate New Labour's wider commitment to the decentralisation of power and the empowerment of local bodies and people to participate in local politics. Indeed, as Stanton notes, the LDEDCA 'represents . . . improved local accountability and increased citizen participation . . . [thus] signify[ing] the reinvigoration of local government and local democracy'.[62]

This section has sought to outline the nature of Labour's local governmental and democratic reforms. Whilst leaving it to later sections to go into greater detail in

v2.0 <http://www.nationalarchives.gov.uk/doc/open-government-licence/version/2/> ('2008 White Paper').

57 Ibid. 1.

58 Ibid. 2.

59 Ibid. i.

60 Ibid. i.

61 Hereinafter LDEDCA.

62 Stanton (n 50) 8.

respect of certain reforms, and there to analyse the extent to which they achieve accountability and encourage citizen participation, Labour's motivation to decentralise to the local level and empower local authorities and individuals is clear to see, with changed attitudes from those that were evident in the mid-1980s helping to put in place reforms attuned with the reinvigoration of local democracy. Indeed, Labour's approach is suitably summed up by Hazel Blears:

> [T]here are few issues so complex, few problems so knotty, that they cannot be tackled and solved by the innate common sense and genius of local people . . . [It] should be the hallmark of the modern state: devolved, decentralised, with power diffused throughout . . . society . . . People should have the maximum influence . . . over the decisions . . . which shape their lives.[63]

The extent to which this was the case in practice will become evident later in the chapter. For now, however, it is necessary to explore more recent local governmental reforms, as set out by the Coalition government, to examine the extent to which they continued this trend.

Local government and the Coalition government: the Big Society and the Localism Act

In May 2010, the General Election produced, for the first time since 1974,[64] a hung parliament. The Labour Party that had been in government for 13 years was replaced by a Conservative–Liberal Democrat Coalition government. From its early days, this was committed to the 'radical devolution of power to [the] local level, [and the] giving [of] new powers and opportunities to councils, communities, neighbourhoods and individuals'.[65] In terms of local governmental and democratic reform, this brought to the fore, *inter alia*, the Big Society – a policy that had become a pillar of the Conservative Party manifesto during their period in opposition and in the run up to the election. In terms of what the Big Society represented, David Cameron noted in 2009 his desire to create:

> [A] transition 'from Big Government to Big Society' – taking power, responsibility and decision making from the state and giving it to individuals, neighbourhoods, or 'the lowest possible tier of government'. Such ambitions are perhaps more traditionally described as decentralisation or devolution, and also find expression with the new administration in the term 'localism'.[66]

63 The 2008 White Paper (n 56) iii.

64 See V Bogadnor, *The Coalition and the Constitution* (Oxford: Hart Publishing, 2011) xi and generally.

65 Communities and Local Government Committee, *Localism* (HC 2010–2012, 547-I) 3.

66 K Evans, '"Big Society" in the UK: A Policy Review' (2011) 25 *Children and Society* 164 at 164.

It was, on the face of it, a reformulation of policies and promises that had been introduced and suggested during Labour's time in government, though the finer details and the manner in which the Coalition set out to achieve such objectives differed in key respects, as will be explored later. Nonetheless, it represents a fundamental commitment to ensuring that there is the promotion of decentralisation, increased empowerment of communities and greater encouragement of local participation.[67] Indeed, as the Coalition's Deputy Prime Minister, Nick Clegg, noted, there is

> a new approach from government, ending the culture of Whitehall knows best. We are looking across the board at how we can hand power back to people . . . For too long government has talked about this but failed to deliver . . . Our aim is powerful local communities, working with government, allowing the whole country to thrive.[68]

On this basis, the government's short White Paper entitled *Local Growth: Realising Every Place's Potential* (2010) built upon a foundation of subsidiarity[69] and recognised the value of local decision-making, pledging to 'shift power to local communities'.[70] Indeed, it stressed that every locality is unique and is best placed to understand local issues affecting their development.[71] Whilst predominantly centred around a focus on local business growth and prosperity, this White Paper nonetheless demonstrated an enthusiasm on the part of central government to foster local input and to ensure that communities themselves can drive forward local development.

The most significant development of the Big Society policy, however, was the enactment of the Localism Act 2011. A lengthy and complex piece of legislation, it covered a range of local issues.[72] Most notably, it repealed, in schedule 1, the 'well-being power' introduced in the Local Government Act 2000 and replaced it, in s 1, with a welcome 'general power of competence',[73] intended to be broader and to give local authorities the power to do anything an individual can do.[74] Though it repealed the duty to promote democracy and the provisions relating to

67 Cabinet Office, *Building the Big Society*, 18 May 2010, London: Cabinet Office <https://www.gov.uk/government/uploads/system/uploads/attachment_data/file/78979/building-big-society_0.pdf> accessed 10 November 2013.

68 DBIS, *Local Growth: Realising Every Place's Potential* (White Paper, Cm 7961) (London: HMSO, 2010) ('2010 White Paper').

69 See Chapter 2 (n 18) and Consolidated Version of the Treaty on European Union [2012] OJ C326/15, Article 5(3). The White Paper stated that '[d]ecision-making and delivery mechanisms should operate at the most appropriate geographical levels' (ibid. para. 2.1).

70 The 2010 White Paper (n 68) 5.

71 Ibid. para. 1.19.

72 A Layard, 'The Localism Act 2011: What Is "Local" And How Do We (Legally) Construct It?' (2012) 14(2) *Environmental Law Review* 134 at 134.

73 See N Dobson, 'General Competence to Restore *Vires* Confidence?' (24 March 2010) 107(12) *Law Society Gazette* 18 at 18.

74 Localism Act 2011, s 1.

the holding of local authority petitions, brought in by the LDEDCA, it sought to further local democratic engagement and empowerment by way of certain community rights and powers, including a 'community right to challenge' and a 'community right to build'. It also enabled ministers to devolve public services from centralised government to local authorities,[75] and, with a particular focus on planning and community development, it empowered 'communities to make neighbourhood plans and neighbourhood developments orders',[76] as Chapter 5 will go on to discuss. The Localism Act, therefore, is an important piece of legislation, and one that potentially has a key role to play in determining local governmental and community authority. Continuing the trend started by New Labour, it sets out extensive decentralising powers and makes provision for the broad empowerment of local people, communities and authorities, though the extent to which these are starting to work in practice will be considered later, with a particular focus there on the achievement of accountability and the encouragement of citizen participation.

This big section has explored the development of local government since the late nineteenth century and outlined various policies, proposals, reforms and promises that have – since New Labour came to government in 1997 – continued to shape the powers of local government and the strength of local democracy more widely. Strong leadership, the decentralisation of power and the empowerment of local citizens and people are constantly recurring themes here, and underline the constant objectives on which recent successive governments have focused to reinvigorate local democracy in the UK. These provide a framework for the next section to consider accountability and citizen participation in light of this recent local governmental reform, thus providing a foundation for the chapter later to consider the extent to which the achievement of local sustainability has been enhanced as a result.

Accountability and citizen participation in local government

Chapter 3 identified the concept of accountability, defining it both in terms of what it signifies and in respect of wider features and distinctions. In particular, it explored the relationship between accountability, representation and citizen participation, and considered that 'where there is a strong culture of participation, then accountability will occur naturally'.[77] The reasoning behind this is that a culture of participation can give rise to greater mechanisms for accountability, ensure responsive and relevant decision-making and mean that citizens can, more easily, question and scrutinise the process as they will have had the opportunity

75 DCLG, *A Plain English Guide to the Localism Act*, 15 November 2011, London: DCLG <https://www.gov.uk/government/uploads/system/uploads/attachment_data/file/5959/1896534.pdf> accessed 10 November 2013.

76 A Layard, 'Law and Localism: The Case of Multiple Occupancy Housing' (2012) 32(4) *Legal Studies* 551 at 557.

77 J Onyx and B Dalton, 'Accountability and Advocacy' (2006) 12(1) *Third Sector Review* 7 at 15.

to be a part of it. With this in mind, this section considers the three key and relevant themes of recent local governmental reform in the UK, as identified above. It explains the manner in which local governmental reform creates strong local leadership, facilitates the decentralisation of power and empowers citizens and, as a result, can be said to achieve accountability and citizen participation at the local level.

Strong leadership

Strong local leadership is at the very core of accountability. Without a clearly identifiable, strong local leader, the principle would fail to operate effectively as there would be no clear person or body 'to suffer the consequences, take the blame or undertake to put matters right if it should appear that errors have been made',[78] or to explain, justify and answer for errors in decision-making.[79] Indeed, this need is evident from Moncrieffe's suggestion that accountability refers to the notion of holding public officials accountable and the need for such officials to act effectively and in the best interests of the community and its citizens.[80] Without such officials in prominent and strong leadership positions, the system would lack clarity and transparency of process and citizens would not know whom to hold to account. Indeed, and bearing in mind the increased decentralisation of power that is later considered, the 2006 White Paper notes that it is a clear, overriding principle that the greater the powers being devolved, then the greater the premium on clear, transparent and accountable leadership.[81] Strong local leadership, therefore, is essential not only to achieving local accountability but, more widely, also to ensuring the appropriate exercise of powers decentralised for the benefit of local areas.

With this in mind, it is hardly surprising that 'the main thrust of Labour thinking on local government reform was to strengthen leadership at the local level'.[82] Indeed, it was a theme running through the 2006 White Paper's proposals and the LGPIHA's provisions,[83] the reforms there considering the need for an enhanced role for councils as strategic leaders and place-shapers for communities, and emphasising that local councillors acting as champions for their communities is an idea at the heart of our democracy.[84] This was only the beginning, however, with the prioritisation of strong local leadership growing in prominence over the

78 See D Oliver, *Constitutional Reform in the UK* (Oxford: OUP, 2003) 48.

79 See R Mulgan, 'Accountability: An Ever-Expanding Concept' (2000) 78(3) *Public Administration* 555 at 569.

80 JM Moncrieffe, 'Accountability: Idea, Ideals, Constraints' (2001) 8(3) *Democratization* 26 at 27.

81 The 2006 White Paper (n 5) para. 4.10.

82 V Bogdanor, *The New British Constitution* (Oxford: Hart Publishing, 2009) 259.

83 See the 2006 White Paper (n 5) chapters 3 and 5, and further LGPIHA, s 62.

84 Ibid. chapter 5 generally and also paras. 3.10–3.12. Also see M Purdue, 'Current Topics (February): The Local Government White Paper and Planning' (2007) *Journal of Planning and Environmental Law* 157 at 162.

following years, and further developments seeking to build on the initial intentions of the Labour government, as this section now goes on to illustrate.

Changes to executive arrangements have perhaps been most significant in this regard, with Harrison noting, with respect to the LGPIHA, the extent to which they focus on the 'strengthen[ing of] local leadership by making it more visible and effective'.[85] The Local Government Act 2000 set out in detail the possible arrangements available to local authorities and, since then, further provisions have made changes to these and worked to refine the models within which local authorities can operate most effectively and democratically. Indeed, building on the provisions of the 2000 Act, Part 3 of the LGPIHA adds that councils are required to adopt models made up of either an executive leader and cabinet executive or a directly elected mayor and cabinet executive,[86] whilst the Localism Act 2011 also gives options to major cities in the UK to hold referenda to decide on the implementation of directly elected mayors.[87]

Whilst either an executive leader or a directly elected mayor would fulfil the role of a clearly identifiable leader, it is felt that directly elected mayors bring a valuable democratic advantage over executive leaders in that they are chosen by the electorate rather than by the council itself. As Larsen notes, 'it seems . . . a reasonable assumption that a mayor elected directly by the citizens could enjoy and would make claims to a different and stronger legitimacy than one indirectly elected by the councillors'.[88] Indeed, in terms of the effect this has with regard to local power, the government itself notes that 'elected mayors can provide democratically accountable strong leadership . . . [and are] able to instigate real change'.[89] The ability to instigate such change was enhanced, in this instance, by the government's promise to 'give these new mayors "significant clout"' and, potentially, 'authority over all public services delivered locally'.[90]

The democratic benefits, therefore, are clear to see. Directly elected mayors can not only provide the strength of leadership necessary to bring change to a local area but also, through their clear position and direct answerability to those citizens who elected them, they can be clearly accountable to local people. Despite this, however, in reality, directly elected mayors have not been widely introduced in the UK. There are only 15 across England and Wales, and whilst the option set out in the Localism Act 2011 to hold mayoral referenda was widely taken up, it resulted in overwhelming rejection.[91]

85 A Harrison, 'The Cult of Cabinet', 29 January 2008, *Solicitors Journal* 12 at 13.

86 Explanatory Notes to the LGPIHA, para. 155.

87 Localism Act 2011, Sch 2, Pt 1, which inserts a new s 1A to the Local Government Act 2000, making provision for the introduction of these mayors.

88 HO Larsen, 'Directly Elected Mayors – Democratic Renewal or Constitutional Confusion?' in J Caulfield and HO Larsen (eds) *Local Government at the Millennium* (Wiesbaden: Springer Fachmedien Wiesbaden, 2002) 111 at 113.

89 *A Plain English Guide to the Localism Act* (n 75).

90 R Hambleton, 'A Jekyll and Hyde Localism Bill?' (2011) 80(1) *Town and Country Planning* 15 at 17.

91 There were initially 16; see generally M Sandford, House of Commons Library, *Directly Elected Mayors* (Standard Note SN/PC/5000, 16 July 2013).

Recent legislation shows, therefore, that local authorities have limited options when it comes to selecting executive arrangements and are very much restricted by higher government policy – something which is arguably indicative of wider local governmental and democratic reform, as this chapter later goes on to discuss. Nonetheless, through having the opportunity to select a directly elected mayor or an executive leader, local authorities are at least able to ensure that a single, clearly identifiable leader can be at the helm of local decision- and policy-making, thus creating strong local leadership and local accountability. Indeed, this is reflected by Fenwick and Elcock, who note that earlier reforms focusing on directly elected mayors were part of 'a New Labour culture where strong individual leadership . . . replaced old-style collectivism'.[92] In the form of the Localism Act, the Coalition government has sought to continue this culture.

Another reform relating to the structure of local government that has, in recent years, affected the clarity and strength of local leadership relates to the creation of unitary authorities. It was noted above that plans to introduce single-tier local government in the UK were first discussed in the Redcliffe-Maud Commission's Report in 1969.[93] However, it was not until the early 1990s and the Local Government Commission's consideration of the two-tier structure introduced in 1972 that their widespread adoption was considered. Though only 46 unitary authorities were then introduced,[94] the Labour government legislated in 2007 to empower the Secretary of State to invite certain areas to move from two-tier local government to unitary status.[95] As a result, there are now 77 unitary authorities across England and Wales.[96] Indeed, with regard to continuing previous and sporadic development and introduction of unitary authorities, Wilson and Game note that Labour appeared very much of the view that 'bigger . . . means more efficient and therefore better'.[97]

However, the Coalition government's attitude towards single-tier government is reflected in the swiftly enacted Local Government Act 2010, which provided that 'no further relevant order may be made under section 7 of the [LGPIHA] . . . (power to implement proposals for a single tier of local government for an area)'.[98]

92 J Fenwick and H Elcock, 'New Development: The Elected Mayor and Local Leadership' (2005) 25(1) *Public Money and Management* 61 at 61.

93 See King (n 8) 158 and n 24 above.

94 See Wilson and Game (n 9) 69. They there note that the public were not convinced about the prospect of unitary authorities, with many opposing the Commission's proposals.

95 LGPIHA, s 2.

96 See Office for National Statistics, *Counties, Non-metropolitan Districts and Unitary Authorities* <http://www.ons.gov.uk/ons/guide-method/geography/beginner-s-guide/administrative/england/counties/index.html> accessed 10 November 2013.

97 Wilson and Game (n 9) 16.

98 Local Government Act 2010, s 1(1). Through enacting this provision, the Coalition halted plans that were already taking shape for unitary authorities in Norwich, Suffolk and Devon. See I Leigh, 'The Changing Nature of Local and Regional Democracy' in J Jowell and D Oliver (eds), *The Changing Constitution* (7th edn, Oxford: OUP, 2011) 237 at 239. Also see HM Government, *The Coalition: Our Programme for Government* (London: Cabinet Office, 2010) 12 <https://www.gov.uk/government/publications/the-coalition-documentation> accessed 10 November 2013.

Though the primary rationale here was to release local authorities from 'the consequences of the previous Government's command-and-control approach to local government . . . [and] to make local authorities genuine leaders of their local communities',[99] it is evident from statements in the House of Commons that the Coalition government sees moves to unitary authorities as being overly expensive and not necessary to achieve the aims of decentralisation.[100]

Whilst not necessarily a current priority in terms of local governmental reform, therefore, the creation of some unitary authorities during the late 1990s and the later years of Labour's government means that many are still very much in operation in some parts of England and Wales, though some feel that their more widespread implementation remains unfinished – there could be more to come.[101] Nonetheless, for the time being, we are left with a local government that contains a hybrid structure – two tiers in some areas, a collection of unitary authorities and a number of metropolitan and borough councils.

In terms of the effect that unitary authorities have on the strength of local leadership, they bring both benefits and disadvantages. On the one hand, having a single-tier of local government could, in some instances, reduce confusion relating to the different and occasionally conflicting responsibilities of district and county councils. Indeed, emphasising that local councillors should be champions for their local communities and that strong local councillors, representing their communities, are at the very heart of our democracy,[102] the 2006 White Paper suggested that in two-tier areas, where strong leadership and clear accountability were harder to establish, councils having the opportunity to seek unitary status would overcome risks of duplication, confusion and inefficiency of governance.[103] This would strengthen local leadership and ensure greater prominence, clarity and transparency in that it would be easier to see how and where decisions are made and, therefore, to see who is accountable for those decisions. Indeed, Wilson and Game quote the White Paper in noting 'a widely held view that moving to unitary structures would be the best way [to] improve accountability and leadership, increase efficiency, and improve outcomes for local people'.[104]

On the other hand, however, where unitary authorities have been established, it has often been the case that they have replaced a large number of county and district councils. This means that the areas covered by single-tier local authorities are much larger, with a greater number of wards and citizens being affected by the decisions of that one authority.[105] Consequently, the effectiveness and respon-

99 HC Deb 21 October 2010, vol 516, col 1155.

100 Ibid. col 1155–1156.

101 Wilson and Game (n 9) cite a headline from 2009 noting that civil servants told 'a private meeting of council leaders that, on efficiency grounds, "two-tier local government is unsustainable" and further unitary reorganisation is likely to prove necessary' (16).

102 The 2006 White Paper (n 5) para. 3.5 and see Purdue (n 84) 162.

103 Ibid. para. 3.55.

104 Ibid. para. 3.55, cited in Wilson and Game (n 9) 73.

105 See, further, C Copus, 'British Local Government: A Case for a New Constitutional Settlement' (2006) 21(4) *Public Policy and Administration* 4 at 12 and 13.

siveness of that authority's decision-making will be reduced and the manner in which such authorities operate would be directly at odds with the concepts of decentralisation and subsidiarity. Power would be exercised at a level far removed from citizens, making the provision of strong, identifiable local leadership harder, and, as a result, citizens would find it increasingly difficult to exercise their rights of accountability in the event of errors in decision-making. The gravity of this issue is highlighted by Wilson and Game, who note that in nine new unitary authorities created in 2009 residents were served by 64 per cent fewer councillors than they had been previously, with each councillor representing an average of 4,200 individuals.[106] This, they suggest, makes the use of the term 'local' in this context somewhat ironic, with the dramatic reduction in local councillor numbers signifying weaker local leadership and a democratic deficit between citizens and their local representatives.[107]

Analysis of the strength of unitary authorities' local leadership, therefore, shows mixed conclusions. On the one hand, they can bring clarity and transparency of process and, as a result, make it easier for citizens to exercise accountability. On the other hand, however, the replacing of county and district councils by fewer unitary authorities means that there are more citizens under the jurisdiction of one local authority. Consequently, effectiveness and responsiveness are reduced, with the result that accountability is not so easily achieved and the strength of their wider leadership is called into question.

Linked to the strength of local leadership is the promotion of local partnerships. Indeed, the 2006 White Paper noted that an enhanced role for councils as strategic leaders and place-shapers of their communities can be achieved through stronger local partnerships.[108] Such partnerships are important as they enable local bodies and organisations to work with citizens and other localised authorities, meaning that resources can be put to the best possible use in order to achieve the objectives in a given area. Indeed, the importance of partnerships in the wider process of local leadership is echoed by Arden *et al.*, who state that 'modern local government may . . . be characterised as one with a leadership . . . role within each area, through a partnership approach involving a range of other bodies'.[109]

Part 5 of the LGPIHA created a statutory basis for the strategic role that authorities had already begun to play through partnerships between authorities and other local bodies, using the Local Area Agreement[110] as a framework.[111] As the Act's Explanatory Notes illustrate, the LAA is an agreement between local authorities and certain other partner authorities encouraging consultation and cooperation with regard to local improvement and the development of 'Sustainable Community Strategies'.[112] These 'Sustainable Community Strategies', mentioned

106 Wilson and Game (n 9) 74.
107 Ibid. 74 and 76.
108 See the 2006 White Paper (n 5) 10.
109 Arden *et al.* (n 6) para. 1.6.43.
110 Hereinafter LAA.
111 C Baker, 'Update: Local Government', 30 November 2007, *Solicitors Journal* 1529 at 1530.
112 Explanatory Notes to the LGPIHA, para. 228.

in brief in Chapter 2, set out the long-term vision and strategic direction for an area's environmental, economic and social well-being,[113] ensuring that sustainable development can be very much at the heart of local decision-making.[114] Now abolished,[115] the LAAs have been replaced by Total Place, a government initiative designed further to inspire local partnership working through bringing together members of the public, local businesses and voluntary sector organisations to consider how spending might be organised most efficiently.[116]

The importance of local partnerships, particularly in view of strengthening how a local authority operates, rests on the way in which they can promote communication between local institutions and people, meaning that ideas and resources can be shared and experience and knowledge valued. Indeed, Mohr and Spekman go so far as to suggest that communication is central to the success of partnership working.[117] In this sense, it promotes a key aspect of the accountability principle which Mulgan notes as involving a dialectical activity through which citizens can question and scrutinise those making decisions.[118]

This section has highlighted just a few ways in which recent local governmental reform and policy has sought to strengthen local leadership, focusing in particular on changes to executive arrangements, the sporadic and inconsistent introduction of unitary authorities as well as the importance of local partnerships. These are just a few examples, however, with wider aspects of reform and policy also having an impact here. Indeed, recalling the importance of transparency in achieving accountability and that without the means through which to see what decisions are made and the process through which they are implemented, citizens have no basis on which to hold decision-makers to account. Policies encouraging what the Local Government Association labels as the unbundling of accountability,[119] and those giving local people improved access to information and data, including 'information about how public funds are being spent . . . and what they are achieving',[120] have also worked to ensure that citizens can know how local decision-making procedures operate. In addition, overview and scrutiny committees – introduced in 2000 and developed by legislation in 2007 – continue to oversee and scrutinise local decision-makers within local authorities themselves.[121]

113 Wilson and Game (n 9) 161.

114 Arden *et al.* (n 6) para. 1.6.33.

115 HC Deb 13 October 2010, vol 516, cols 20WS and 21WS.

116 See Wilson and Game (n 9) 162.

117 J Mohr and R Spekman, 'Characteristics of Partnership Success: Partnership Attributes, Communication Behaviour and Conflict Resolution Techniques' (1994) 15 *Strategic Management Journal* 135 at 137.

118 Mulgan (n 79) 569.

119 Local Government Association, *Essential Localism: A Local Government Group Response to Decentralisation and the Localism Bill: An Essential Guide* (2010) 23 <http://www.local.gov.uk/c/document_library/get_file?uuid=33734989-4b6f-40dd-838f-25d267e03600&groupId=10180> accessed 10 November 2013.

120 Ibid. 20.

121 These have a key role to play in developing and reviewing policy and in holding the executive to account (Arden *et al.* (n 6) para. 1.4.206).

This motivation to provide a strong base of local leadership and decision-making in UK local government, therefore, goes much deeper than a few specific policy areas; it runs through wider aspects of local democratic development. Improved access to information and the continued operation of overview and scrutiny committees seek to strengthen local leadership and decision-making, thus laying the foundations for greater accountability.

It is clear to see, therefore, that the strength of local leadership has for many years been a priority of local governmental reform. It is essential to ensuring clear, transparent and accountable decision-making at the local level, allowing the public and other affected bodies sufficient scrutiny of local authorities' decisions and policies. The extent to which it has achieved this, however, highlights a number of issues.

Efforts to increase the number of directly elected mayors should have been a step in the right direction, with successive governments over many years seemingly committed to their obvious democratic benefits and the clear accountability that they can bring to a process.[122] The rejection of the policy at the local ballot box, however, means that their widespread implementation has yet to be fully realised, with the system still being very much founded on a mixture of executive leaders and these directly elected mayors. Furthermore, whilst the introduction of unitary authorities can potentially bring both advantages and disadvantages to local governmental leadership, the fact that we still have what is described as a hybrid model of local government is a separate cause for concern in relation to clarity of process.

The strength of local leadership, therefore, whilst integral to achieving accountability, has perhaps failed to reach its full potential in the context of UK local government. Despite a range of promises and reforms over the years, it seems that more needs to be done to strengthen local leadership and ensure that accountability can be achieved more effectively. As Chapter 6 further discusses, this should perhaps come in the form of according greater structural choice to local authorities and moving away from what Jones and Stewart describe as being a system where 'central government thinks it knows better than the local authorities concerned and their citizens'.[123] For now, however, it is clear that consideration of the strength of local leadership raises a few issues which, as will later be explored, affect the appropriate achievement of local sustainability in the UK.

Decentralisation of power

The second theme running through recent local governmental reform and policy relates to the decentralisation of power to the local level. Chapter 3 has already

122 It has already been noted that the Local Government Act 2000 set out the option for authorities to adopt directly elected mayors. See further Arden *et al.* (n 6) paras. 1.4.142 and 1.4.143.

123 G Jones and J Stewart, 'Local Government: The Past, the Present and the Future' (2012) 27(4) *Public Policy and Administration* 346 at 359.

discussed the fact that one of the reasons underlying a lack of accountability in the UK's representative democracy has been the mass centralisation of power during the 1970s and 1980s that led to what Bogdanor and Loughlin label 'the demise of local government'.[124] Recent local governmental reform, however, and the increasing emphasis on localism, have brought with them a wave of decentralisation from central government to a level closer to citizens and communities and, as this section will argue, a potential increase in local accountability and the facilitation of citizen participation.

The benefits and relevance of decentralisation have already been noted – without appropriate decision-making powers being exercised at the local level, citizens would not be able either to involve themselves actively in decision-making or to exercise their rights of accountability adequately due to there being too great a distance between decision-makers and affected persons. As a result, decision-making processes would be insufficient to ensure relevant and responsive decisions, appropriate for and in the best interests of local people. Indeed, Fauget notes the wide range of literature demonstrating the extent to which 'decentralization makes government more responsive to local needs'.[125]

More broadly, however, the need to decentralise power to a local level is also justified on the basis of subsidiarity, a principle previously discussed in Chapter 2.[126] As was there noted, it has its roots in European Union law and states that:

> [I]n areas which do not fall within its exclusive competence, the Union shall act only if and in so far as the objectives of the proposed action cannot be sufficiently achieved by the Member States, either at central level or at regional and local level, but can rather, by reason of the scale or effects of the proposed action, be better achieved at Union level.[127]

This means that action must be taken and power exercised at the most appropriate level and sensibly close to those affected by that action. Though the Treaty itself implies that subsidiarity is justified on the basis of effectiveness and efficiency of process, in terms of local democracy it is important that local institutions have the ability to make local decisions and policies as, without that power, it would be more difficult for local citizens to exercise accountability and for resultant decisions and policies to be responsive to local needs and issues. Indeed, as Collier notes, it is in 'keeping with the "subsidiarity" concept [that] the local level might . . . in some instances, be the most appropriate one for policy making, with action as close to the citizen as possible'.[128] It would, for example, be impractical

124 See generally Loughlin (n 7).

125 J-P Fauget, 'Does Decentralization Increase Government Responsiveness to Local Needs?' (2004) 88 *Journal of Public Economics* 867 at 867.

126 See Chapter 2 (n 18).

127 Consolidated Version of the Treaty on European Union [2012] OJ C326/15, Article 5(3).

128 U Collier, 'Local Authorities and Climate Protection in the European Union: Putting Subsidiarity into Practice' (1997) 2(1) *Local Environment* 39 at 39–40. She there cites: U Collier 'Developing

if central government spent a long time making decisions relating to local regeneration issues affecting a particular local community. Instead, these might more reasonably be made by local government or decision-makers closer to that community itself. Having such issues being decided at the central level is not only impractical and a waste of central executive resources, but it also means that decisions would likely be less responsive and relevant to specific local issues and problems. Decentralisation, therefore, plays an important role in ensuring local accountability, as Chapter 3 emphasised and as consideration of the principle of subsidiarity here further demonstrates. Indeed, as the Local Government Association notes, 'the whole point of localism – or decentralisation – is better accountability'.[129]

In addition to this, decentralisation also facilitates citizen participation in that if citizens are to become actively involved in decision-making processes that affect them, those processes and their related powers need to be exercised at a level close to those citizens to make such citizen participation possible. As Bailey and Elliott note, 'local government can enable citizens to *participate* in governance more readily and to a greater extent than would be possible if all governance occurred at a national level'.[130] Indeed, by contrast, where power rests with centralised government, it becomes more difficult for people to participate in the process as decisions are made at a higher level, and they are confined to relying on a purely representative system to make decisions affecting local lives. Decentralisation, therefore, is essential in affording local people greater access to processes affecting their lives and, consequently, in facilitating citizen participation. With this in mind, this section now explores the plethora of measures and reforms that have been introduced in recent years with the aim of decentralising power to the local level, in order that it can examine the extent to which they achieve this accountability and facilitate citizen participation.

Promises to decentralise have been made consistently by successive governments. Ruth Kelly, for instance, noted in 2006 the government's aim to 'give local people and local communities more . . . power to improve their lives', acknowledging that 'we must have the courage at the centre to let go. The challenges we face are too complex, the needs often too local, for all solutions to be imposed at the centre.'[131] Just two years later this was echoed further by Hazel Blears' White Paper, which stressed the need to 'shift power, influence and responsibility away from existing centres of power and into the hands of communities and citizens'.[132]

More recently, introducing the Localism Bill for its second reading in the House of Commons, the Coalition's Secretary of State for Communities and Local

Responses to the Climate Change Issue in the EU: The Role of Subsidiarity and Shared Responsibility' (1996) in U Collier, J Golub and A Kreher (eds) *Subsidiarity and Shared Responsibility: New Challenges for EU Environmental Policy* (Baden-Baden: Nomos Verlag, 1997) 177.

129 *Essential Localism* (n 119) 23.

130 Bailey and Elliott (n 2) 438–9 (emphasis added).

131 The 2006 White Paper (n 5) 4.

132 The 2008 White Paper (n 56) para. 1.3.

Government, Eric Pickles, noted that 'the Bill will reverse the centralist creep of decades and replace it with local control. It is a triumph for democracy over bureaucracy. It will fundamentally shake up the balance of power in this country, revitalising local democracy and putting power back where it belongs, in the hands of the people.'[133] The desire and motivation to decentralise, therefore, are self-evident, with the last three governments stating the need to push power down to communities and local government. It is the purpose of this section, therefore, to explore recent examples of efforts to decentralise and to consider the extent to which the reforms and policies promote accountability and facilitate citizen participation.

The first such example relates to the broad, general powers with which local government has been empowered over the years. The Local Government Act 2000 introduced, in s 2, a 'well-being power', which provided that local authorities had the power to do anything which they considered likely to achieve the promotion or improvement of the economic, social and environmental well-being of their local area.[134] The intention was to enable local authorities to act in a manner beneficial to their local area.[135] Indeed, noting the power's breadth, Arden cites guidance published in 2001 that states that 'the Government's purpose in introducing the well-being power is to reverse that traditionally cautious approach and to encourage innovation and closer joint working between local authorities and their partners to improve communities' quality of life'.[136] This is evident from a couple of cases where, as Leigh notes, 'some judges have given the provision a wide and generous interpretation'.[137] The decentralisation envisaged in the 2000 Act, therefore, was realised in a big way. Local authorities had broad powers to act in a way that could develop and improve local areas.

This did not last long, however, as powers under the provision were soon curtailed by the Court of Appeal in *R (Brent LBC) v Risk Management Partners*,[138] leading to what some have described as a 'massive loss of confidence'.[139] In the case, 'a consortium of local authorities formed a mutual insurance company with which one of them entered into a contract of insurance' to save costs.[140] This was found to be too wide to fall within s 2(1) of the Act and was consequently deemed *ultra vires*. Moore-Bick LJ noted that a local authority could not 'lawfully embark on any scheme that [might] . . . reduce its costs',[141] adding that 'section 2 gives a

133 HC Deb 17 January 2011, vol 521, col 558.

134 Local Government Act 2000, s 2(1).

135 Explanatory Notes to the Local Government Act 2000, para. 1.5.

136 DETR, *Power to Promote or Improve Economic, Social or Environmental Well-Being* (2001) <http://webarchive.nationalarchives.gov.uk/+/; http:/www.communities.gov.uk/index.asp?id=1133749> accessed 10 November 2013, cited in A Arden, 'Whose Well-Being: Central or Local Government?' (2002) 5(3) *Journal of Local Government Law* 51 at 53.

137 Leigh (n 98) 245. Leigh there notes *R (J) v Enfield LBC* [2002] EWHC 432 (Admin) and *R (Khan) v Oxfordshire County Council* [2004] EWCA Civ 309 as exemplifying this.

138 [2009] EWCA Civ 490.

139 Dobson (n 73) 18.

140 Leigh (n 98) 245.

141 [2009] EWCA Civ 490, para. 178.

local authority power to take steps that have as their object, direct or indirect, some reasonably well defined outcome which it considers will promote or improve the well-being of its area'.[142] The judgment was significant and served, as Layard notes, to undermine the credibility of the 'well-being power', limiting further innovation on the part of local authorities.[143] The limitation of this further innovation would, in turn, have served to restrict the extent to which local authorities could make relevant and responsive decisions at a level close to citizens. Consequently, accountability would have been affected and opportunities for citizen participation reduced. Change was needed, therefore, to re-empower local government and to ensure sufficient decentralisation to enable authorities to act in the best interests of local people and provide adequate opportunity for local accountability and citizen participation. Indeed, Dobson cites a Local Government Association meeting at which the impact of the *Brent* judgment was discussed and where it was argued that:

> There is a pressing need . . . for local government to be given a general power of competence to achieve excellence for the public. All local and regional partnerships will demand – and benefit from – the greater clarity and certainty of powers that would flow from a general power of competence and help local governance to be fit for purpose for the 21st century.[144]

This desire was finally realised by the Localism Act 2011, which repealed the 'well-being power' contained in s 2 of the Local Government Act 2000 and introduced, in its place, the longed for 'general power of competence'.[145] This now provides that a local authority can do 'anything an individual generally may do' within the boundaries of certain express limitations.[146]

The breadth of this power is self-evident. Part of the Coalition's 'broader prospectus of decentralisation',[147] it is, as Leigh cites, intended to empower authorities 'to act in the best interest of their voters, unhindered by the absence of specific legislation'.[148] The result is that, *inter alia*, local authorities can be potentially more accountable to local people, who don't have to look very far in terms of questioning or scrutinising decision- and policy-making and who potentially have greater participatory opportunities since that increased power is at a

142 [2009] EWCA Civ 490, para. 180, cited in Leigh (n 98) 245.

143 Layard (n 72) 136.

144 Dobson (n 73) 18.

145 See Localism Act 2011, s 1 and sch 1. The 'well-being power' remains in force in Wales.

146 Ibid. s 1. These express limitations include: an authority cannot do anything that they are unable to do by virtue of a pre-commencement or post-commencement limitation (s 2(2)), and an authority cannot make or alter contracting-out arrangements (s 2(3)).

147 N Randall and D Seawright, 'Territorial Politics' in T Heppell and D Seawright (eds), *Cameron and the Conservatives: The Transition to Coalition Government* (London: Palgrave Macmillan, 2012) 105 at 108.

148 Conservative Party, *Control Shift: Return Power to Local Communities* (2009) Responsibility Agenda, Policy Green Paper No. 9, cited in Leigh (n 98) 244.

lower level. In short, though the 'general power of competence' is still relatively new, on paper it reflects a vital decentralisation of autonomy and consequently provides a firm foundation for improved local accountability and citizen participation, ensuring as it does the exercise of power at a local level and on the potential basis that it can be used for more relevant and responsive decision-making.

Another way in which recent local governmental reform has attempted to facilitate the decentralisation of power is through changes to parish councils. Parishes, as 'units of ecclesiastical administration', date back to Anglo-Saxon times, historically having responsibility for various aspects of local life.[149] In their modern form, generally overseen by parish councils, they date back to the Local Government Act 1894 which provided that a 'Parish Council for a rural parish shall be elected from among the parochial electors of that parish'.[150] Though the Local Government Act 1972 made some changes, seeking actively to introduce further parishes and to change some existing boroughs into parishes,[151] it is the LGPIHA that is most recently significant.

Section 77 of the LGPIHA introduced changes to the powers of parish councils by widening the scope of the aforementioned 'well-being power', enacted in s 2 Local Government Act 2000, to apply also to parish councils. In short, this gave the locally constituted councils the power to do anything which they considered likely to achieve the promotion of improvement to the economic, social or environmental well-being of their area.[152] Repeal of this power has already been noted and discussed; however, the spirit behind parish councils' inclusion in its remit lives on through the Localism Act 2011, under which the new 'general power of competence' applies to 'eligible parish councils'.[153] Such decentralisation, therefore, is notable in that it affords the lowest level of local government considerable discretion and scope to make important decisions affecting a local area, with only a few restrictions.[154]

Due to the way in which parish councils operate, and the fact that they are composed of local people, the decentralisation of power set out in the LGPIHA and Localism Act creates the potential for effective accountability and widespread citizen participation. Indeed, the reforms provide a fundamental opportunity for local people to be directly involved in decision-making, whilst the exercise of that power at the most appropriate level and as close to the people as possible not only demonstrates an appreciation of the subsidiarity principle, but also serves to make local decision-making potentially more accountable, with decisions and policies being formulated closer to citizens and a process in place that can respond more

149 Wilson and Game (n 9) 55.
150 Local Government Act 1894, s 3(1).
151 Arden *et al.* (n 6) para. 1.4.47.
152 A Harrison, 'Power to the People', 15 January 2008, *Solicitors Journal* 16 at 16.
153 See Localism Act 2011, s 8(1)(f).
154 This power cannot be used where there is an existing prohibition, nor used to raise money, and regard must be had to the Secretary of State's guidance in the exercise of the power. See Harrison (n 152) 16.

easily and with greater relevance to local issues. As Jones notes, the 'intention of stimulating community engagement and strengthening local leadership' was a key factor underlying the Labour government's renewed interest in town and parish councils.[155]

In addition, it is worth noting here that the manner in which parish councils encourage citizen participation also serves to maintain the 'minimal degree of representation' that reflects the most suitable degree of participation, as discussed in Chapter 3. This is ensured by virtue of the fact that citizens who sit on the councils are elected by members of the local community. Consequently, citizens' involvement is not merely on the basis of total citizen control, but is determined by democratic process on the basis of which local individuals, acting as parish councillors, can play an important representative role. As Yarwood notes, 'comprised of lay members of the public . . . parish councils have the potential to represent local interests and opinion'.[156] As a result, local knowledge and expertise are input into the process in a more measured and organised fashion, whilst accountability can operate more effectively on the basis of those elections.

Recent local governmental reform, therefore, has set out key provisions seeking to decentralise power to local authorities, as the 'general power of competence' and the development of parish councils serve to illustrate.[157] Such decentralisation, consistent with considerations above, does much to promote local accountability and facilitate citizen participation through ensuring that power is exercised at a level close to citizens, thus making it more accessible and visible and potentially making resultant decisions more responsive and relevant.

In reality, however, and despite the clear potential of these most recent reforms, the lack of success of past governmental efforts to decentralise to the local level is reflected in the very fact that successive governments have constantly stressed this need to decentralise. This section opened by noting the words of Ruth Kelly, Hazel Blears and Eric Pickles and their promises to push power down to the local level, and there are many examples – going further back – that echo the same proposals.[158] Whilst the achievement of a reinvigorated democracy is by no means a quick and easy task, these ongoing statements, made years apart, are perhaps

155 A Jones, 'New Wine in Old Bottles? England's Town and Parish Councils and New Labour's Neighbourhood Experiment' (2007) 22 *Local Economy* 227 at 229.

156 R Yarwood, 'Parish Councils, Partnership and Governance: The Development of "Exceptions" Housing in the Malvern Hills District, England' (2002) 18 *Journal of Rural Studies* 275 at 277. He there cites: M Tewdwr-Jones, 'Rural Government and Community Participation: The Planning Role of Community Councils' (1998) 14 *Journal of Rural Studies* 369.

157 These are just two examples, however, with further provisions also seeking to decentralise power. The Localism Act 2011, for example, also gives the Secretary of State the power to transfer a local public function from a public authority to a permitted authority, including district or county councils (s 15(1)). The government's intention here is that ministers will be able to devolve powers affecting local people and local areas currently exercised by 'central government and remote quangos to local authorities' with the justification that this would 'improve local accountability' (*A Plain English Guide to the Localism Act* (n 75) 6).

158 John Prescott in the foreword to *Modern Local Government – In Touch with the People* (n 30).

indicative of continued reluctance at the centre to 'let go' and realise the potential for decentralisation harboured by local authorities. Indeed, this reluctance is further evident from the overly prescriptive supervision of local government and the limitations that have, over the years, been imposed on the exercise of its power. Davies, for instance, notes the extent to which, during the 1990s, central government adopted something of an overly prescriptive approach to local government.[159] In addition, however, and more recently, provisions set out in the LDEDCA relating to the duty to hold and respond to local petitions were, on the face it, democratic and sought to give freedom of choice to local authorities. In the finer details, however, central government sought meticulously to prescribe when local petitions could be held, the form they should take and the requirements necessary for them to be entertained by a local authority.[160] Indeed, even in respect of the Localism Act's 'general power of competence', Hambleton notes that 'central government has retained the power to stop local authorities using the power to do things the Government dislikes', questioning the manner in which this can be said to be 'a bold step in the direction of community empowerment'.[161] Recent legislation, therefore, demonstrates a clear tendency, on the part of central government, to over-prescribe the manner in which local powers can be used.

In addition, judicial limitations on local power and input also seek to demonstrate this reluctance to 'let go'. Whilst the impact of the *Brent* judgment on the scope of the 'well-being power' has already been discussed, the effects of the judgment in *R (Shrewsbury and Atcham B.C, Congleton B.C) v Secretary of State for Communities and Local Government*[162] were also such as to limit central engagement with the localities on key local issues.[163] Though the case itself concerned a judicial review in respect of decisions to replace two-tier local government with unitary authorities in parts of Shropshire and Cheshire,[164] it is notable that, in its aftermath, the possibility for the Secretary of State to consult with local citizens as regards the creation of unitary authorities was removed from the Local Government and Public Involvement in Health Bill, thus potentially limiting the extent to which local innovation could drive forward local governmental reform.[165]

If the more recent reforms seeking to decentralise to the local level are to be fully realised, therefore, there needs to be less prescription and direction from central government. Whilst, of course, the nature of our unitary constitution

159 Davies (n 32) 4.

160 J Stanton, 'Localism in Action?' *UK Constitutional Law Group*, 14 March 2013 <http://ukconstitutionallaw.org/2013/03/14/john-stanton-localism-in-action/> accessed 10 November 2013.

161 Hambleton (n 90) 16.

162 [2007] EWHC 2279 (Admin).

163 Arden *et al.* (n 6) para. 1.4.102.

164 See M Purdue, 'Secretary of State for Communities and Local Government Proposals to Replace Two-Tier Local Government with Unitary Authorities' (2008) *Journal of Planning and Environmental Law* 1651.

165 See Arden *et al.* (n 6) para. 1.4.102 and, there, note 4.

demands that local authorities operate on the basis of centralised policy, if these constant promises to ensure 'power to the people' are to come to fruition, then local authorities need to be able to use local power in a way that is suitable for their local areas. This, as is discussed further below and in Chapter 6, is a key challenge for local sustainability.

Citizen empowerment

The final theme running through recent local governmental reform stems from the decentralisation of power to the local level and relates to citizen empowerment. Chapter 3 has already discussed the effect that citizen participation has on accountability, noting that where citizens participate in local decision-making, there is improved transparency and communication, as well as the potential for an increase in mechanisms for accountability. As a result, decisions and policies stemming from the process can be more responsive to local needs and issues. Indeed, and further, as Onyx and Dalton were there cited as stating, 'where there is a strong culture of participation, then accountability will occur naturally . . . [as] those most affected by the decision have been a part of making it, and will be immediately aware of its implementation'.[166] In terms of sustainability too, as well as being a key principle of environmental decision-making, citizen participation also ensures that local needs and desires can effectively input into the sustainability process, contributing local knowledge and expertise of an area to ensure that the resultant changes are relevant, responsive and appropriate. On this basis, therefore, it is the purpose of this section to examine recent local governmental reform to consider the extent to which it ensures this empowerment of local citizens, before then analysing the extent to which this ensures citizen participation and achieves local accountability.

The importance of empowering citizens to participate in local affairs is reflected throughout recent local governmental reform. Indeed, Hazel Blears has already been quoted as stating that 'there are few issues so complex, few problems so knotty, that they cannot be tackled and solved by the innate common sense and genius of local people . . . People should have the maximum influence . . . over the decisions . . . which shape their lives.'[167] This is reiterated throughout early proposals, with the 2006 White Paper noting that citizens and communities should have a bigger say in the public services they receive and play a more prominent role in shaping the places in which they live and work.[168] It suggested giving citizens greater control over their lives through increased consultation and involvement as regards the running of local areas.[169] On this basis, it proposed the creation of a stronger legal framework, requiring local authorities to secure the

166 Onyx and Dalton (n 77) 15.
167 The 2008 White Paper (n 56) iii. Also see n 63 above.
168 The 2006 White Paper (n 5) para. 2.7.
169 Ibid. para. 2.7.

participation of local citizens and communities, and promising that local people would receive more information about service standards and be able to turn to their local councillor to demand answers through a Community Call for Action scheme.[170] Two years later the 2008 White Paper emphasised that citizens and communities are capable of taking difficult decisions and being the authors of their own destiny, stressing that central government 'should be a platform under people's feet, not a weight holding them down'.[171] Early proposals, therefore, reflect the government's commitment to empowering local citizens and indicate the manner in which they could be given a bigger say in the services they receive, the decisions and policies that affect them and the way in which their local areas are run more generally. There was a clear desire to give local people the chance to shape their own localities and to mould them into areas in which they would be happy to live and work. The purpose of this section is to analyse the extent to which this materialised in practice, through examining certain key aspects of recent reforms.

A key aspect of the Labour government's empowerment of local citizens were the duties to promote democracy and to secure involvement, proposed in the 2008 White Paper and enacted in the LDEDCA.[172] Imposed on local authorities, these duties were justified on the basis of the government's view that 'political participation and democratic control . . . [should not be seen] as a privilege begrudgingly bequeathed to the citizenry by those with power, but as an activity fundamental to the definition of "citizen", to be claimed as a right'.[173]

The duty to promote democracy, contained within s 1 of the LDEDCA, though now repealed,[174] meant that a 'local authority [had] a duty to promote understanding of the . . . functions of the authority; . . . the democratic arrangements of the authority; . . . [and] how members of the public [could] . . . take part in those democratic arrangements and what is involved in taking part'.[175] Through such a duty, the government was aiming to ensure that local power could extend beyond the town hall to the doorstep of every citizen.[176] Indeed, it exemplifies Bailey and Elliott's suggestion, noted above, that 'local government can enable citizens to *participate* in governance more readily and to a greater extent than would be possible if all governance occurred at a national level',[177] as it provides the means through which local people can better understand local decision-making and

170 Ibid. para. 2.7. The Community Call for Action scheme first established by the Police and Justice Act 2006 makes it possible for citizens to turn to their local councillor and demand answers. It operates by way of councillors taking up the concerns of local residents and finding ways in which the problems can be resolved (Ibid. paras. 2.29–2.32).

171 The 2008 White Paper (n 56) para. 1.3.

172 See LDEDCA, s 1 and s 23.

173 The 2008 White Paper (n 56) para. 1.9.

174 Section 45 of the Localism Act 2011 repealed this duty as part of a wider effort to reduce 'radically the burden of regulation on local government' (HC Deb 17 January 2011, vol 521, col 520).

175 LDEDCA, s 1.

176 The 2008 White Paper (n 56) para. 1.44.

177 Bailey and Elliott (n 2) 438–9 (emphasis added).

participate in it. As Stanton notes, this duty 'facilitate[s] the effective working of the accountability principle between the electorate and the locally elected . . . [and] should . . . empower citizens to become involved in local governance procedures [enabling them to] make a valuable contribution to the state of local democracy'.[178] Whilst in force, therefore, this duty underlined the importance of ensuring that local people be made aware of the way in which local processes operate, affording them greater understanding of the opportunities to participate and to hold local authorities accountable.

The duty to secure involvement, whilst also repealed in 2011, is worth discussing here too. This built upon provisions contained in s 138 of the LGPIHA which added s 3A to the Local Government Act 1999 and set out the instances in which 'representatives of local persons (or of local persons of a particular description) [could] . . . be involved in the exercise of [local authority] . . . functions'.[179] The duty, contained within s 23 of the LDEDCA, provided that 'where an authority . . . considers it appropriate for representatives of interested persons (or of interested persons of a particular description) to be involved in the exercise of any of its relevant functions', then they can provide information about the exercise of that function, consult with such persons as to the exercise of that function or encourage them to be involved in some other way.[180] Citizen participation in respect of this duty perhaps rested a little lower down Arnstein's 'ladder of citizen participation' than is typified by involvement on parish councils,[181] due to the emphasis it placed on transparency and consultation, as well as more active involvement. It was nonetheless notable and served to illustrate the extent to which recent reforms have been motivated to include local people more actively. Indeed, as Stanton notes, this duty ensured that citizens could be 'given more ways through which their local knowledge and experience [could] influence the way in which local areas are governed and how they operate'; it is a broad duty 'which encourages participation in a broad range of areas'.[182] In addition, the inclusion of local people in this way also serves to demonstrate healthy accountability. Through greater access to information, a more visible process and the opportunity to get involved, citizens can more easily exercise their rights of accountability.[183] The duty to secure involvement, therefore, is a provision that covers a wide range of bodies,[184] and that demonstrates both a clear encouragement of citizen participation across a range

178 Stanton (n 50) 4.

179 LDEDCA, s 23.

180 Ibid.

181 S Arnstein, 'A Ladder of Citizen Participation' (1967) 35(4) *Journal of American Institute of Planners* 216.

182 Stanton (n 50) 5.

183 Onyx and Dalton (n 77) 15.

184 The concerned authorities, listed in LDEDCA, s 23(2), include: the Arts Council of England, the Environment Agency, the Health and Safety Executive, the Homes and Communities Agency, regional development agencies, police authorities and the Secretary of State.

of services that local areas have to offer, as well as improved accountability in respect of local decision-making.

Both of these duties, therefore, proposed in the 2008 White Paper and enacted by the LDEDCA, are motivated by a strong sense of the benefits that participating citizens can bring to local decision- and policy-making processes. The duty to promote democracy encourages greater transparency, communication and accountability, whilst the duty to secure involvement both encourages citizen participation and ensures healthier local accountability. Indeed, as the 2008 White Paper itself noted, 'by engaging in politics people can enact beneficial change, serve their communities . . . and contribute to a strong society and nation'.[185] In this way, therefore, citizen empowerment has been at the forefront of the government's recent localism agenda and has very much underlined local authorities' day-to-day activities.

The enthusiasm to place citizens at the heart of local governmental practice is evident in more specific aspects of recent reform as well. The LDEDCA, discussed in brief below, imposed a duty on local authorities to consider and investigate petitions from local communities, guaranteeing petitioners a response on issues which can be raised.[186] The Act required that a local authority set out a scheme for the handling of petitions and, provided that certain conditions are met concerning the process and the number of signatories, local authorities must acknowledge receipt of the petition, take steps and even debate the issue in council.[187] The democratic benefits of petitions are self-evident. They allow citizens to input their views into the local democratic system and enable them to play an active role in the process. Indeed, as Stanton notes, the provisions in the LDEDCA had the effect of 'empower[ing] citizens to become involved in local governance procedures', meaning that they would be 'directly affecting local decision-making'.[188]

As with the duty to promote democracy, however, the duty to hold and respond to petitions was repealed by the Localism Act 2011 on the basis that the provisions were felt to be an unnecessary over-prescription of local autonomy.[189] In their place, the initial Localism Bill laid out provisions detailing the implementation of local referenda. Indeed, July 2011's draft of the Localism Bill provided that 'a principal local authority must hold a referendum . . . if any of the following conditions is met'.[190] The conditions that followed were largely administrative, though did include the requirement that the petition be signed by 5 per cent of local electors.[191] Whilst, on the face of it, the proposed reforms seemed to lay down

185 The 2008 White Paper (n 56) para. 1.3.
186 LDEDCA, Pt 1, Ch 2.
187 Ibid.
188 Stanton (n 50) 5.
189 DCLG, *Localism Bill: Local Referendums – Impact Assessment* (2011) <http://www.communities.gov.uk/documents/localgovernment/pdf/1829672.pdf>, at 2 accessed 10 November 2013. Also see n 196 below.
190 Localism HL Bill (2010–12) 90-I, cl 42.
191 Ibid. cls 42(2)(a), 43 and 44.

provisions according a greater degree of choice to local authorities, doing away with the formerly overly bureaucratic, centrally prescribed petitions,[192] and giving localities free rein to consider local issues independently, the provisions did not make the final Act, being deleted from the Bill by the House of Lords a month prior to Royal Assent. It was the view of the Lords that provisions elsewhere – in both the Localism Act and wider legislation – provided suitable opportunity for local referenda and, whilst broad in scope, those in clause 42 of the Localism Bill would have been of little use in practice.[193] Indeed, and on the point of wider referenda in the Localism Act, the Local Government Association noted at an earlier stage that 'it is worth debating . . . why the Bill needs to contain four separate referendum mechanisms and whether that variety will not obscure the improvement in accountability in a fog of procedural confusion for local voters'.[194] Due to the clause 42 provision not making the final Act, however, referenda on council tax levels, governance changes and community planning are all that remain.[195] Whilst the last of these will be discussed in Chapter 5, other referenda contained in the Act ensure that citizens can have their say on key local issues. Despite the withdrawal of this reform, therefore, other provisions serve to ensure that referenda can be used at the local level as a key mechanism for accountability, ensuring that decisions can be potentially responsive to the needs and desires of individuals.

Recent local governmental reform, therefore, demonstrates a clear motivation to empower local citizens to participate in decision- and policy-making. Whilst some reforms introduced by the LDEDCA have since been repealed, those that remain in force, and in particular those introduced by the Localism Act 2011, do much to provide some sort of foundation for the participation of citizens in local affairs and a platform for healthier accountability.

The success of recent reforms aimed at empowering local people also hinges very much on the provisions seeking to decentralise power to the local level. The discussion above has already noted the extent to which these have perhaps not been wholly successful in practice due to a general reluctance on the part of central government to 'let go' and their imposition of heavily prescribed supervision over local activity, and it is a similar story here. Indeed, in repealing the duty to hold and respond to petitions, the DCLG stated in January 2011 that:

> [T]he duty to have a petitions scheme which meets centrally prescribed requirements is unnecessarily bureaucratic for local authorities. By repealing

192 See n 189.

193 'Not only are there the council tax referendums, there are the right-to-build referendums and the neighbourhood planning referendums. Those complement the provisions for referendums which are already open to councils to carry out on governance. Any council may carry out parish polls and informal polls which are to do with its services and functions. We believe that there is pretty good coverage of this, and that there is the chance for people to have their voice heard without these provisions' (Baroness Hanham, HL Deb 10 October 2011, vol 730, col 1412).

194 *Essential Localism* (n 119) 23.

195 Ibid. 23.

> the legislation that requires councils to set up and operate a scheme for responding to all petitions the Government will be contributing to the removal of unnecessary and bureaucratic central prescription and giving councils more freedom to determine how they respond to petitions (other than those calling for a referendum) according to their circumstances.[196]

Issues relating to the manner in which citizens can be empowered, however, run much deeper than concerns about centralised over-prescription and relate to both constantly shifting policies and reforms as well as questions regarding the motivation of local people to engage and participate.

As regards the first of these issues, the argument is that, due to the constantly shifting policies and reforms relating to local empowerment, the opportunities for involvement have constantly been changing, giving rise to potential confusion and disenchantment with the system. For example, whilst the LDEDCA set out a duty relating to the holding of local petitions and a duty to promote democracy and to secure involvement, giving individuals a number of potential mechanisms through which they could become more engaged in local democracy, these provisions lasted only two years before the Localism Act saw fit to repeal them. Though its justifications are not here questioned, constantly changing the opportunities available to citizens to seek accountability and involvement in local decision-making could lead to confusion, potential disenchantment and frustration.[197]

Stemming from this, and indeed perhaps as a consequence of it, are the broader issues relating to trends in citizen participation and concerns that it is the 'usual suspects' who take up the opportunities to get involved. The suggestion here is that, where local governmental reform opens up opportunities for citizen participation in local affairs, it is the same sort of people who engage and take up these opportunities. Indeed, as regards citizen participation on parish councils, for instance, Abram *et al.*'s interview-based research reveals that citizens who participate 'are usually either working full-time or part-time and have busy responsible jobs, or they run their own businesses and possibly they are involved in other areas of voluntary work. It's very common for a parish councillor to be a magistrate, it's very common for a parish councillor to be on the parochial church council.'[198] Though this view pre-dates Labour's reforms relating to parish councils, it illustrates the type of people who are inclined to participate in local governance and is perhaps indicative of a wider picture as regards patterns of citizen participation, as Lee and Abbot also discuss in exploring public participation in environmental issues under the Aarhus Convention.[199] Whilst it is a

196 *Localism Bill: Local Referendums – Impact Assessment* (n 189).

197 On this, see further 'Issues underlying citizen participation' section, p. 158 below.

198 S Abram, J Murdoch and T Marsden, 'The Social Construction of "Middle England": The Politics of Participation in Forward Planning' (1996) 12(4) *Journal of Rural Studies* 353 at 359. Their study related to the way in which social actors represent rural communities and environments in the context of the planning system.

199 See M Lee and C Abbot, 'The Usual Suspects? Public Participation under the Aarhus Convention' (2003) 66(1) *Modern Law Review* 80.

concern that runs much deeper than participation in local sustainability, therefore, more needs to be done to inspire greater motivation amongst a wider range of local people, as Chapter 6 will further discuss.

Whilst on the face of it, therefore, provisions aimed at citizen empowerment seem committed to ensuring the involvement of local people and the achievement of local accountability, wider issues and concerns mean that their full potential has perhaps not been realised. Citizens need to be given a more stable basis on which to build a culture of participation and that base needs to be more appealing to a great number of local people, as Chapter 6 goes on to discuss further.

Conclusion in respect of accountability and participation in local government

This section has explored three key aspects of recent local governmental reform and has considered the extent to which it adheres to the principle of accountability and encourages citizen participation. It has identified a range of promises and demonstrated a clear motivation to strengthen local leadership, decentralise power and empower citizens to participate in local affairs and has shown that, on paper at least, the policies and reforms demonstrate a foundation on which accountable local leadership and the encouragement of citizen participation can thrive. In practice, however, whilst progress has unquestionably been made in comparison with the state of local government in the early 1990s, issues remain. Central prescription of local authorities has not only meant that the strength of local leadership is compromised by a limitation of choice over appropriate structures; it has also indicated that, in terms of decentralisation, central government seems rather reluctant to 'let go' of autonomy that might better sit at the local level. In addition, and stemming from this, the base for citizen empowerment is an unstable one, plagued by constantly shifting policies and opportunities which, in practice, only a select group of citizens seem willing to take up. The result is, therefore, that whilst accountability and citizen participation are achieved in part, local government is perhaps not as accountable as it could be, with the potential for citizen participation not being fully realised. It is the purpose of the final part of this chapter to consider the extent to which these reforms and their limited achievement of accountability and encouragement of citizen participation affect local government's pursuit of local sustainability.

The model of local sustainability and local governmental reform

In light of the hypothesis that this book sets out to test, it is the purpose of this section to bring this chapter's analysis of recent local governmental reform together with the 'model of local sustainability' set out in Chapter 2. This will facilitate evaluation of the extent to which the accountability and citizen participation set out in those reforms, though not fully realised in practice, affect the achievement of local sustainability.

The important role that local government can play in the achievement of sustainability has already been discussed in Chapter 2.[200] Whilst the *Johannesburg Declaration* and *Agenda 21* provide a wide authoritative base for the local focus on sustainability, specific provisions and policies within the UK government's Strategies for Sustainable Development as well as recent legislation set out the way in which local authorities can pursue particular objectives relating to sustainability. Worth recalling here are the duties contained in the Local Government Act 2000 and the Sustainable Communities Act 2007, to name just two examples. These duties ensure that local authorities prepare strategies for the promotion of the economic, social and environmental aspects of a local area[201] and encourage the promotion of sustainability at the local community level.[202] On the established premise, therefore, that local authorities work towards the achievement of sustainability, this section now applies the 'model of local sustainability' and explores the way in which recent local governmental reform, in the context of the above discussion as regards accountability and citizen participation, can be said to enhance local sustainability. In doing this, it considers each of the model's aspects of sustainability in turn.

Needs of the people

The first aspect of the 'model of local sustainability' relates to meeting the needs of local people, and Chapter 3 has already noted the extent to which accountability and citizen participation play a key role in determining such needs. Accountability, particularly in the sense reflected by Moncrieffe's notion of *ex-ante* accountability, encourages decision-makers to take account of local interests, whilst the dialectical nature of the principle more widely ensures that citizens can communicate with those in power and input their needs and desires into the process. It means, as explored in Chapter 3, that accountability can be a mechanism for responsiveness, ensuring as it does that resultant decisions, policies and actions meet the needs of individuals and take into consideration issues and problems that affect a particular area. Accountability, therefore, plays a vital role in enhancing the achievement of local sustainability. In addition, and more significantly, the needs and desires of local individuals can be determined through encouraging their direct participation in decision-making procedures. Indeed, it is recalled that Baker *et al.* cite Achterberg in noting that 'participation in the decisions which affect one's own life is a central political value of democracy . . . the required changes of lifestyle connected with a shift to sustainable development can never be lasting if they are imposed in an authoritarian way'.[203] Citizen participation, therefore, is also crucial

200 See 'Local sustainability in the UK' section, p. 17 above.

201 Local Government Act 2000, s 4.

202 Sustainable Communities Act 2007, s 1(1) and s 1(2).

203 S Baker, M Kousis, D Richardson and S Young (eds), *The Politics of Sustainable Development: Theory, Policy and Practice within the European Union* (London: Routledge, 1997) 23–4, who there cite: W Achterberg, 'Can Liberal Democracy Survive the Environmental Crisis? Sustainability,

to understanding the needs of local people and in ensuring the responsiveness of decisions aimed at meeting those needs. With all this in mind, however, it is necessary to consider the way in which recent local governmental reform fits in here; this section does this, considering each of the above themes in turn.[204]

Strong local leadership is a fundamental requirement of local decision-making and is vital in providing a foundation for the accountability that is so important to local sustainability. In terms of the reforms discussed above, the widespread introduction of directly elected mayors and the potential adoption of unitary authorities, for example, could possibly serve to provide a stronger platform for local authorities' pursuit of sustainability. The simpler structures offered by unitary authorities can offer a firmer base for accountability and clearer avenues through which citizens can hold local decision-makers to account,[205] whilst the implementation of directly elected mayors would have ensured that local people could choose strong, local leaders who are held to account more easily.[206]

Recall, at the same time, the words of the *Johannesburg Plan of Implementation*, which noted that, in promoting sustainable development, 'all countries should strengthen governmental institutions . . . by providing necessary infrastructure and by promoting transparency, accountability and fair administrative and judicial institutions'.[207] Through encouraging clearer and more visible leadership by the introduction of unitary authorities, as well as promoting the widespread adoption of directly elected mayors, therefore, local authorities could ensure strengthened governmental institutions and provide the necessary infrastructure to ensure accountability and, consequently, meet the needs of local people more effectively.

In addition to this, the manner in which the reforms proposed and encouraged greater partnership working at the local level would have satisfied Moncrieffe's consideration of *ex-ante* accountability – that which emphasises the importance of understanding local needs and interests.[208] Bearing in mind the LAA's aforementioned role in developing 'Sustainable Community Strategies', it would have been central to the work of these partnerships to engage with local people and other local institutions in setting out a vision for the improvement and development of a local area, and to appreciate and satisfy their needs and interests.[209] As Wilson and Game note, the identification of community needs and aspirations were key to these Strategies' broader role in pushing forward the development of a local area.[210]

Liberal Neutrality and Overlapping Consensus' in A Dobson and P Lucardie (eds), *The Politics of Nature: Explorations in Green Political Theory* (London: Routledge, 1993) 81 at 82.

204 Strong local leadership; the decentralisation of power; and the empowerment of local citizens.

205 See n 104 above and Wilson and Game (n 9) 73.

206 See Larsen (n 88) 113.

207 UN, *Johannesburg Plan of Implementation*, Annex to Resolution 2 of the *World Summit on Sustainable Development*, Johannesburg, 26 August–4 September 2002, A/CONF.199/20, New York: UN, para. 4.

208 Moncrieffe (n 80) 27.

209 Wilson and Game (n 9) 161.

210 Ibid. 161.

Reforms seeking to strengthen local leadership, and the benefits in terms of accountability that these can bring, ensure, therefore, that decision-making procedures working towards local sustainability can more effectively seek to meet the needs and desires of local people.

Local governmental reforms focusing on the decentralisation of power could also have a key part to play in determining the needs of local people. As considered above, the argument here is that if power can be exercised at a level closer to citizens, then it is easier for them to see how and why decisions are made, to hold decision-makers to account and, consequently, to ensure more relevant and responsive decisions in respect of local issues.[211] In addition, it means that the process is more accessible and that it is easier for citizens to involve themselves in decision-making and to input their needs and interests into the process directly. This is best exemplified by reference to reforms to parish councils, especially in the context of their inclusion in the remit of the 'general power of competence'. These bodies of local people not only make decisions on the council but also live and work in the particular local area. As a consequence, experience of their life in the neighbourhood as well as an understanding of its needs and issues can directly inform the local decisions that parish councils make. Whilst their jurisdiction and scope are somewhat limited, inclusion of the 'general power of competence' in the remit of parish councils means that they do retain broad powers to improve a local area and, as a result of their composition, such improvements can be responsive to the needs and desires of local people and a community more widely. Decentralisation, therefore, can bring improved access to accountability and greater opportunity for citizen participation.

Finally, reforms that seek to empower local citizens to participate in local decision-making are perhaps the most notable in terms of ensuring local needs and desires are taken into consideration in the pursuit of sustainability, as through their involvement citizens can input their needs and desires directly into the process. Whilst, as mentioned above, the community rights introduced in the Localism Act 2011 are discussed more appropriately in the next chapter, the duties to promote democracy and to secure involvement, though since repealed, facilitate the discussion here, and provisions introducing local referenda serve to provide an example of the way in which more recent reforms have sought to empower local people.

The duties to promote democracy and to involve local people were notable, whilst in force, in that they encouraged citizen involvement in a range of local authority activities. Though they did not stipulate specific aspects of such activities, they demonstrated a keen willingness to ensure that citizens could play a part in local governmental affairs. In addition, reforms, introduced in the Localism Act, setting out the requirements for referenda are also particularly notable in terms of affording local people an opportunity to get their views across. In particular, bearing in mind that Part 6 of the Act introduces referenda in respect of community development orders,[212] the reforms show a clear encouragement of

211 See Fauget (n 125) 867 and Collier (n 128) 39–40.
212 See Layard (n 76) 557.

citizen participation in gauging the opinions of local people and seeking to understand issues and concerns in improving and developing local areas. Reforms that seek to empower citizens, therefore, demonstrate a clear potential benefit in terms of determining local needs and desires in the process of achieving sustainability.

Recent local governmental reforms, therefore, and the manner in which they set out the potential achievement of accountability and citizen participation, demonstrate the extent to which local government can more effectively seek to meet the needs of local citizens and, bearing in mind the role that it can play, enhance the achievement of local sustainability.

Sustainability

The second aspect of the model relates to sustainability. This is crucial as any improving changes that are introduced must not just meet the needs of existing generations, but also be able to accommodate the requirements of future generations.[213] This involves the implementation of lasting change and, in the local sense, securing communities against, or at least minimising, any further future deprivation. It was noted in Chapter 3 that one way in which sustainability can be ensured is through an ongoing commitment by local governmental bodies and local people working to ensure that standards and achievements attained through developments are maintained for the future. Such a commitment is exemplified in one way by local authorities' engagement with development partnerships and initiatives, examples of which are discussed in the next chapter. In addition, s 4 of the Local Government Act 2000, as amended by s 114 of the LGPIHA, required all local authorities to prepare a community strategy to promote the economic, social and environmental well-being of a particular area. Containing language consistent with the three pillars of sustainability, this exemplifies one way in which local authorities were required to demonstrate commitment to long-term development.

Whilst this commitment depends, to a degree, on the statutory duties imposed on local authorities, it is also reliant on local people constantly playing their part in maintaining the development of local areas. Though this will become clearer in the next chapter, for now the most obvious way through which recent local governmental reform has worked to ensure this commitment for sustainability is through decentralising power to the local level and empowering citizens to participate in decisions that affect their areas. In particular, reforms giving parish councils greater power, expanded by the LGPIHA and the Localism Act 2011,[214] equip local people with the tools necessary to play a part not only in the

213 World Commission on Environment and Development, *Our Common Future* (Oxford: OUP, 1987) 43 ('Brundtland Report').

214 LGPIHA, s 77, extends the 'well-being power' to include parish councils, whilst the Localism Act 2011, s 1, replaces that power with a 'general power of competence' that also includes parish councils.

development of neighbourhoods but also in the ongoing commitment to ensure that such changes can last. Indeed, that commitment can stem both from the legal basis of parish councils' roles, and also from a moral and social desire to ensure that their local areas are pleasant places in which to live and work.[215]

By providing for the decentralisation of power and empowering citizens to participate in local decision-making, therefore, recent local governmental reforms are putting in place measures that provide a foundation for local people to ensure an ongoing commitment to developing local areas and to ensuring the sustainability of those developments.

Three pillars: environmental, social and economic development

The final aspect of the 'model of local sustainability' comprises objectives aligned with the three pillars of sustainable development. The three-pillar approach, as Chapter 2 discussed, has emerged in recent years as a universally accepted definition of sustainability,[216] reflecting as it does the key objectives on which the principle is based. Whilst a focus on particular aspects of these three pillars is partly dependent on certain policies and initiatives, elements of recent local governmental reform and the manner in which the latter sought to achieve accountability and citizen participation at least provide a foundation for their satisfaction. On this basis, this section evaluates the extent to which recent reform, considered in the context of accountability and citizen participation, enhances this aspect of sustainability. It is structured first to explore the impact of decentralisation and empowerment, before then considering social development and community cohesion.

Decision-making in respect of environmental, social and economic aspects of a local area requires, *inter alia*, an understanding of important local issues and the need to be responsive to those issues. Only then can relevant and appropriate decisions and policies be made that benefit a particular area and enrich the lives of those living and working in that area. The most prominent way through which this can be achieved is by the decentralisation of power, the encouragement of citizen participation in the process and the provision of mechanisms to ensure that the wider neighbourhood is able to scrutinise and question such decisions and policies.

This chapter has already identified ways in which recent local governmental reforms seek to promote decentralisation and encourage citizen empowerment and the manner in which these objectives are aligned with accountability and participation. In terms of the effect this then has on the three pillars of sustainability, a

215 This moral desire is echoed by a recent survey which shows that, in Devon, 87 per cent of parish councillors took up the role to ensure that they could work to improve the well-being of their local areas. See G Borne, 'Understanding Town and Parish Council Needs for a Sustainable Devon: Interim Report' (2008) (1) *Promoting Sustainable Communities* 1 at 13.

216 J Holder and M Lee, *Environmental Protection, Law and Policy: Text and Materials* (2nd edn, Cambridge: CUP, 2007) 237.

suitable example is provided by the aforementioned changes to parish councils. Their powers have been developed constantly by legislation over the years, and they cover various environmental, social and economic aspects of a local area.[217] In terms of environmental aspects, they maintain roads, plant trees and lay grass verges; economically they participate in schemes of collective investment and attempt to attract visitors and accommodate tourists; and socially they provide and promote recreational activities whilst working towards the prevention of crime.[218] Having such powers at the local level, coupled with the aforementioned democratic benefits of parish councils, means that from the outset local citizens can, more easily, exercise 'rights of accountability' and participate in decisions affecting the environmental, social and economic aspects of their local areas, all the while ensuring that such decisions benefit from their knowledge and expertise of the locality. Bearing in mind, however, recent changes to create more widespread parish councils and to include them within the remit of the 'general power of competence', it is clear that the reforms provide a platform for the greater decentralisation of autonomy, improved access to accountability and the wider empowerment of local people, and consequently the potential enhancement of the manner in which parish councils can work towards sustainability in a particular neighbourhood.

Parish councils illustrate just one way through which the decentralisation of power and the increased participation of local people can improve the environmental, social and economic development of local areas. The now repealed 'well-being power', introduced in 2000, mirrored the language of the three pillars of sustainability and, in doing so, accorded potentially broad powers to wider local councils to improve their neighbourhoods along its lines. Indeed, such language is still reflected in the Sustainable Communities Act 2007, which, as noted in Chapter 2,[219] invites local authorities to submit proposals to improve the economic, social or environmental well-being of a particular area.[220] In addition, the encouragement of local partnerships, and in particular the now repealed LAA's role in developing 'Sustainable Community Strategies', would have served to set out specific objectives for a local area, in line with the environmental, social and economic aspects of sustainability, and in conversation with local organisations and people. Bearing in mind the manner in which such partnerships satisfy the dialectical aspect of accountability, this provides a further example of the potential for recent reform to enhance local sustainability.

Finally, and with a specific emphasis on the social head of the three pillars, the decentralisation of power and the empowerment of local citizens in decision-making processes pertaining to sustainability would also have a specific benefit in terms of achieving community cohesion – a notion key to social development in

217 DEFRA, *Powers and Duties of Parish Councils*, <http://archive.defra.gov.uk/rural/documents/living/communities/PPow-dutylist.pdf> accessed 11 November 2013.

218 Ibid.

219 See 'Local sustainability in the UK' section, p. 17 above.

220 Sustainable Communities Act 2007, s 1(1) and s 1(2).

particular.[221] The argument here is that where citizens can participate in local affairs and are brought together in partnership with organisations and members of the wider community, then that local area becomes more cohesive. Indeed, Robinson acknowledges that community cohesion occurs 'where participation is taking place across communities, knitting them together into a wider whole'.[222] In terms of recent local governmental reform, strengthened leadership and the encouragement of local partnerships would have the effect of drawing a community together, whilst by decentralising power to that level and empowering citizens to play their part in the process, the interests of a particular community would inform the process and the very act of being collectively involved in decision-making would enhance community cohesion. Indeed, as the Labour government stated in its 2006 White Paper, 'increasing resident participation in decision-making, enhancing the role for community groups, strengthening local leadership . . . empowering councils, in partnership with other public agencies, to take on the place-shaping role will all help to build cohesive and self-confident communities'.[223]

This section has sought to demonstrate, by way of just a few examples, that the potential for accountability and citizen participation harboured by recent local governmental reform offers the opportunity to enhance local sustainability through a focus on each of the three pillars of sustainability. By combining new and existing powers to develop local areas with opportunities for citizen participation and accountability, parish councils demonstrate the extent to which environmental, social and economic objectives can be achieved more democratically, whilst strengthened local leadership and the encouragement of local partnerships help to ensure that communities can become more cohesive and better developed as a result.

Concluding remarks

This chapter has considered accountability and citizen participation in light of recent local governmental reform, and in the context of the 'model of local sustainability'. This has enabled evaluation of the extent to which the accountability and citizen participation achieved through recent reform enhance local sustainability, thus seeking to test the hypothesis that this book sets out in Chapters 2 and 3.

It has been shown that reforms providing for strong local leadership, the forming of local partnerships, the decentralisation of power and the empowerment

221 It was noted in Chapter 2 that cohesion is central to sustainability as it represents the idea that local people should feel a part of and belong to a neighbourhood that is, at the same time, imbued with a sense of community spirit.

222 D Robinson, 'The Search for Community Cohesion: Key Themes and Dominant Concepts of the Public Policy Agenda' (2005) 42 *Urban Studies* 1411 at 1417.

223 The 2006 White Paper (n 5) para. 8.6.

of local people demonstrate, on paper, the potential for local accountability and the encouragement of citizen participation. This, in turn, and in view of consideration of the 'model of local sustainability', can enhance key aspects of the sustainability principle. Accountability and citizen participation ensure that decisions and policies are responsive to local needs and desires, that developing changes are sustainable and that environmental, social and economic developments are appropriate and responsive. The reforms, therefore, demonstrate a step in the right direction – their appreciation of and potential for accountability and citizen participation mean that local government's achievement of sustainability can be enhanced.

The issue that remains, however, is the manner in which these reforms have worked in practice. The final section of this chapter – exploring the 'model of local sustainability' – has been careful in assessing the potential for local governmental reform to achieve the accountability and citizen participation necessary to enhance local sustainability, and indeed, as above, it has shown that – on paper – the reforms are relatively successful in this regard. If this potential is to be realised, however, then the challenges posed by centralised over-prescription of local authorities' executive arrangements, central government's reluctance to 'let go' of powers better suited to the local level and its constantly shifting policies need to be addressed, along with broader concerns relating to the wider participation of individuals. If these reforms do not sufficiently realise the clear potential and motivation that lie at their heart, then they fail adequately to achieve the appropriate accountability or to encourage the citizen participation necessary to enhance local sustainability. The potential is there – this chapter has shown that much. More needs to be done, however, to ensure that this potential can be realised and that local sustainability can be enhanced as a consequence.

Bibliography

Abram, S, Murdoch, J and Marsden, T, 'The Social Construction of "Middle England": The Politics of Participation in Forward Planning' (1996) 12(4) *Journal of Rural Studies* 353.

Achterberg, W, 'Can Liberal Democracy Survive the Environmental Crisis? Sustainability, Liberal Neutrality and Overlapping Consensus' in Dobson, A and Lucardie, P (eds), *The Politics of Nature: Explorations in Green Political Theory* (London: Routledge, 1993) 81.

Arden, A, 'Whose Well-Being: Central or Local Government?' (2002) 5(3) *Journal of Local Government Law* 51.

Arden, A, Baker, C and Manning, J, *Local Government Constitutional and Administrative Law* (2nd edn, London: Sweet and Maxwell, 2008).

Arnstein, S, 'A Ladder of Citizen Participation' (1967) 35(4) *Journal of American Institute of Planners* 216.

Bailey, S and Elliott, M, 'Taking Local Government Seriously: Democracy, Autonomy and the Constitution' (2009) 68(2) *Cambridge Law Journal* 436.

Baker, C, 'Update: Local Government', 30 November 2007, *Solicitors Journal* 1529.

Baker, K, *The Turbulent Years: My Life in Politics* (London: Faber & Faber, 1993).

Baker, S, Kousis, M, Richardson, D and Young, S, (eds), *The Politics of Sustainable Development: Theory, Policy and Practice within the European Union* (London: Routledge, 1997).

Bogdanor, V, *The New British Constitution* (Oxford: Hart Publishing, 2009).

Bogadnor, V, *The Coalition and the Constitution* (Oxford: Hart Publishing, 2011).

Borne, G, 'Understanding Town and Parish Council Needs for a Sustainable Devon: Interim Report' (2008) (1) *Promoting Sustainable Communities* 1.

Cabinet Office, *Building the Big Society*, 18 May 2010 <https://www.gov.uk/government/uploads/system/uploads/attachment_data/file/78979/building-big-society_0.pdf> accessed 10 November 2013.

Chandler, JA, *Local Government Today* (4th edn, Manchester: Manchester University Press, 2009).

Collier, U, 'Developing Responses to the Climate Change Issue in the EU: The Role of Subsidiarity and Shared Responsibility' (1996) in Collier, U, Golub, J and Kreher, A (eds) *Subsidiarity and Shared Responsibility: New Challenges for EU Environmental Policy* (Baden-Baden: Nomos Verlag, 1997) 177.

Collier, U, 'Local Authorities and Climate Protection in the European Union: Putting Subsidiarity into Practice' (1997) 2(1) *Local Environment* 39.

Communities and Local Government Committee, *Localism* (HC 2010–2012, 547-I).

Conservative Party, *1983 Conservative Party General Election Manifesto* <http://www.conservative-party.net/manifestos/1983/1983-conservative-manifesto.shtml> accessed 9 November 2013.

Conservative Party, *Control Shift: Return Power to Local Communities* (2009) Responsibility Agenda, Policy Green Paper No. 9.

Copus, C, 'British Local Government: A Case for a New Constitutional Settlement' (2006) 21(4) *Public Policy and Administration* 4.

Davies, JS, 'Double-Devolution or Double-Dealing? The Local Government White Paper and the Lyons Review' (2008) 34(1) *Local Government Studies* 3.

DBIS, *Local Growth: Realising Every Place's Potential* (White Paper, Cm 7961) (London: HMSO, 2010).

DCLG, *Strong and Prosperous Communities: The Local Government White Paper* (Cm 6939-I, 2006), © Crown Copyright, contains public sector information licensed under the Open Government Licence v2.0 <http://www.nationalarchives.gov.uk/doc/open-government-licence/version/2/>.

DCLG, *Communities in Control: Real People, Real Power* (White Paper, Cm 7427, 2008), © Crown Copyright, contains public sector information licensed under the Open Government Licence v2.0 <http://www.nationalarchives.gov.uk/doc/open-government-licence/version/2/>.

DCLG, *Localism Bill: Local Referendums – Impact Assessment* (2011) <http://www.communities.gov.uk/documents/localgovernment/pdf/1829672.pdf> accessed 10 November 2013.

DCLG, *A Plain English Guide to the Localism Act*, 15 November 2011, London: DCLG <https://www.gov.uk/government/uploads/system/uploads/attachment_data/file/5959/1896534.pdf> accessed 10 November 2013.

DEFRA, *Powers and Duties of Parish Councils* <http://archive.defra.gov.uk/rural/documents/living/communities/PPow-dutylist.pdf> accessed 11 November 2013.

DETR, *A Mayor and Assembly for London* (White Paper, Cm 3897, 1998).

DETR, *Modern Local Government – In Touch with the People* (White Paper, Cm 4014, 1998).

DETR, *Power to Promote or Improve Economic, Social or Environmental Well-Being* (2001) <http://webarchive.nationalarchives.gov.uk/+/; http:/www.communities.gov.uk/index.asp?id=1133749> accessed 10 November 2013.

DoE, *Local Government Review: The Structure of Local Government in England. A Consultation Paper* (London: DoE, 1993).

DTLGR, *Byers Sets out Vision for Stronger Local Government with New Freedoms to Deliver Better Quality Services*, 11 December 2001, News Release 2001/0535.

Dobson, N, 'General Competence to Restore *Vires* Confidence?' (24 March 2010) 107(12) *Law Society Gazette* 18.

Evans, K, '"Big Society" in the UK: A Policy Review' (2011) 25 *Children and Society* 164.

Explanatory Notes to the LGPIHA 2007.

Explanatory Notes to the Local Government Act 2000.

Fauget, J-P, 'Does Decentralization Increase Government Responsiveness to Local Needs?' (2004) 88 *Journal of Public Economics* 867.

Fenwick, J and Elcock, H, 'New Development: The Elected Mayor and Local Leadership' (2005) 25(1) *Public Money and Management* 61.

Hambleton, R, 'A Jekyll and Hyde Localism Bill?' (2011) 80(1) *Town and Country Planning* 15.

Harrison, A, 'The Cult of Cabinet', 29 January 2008, *Solicitors Journal* 12.

Harrison, A, 'Power to the People', 15 January 2008, *Solicitors Journal* 16.

HC Deb 21 March 1991, vol 188, col 401.

HC Deb 13 October 2010, vol 516, cols 20WS and 21WS.

HC Deb 21 October 2010, vol 516, col 1155.

HC Deb 17 January 2011, vol 521, col 558.

HL Deb 10 October 2011, vol 730, col 1412.

HM Government, *The Coalition: Our Programme for Government* (London: Cabinet Office, 2010) <https://www.gov.uk/government/publications/the-coalition-documentation> accessed 10 November 2013.

Holder, J and Lee, M, *Environmental Protection, Law and Policy: Text and Materials* (2nd edn, Cambridge: CUP, 2007).

Jenkins, S, 'Accountable to None' (1996) 16(2) *Public Money & Management* 3.

Jenks, E, *An Outline of English Local Government* (5th edn, London: Methuen, 1921).

Jones, A, 'New Wine in Old Bottles? England's Town and Parish Councils and New Labour's Neighbourhood Experiment' (2007) 22 *Local Economy* 227.

Jones, G and Stewart, J, 'Local Government: The Past, the Present and the Future' (2012) 27(4) *Public Policy and Administration* 346.

King, A, *The British Constitution* (Oxford: OUP, 2007).

Larsen, HO, 'Directly Elected Mayors: Democratic Renewal or Constitutional Confusion?' in Caulfield, J and Larsen, HO (eds) *Local Government at the Millennium* (Wiesbaden: Springer Fachmedien Wiesbaden, 2002) 111.

Layard, A, 'Law and Localism: The Case of Multiple Occupancy Housing' (2012) 32(4) *Legal Studies* 551.

Layard, A, 'The Localism Act 2011: What Is "Local" and How Do We (Legally) Construct It?' (2012) 14(2) *Environmental Law Review* 134.

Lee, M and Abbot, C, 'The Usual Suspects? Public Participation under the Aarhus Convention' (2003) 66(1) *Modern Law Review* 80.

Leigh, I, 'The Changing Nature of Local and Regional Democracy' in Jowell, J and Oliver, D (eds), *The Changing Constitution* (7th edn, Oxford: OUP, 2011) 237.

Local Government Association, 'Prosperous Communities: Beyond the White Paper', *Local Government Association*, 7 June 2006 <http://www.local.gov.uk/publications/-/journal_content/56/10180/3367441/PUBLICATION> accessed 11 November 2013.

Local Government Association, *Essential Localism: A Local Government Group Response to Decentralisation and the Localism Bill. An Essential Guide* (2010) <http://www.local.gov.uk/c/document_library/get_file?uuid=33734989-4b6f-40dd-838f-25d267e03600&groupId=10180> accessed 10 November 2013.

Localism HL Bill (2010–12) 90-I.

Loughlin, M, *Local Government in the Modern State* (London: Sweet and Maxwell, 1986).

Loughlin, M, 'The Demise of Local Government' in Bogdanor, V (ed.), *The British Constitution in the 20th Century* (Oxford: OUP, 2004) 521.

Lowndes, V, 'Rescuing Aunt Sally: Taking Institutional Theory Seriously in Urban Politics' (2001) 38(11) *Urban Studies* 1953.

Ministry of Justice, *Governance of Britain*, Cm 7170 (London: HMSO, 2007).

Mohr, J and Spekman, R, 'Characteristics of Partnership Success: Partnership Attributes, Communication Behaviour and Conflict Resolution Techniques' (1994) 15 *Strategic Management Journal* 135.

Moncrieffe, JM, 'Accountability: Idea, Ideals, Constraints' (2001) 8(3) *Democratization* 26.

Mulgan, R, 'Accountability: An Ever-Expanding Concept' (2000) 78(3) *Public Administration* 555.

Newton, K and Karran, T, *The Politics of Local Expenditure* (London: Macmillan, 1985).

Office for National Statistics, *Counties, Non-metropolitan Districts and Unitary Authorities* <http://www.ons.gov.uk/ons/guide-method/geography/beginner-s-guide/administrative/england/counties/index.html> accessed 10 November 2013.

Oliver, D, *Constitutional Reform in the UK* (Oxford: OUP, 2003).

Onyx, J and Dalton, B, 'Accountability and Advocacy' (2006) 12(1) *Third Sector Review* 7.

Parry, K and Roll, J, House of Commons Library, *Local Government and Public Involvement in Health Bill*, 10 January 2007, Research Paper 07/01.

Pimlott, B and Rao, N, *Governing London* (Oxford: OUP, 2002).

Purdue, M, 'Current Topics (February): The Local Government White Paper and Planning' (2007) *Journal of Planning and Environmental Law* 157.

Purdue, M, 'Secretary of State for Communities and Local Government Proposals to Replace Two-Tier Local Government with Unitary Authorities' (2008) *Journal of Planning and Environmental Law* 1651.

Randall, N and Seawright, D, 'Territorial Politics' in Heppell, T and Seawright, D (eds), *Cameron and the Conservatives: The Transition to Coalition Government* (London: Palgrave Macmillan, 2012) 105.

Robinson, D, 'The Search for Community Cohesion: Key Themes and Dominant Concepts of the Public Policy Agenda' (2005) 42 *Urban Studies* 1411.

Royal Commission on Local Government in England, Cmnd 4040 (London: HMSO, 1969).

Royal Commission on Local Government in Greater London, Cmnd 1164 (London: HMSO, 1960).

Sandford, M, House of Commons Library, *Directly Elected Mayors* (Standard Note SN/PC/5000, 16 July 2013).

Stanton, J, 'Local Democracy, Economic Development and Construction Act 2009: A Reinvigorated Local Democracy?' (2011) *Public Law* 1.

Stanton, J, 'Localism in Action?' *UK Constitutional Law Group*, 14 March 2013, <http://ukconstitutionallaw.org/2013/03/14/john-stanton-localism-in-action/> accessed 10 November 2013.

Stoker, G, *Transforming Local Governance. From Thatcherism to New Labour* (Basingstoke: Palgrave, 2004).

Stoker, G, *What Is Local Government For?* (London: New Local Government Network, 2005).

Tewdwr-Jones, M, 'Rural Government and Community Participation: The Planning Role of Community Councils' (1998) 14 *Journal of Rural Studies* 369.

UN, *Agenda 21*, 1992, A/CONF.151/26, Vol. III, New York: UN. Made available by the UN Division for Sustainable Development at <http://sustainabledevelopment.un.org/content/documents/Agenda21.pdf> accessed 7 November 2013.

UN, *Johannesburg Plan of Implementation*, Annex to Resolution 2 of the *World Summit on Sustainable Development*, Johannesburg, 26 August–4 September 2002, A/CONF.199/20, New York: UN.

Wilson, DJ, 'The Local Government Commission: Examining the Consultative Process' (1996) 74 *Public Administration* 199.

Wilson, D and Game, C, *Local Government in the United Kingdom* (5th edn, Basingstoke: Palgrave Macmillan, 2011).

World Commission on Environment and Development, *Our Common Future* (Oxford: OUP, 1987).

Yarwood, R, 'Parish Councils, Partnership and Governance: The Development of "Exceptions" Housing in the Malvern Hills District, England' (2002) 18 *Journal of Rural Studies* 275.

5 The New Deal and the Big Society

Democracy, decision-making and sustainability

Introduction

A key feature of local sustainability in the UK is the emphasis on community-led regeneration. Whilst, as Chapter 4 has set out, local government can have a key role to play in leading the development of local areas, it is consistent with the justifications for local sustainability that local communities should also have the opportunities and means through which to drive forward local development. Based on this premise, therefore, it is the purpose of this chapter to seek to explore the way in which accountability and citizen participation affect the achievement of sustainability at this level.

Governments have – for many years now – introduced a range of initiatives and policies aimed at the regeneration of local communities, as Foley and Martin illustrate.[1] Whilst many of these have existed within top-down structures, with central government setting the nature of the regeneration and the objectives that local areas should strive to meet, in more recent years the emphasis has been on a community-led approach to local regeneration, and it is this approach with which this chapter is chiefly concerned.[2] Community-led sustainability is justified on the basis that, as Chapter 2 explained, 'local decision-makers should "shape the place" because they "know best"'.[3] Indeed, consistent with the principle of subsidiarity, where development focuses on a particular community, the most appropriate level of decision-making is that which operates as closely as possible to members of that community and preferably with their involvement.[4]

With this in mind, the chapter is structured to discuss examples of bottom-up, community-led approaches to local regeneration in the UK. It first considers the New Deal for Communities[5] programme, established under the 1997–2010 Labour

1 P Foley and S Martin, 'A New Deal for the Community? Public Participation in Regeneration and Local Service Delivery' (2000) 28(4) *Policy & Politics* 479 at 480–2.

2 Ibid. 480.

3 A Layard, 'Law and Localism: The Case of Multiple Occupancy Housing' (2012) 32(4) *Legal Studies* 551 at 552.

4 See Chapter 2 (n 18) and Consolidated Version of the Treaty on European Union [2012] OJ C326/15, Article 5(3).

5 Hereinafter NDC.

government, and then explores aspects of the Coalition's Big Society policy. The community-led approach is central to the achievement of accountability and the encouragement of citizen participation as it ensures that decisions can be made at a level closer to citizens, making the process easier to scrutinise and more accessible to involvement. Consequently, following application of the 'model of local sustainability', the chapter concludes that not only do accountability and citizen participation enhance the achievement of sustainability at this level, but also the community-led approach is crucial to tackling local deprivation. Despite this, though, it does also highlight that concerns relating to citizen participation and the willingness of centralised authorities to 'let go' of locally focused powers have perhaps hindered the success of community-led sustainability in practice. This will be further discussed in Chapter 6.

Sustainability in local communities under Labour: the New Deal for Communities

Community regeneration and sustainability were priorities from the early days of Labour's period in government, with the Social Exclusion Unit being tasked to 'develop integrated and sustainable approaches to the problems of the worst housing estates, including crime, drugs, unemployment, community breakdown, and bad schools etc.'.[6] This culminated in a report in 1998 entitled *Bringing Britain Together*, which set out the foundations for the government's national strategy for neighbourhood renewal.[7] It outlined the way in which progress during Labour's first year in power would be built on through increased funding to tackle local regeneration as well as through ensuring coherent policies could effectively tackle local problems.[8] It set out a strategy for tackling poor neighbourhoods, which emphasised a focus on local people, the involvement of communities, the development of an integrated approach with clear leadership, the need for mainstream policies to work within the poorest neighbourhoods and the making of long-term commitments with sustained political priority.[9] In the report, Tony Blair emphasised the severity of local deprivation:

> [W]e all know the problems of our poorest neighbourhoods – decaying housing, unemployment, street crime and drugs . . . over the last two decades the gap between these 'worst estates' and the rest of the country has grown. It has left us with a situation that no civilised society should tolerate.[10]

6 Social Exclusion Unit, *Bringing Britain Together: A National Strategy for Neighbourhood Renewal*, Cm 4045 (London: HMSO, 1998) 1, © Crown Copyright, contains public sector information licensed under the Open Government Licence v2.0 <http://www.nationalarchives.gov.uk/doc/open-government-licence/version/2/> ('*Bringing Britain Together*').

7 Ibid. generally.

8 Ibid. paras. 11, 12 and 13.

9 Ibid. para. 10.

10 Ibid. foreword.

The report was built on over the next few years, with a more concrete National Strategy for Neighbourhood Renewal being published in 2001. This set out 'to narrow the gap between outcomes in deprived areas and the rest'[11] of the country through harnessing government funding, rather than relying on one-off spending, and ensuring that local partnerships and empowered residents could play a part in tackling a range of problems that affect severely deprived neighbourhoods.[12]

One of the most prominent ways in which this developed in practice was through the introduction of new area-based programmes, set up by the government to 'turn around' deprived areas.[13] It is the purpose of this section to consider such area-based programmes and to explore the nature of the Labour government's commitment to community-led regeneration and its achievement of local sustainability in this way. Wary of the vast network of initiatives, programmes and partnerships that were set up as part of the Strategy and wider policies,[14] however, this chapter focuses on the NDC, seeking to take that programme as an example of Labour's drive for community-led regeneration. This can be justified on the basis that it was set up as a pathfinder project to determine the opportunity for community-led neighbourhood renewal and the extent to which it might work in practice. Over the years that followed the NDC came to be one of Labour's flagship regeneration policies and, as such, it provides a suitable example here of efforts to pursue local community sustainability.

The NDC programme was developed by a number of Whitehall departments alongside the Social Exclusion Unit, and launched by the Office of the Deputy Prime Minister in 1999.[15] Set up in 39 of the most deprived neighbourhoods across England, the NDC programme was an experiment in local regeneration, intended to give communities and local people greater influence over the way in which 'funds are used to achieve neighbourhood renewal'.[16] As Stanton acknowledges, 'whereas previous regeneration programmes had seen monies being paid to central and local government bodies for the purposes of regeneration . . . the NDC involved monies being allocated directly to particular neighbourhoods for them to manage, under the direction of a Partnership Board, chiefly made up of local representatives'.[17] The extent to which the NDC community-led regeneration programme was aligned with broader objectives relating to sustainability is noted by Humphreys, who, writing in the context of the NDC, notes that 'regeneration

11 Social Exclusion Unit, *A New Commitment to Neighbourhood Renewal* (London: Cabinet Office, 2001) foreword.

12 Ibid. foreword.

13 See *Bringing Britain Together* (n 6) para. 4.2.

14 Examples of other initiatives and programmes include: Sure Start, the Single Regeneration Budget, the Neighbourhood Renewal Fund, Neighbourhood Warden Schemes and Neighbourhood Management Programmes, to name just a few. See further ibid. chapters 4 and 5.

15 See Committee of Public Accounts, *An Early Progress Report on the New Deal for Communities Programme* (HC 2003–04, 492) 3. Also see J Stanton, 'Local Sustainable Development: Lessons Learned from the New Deal for Communities' (2012) 14(1) *Environmental Law Review* 26 at 26.

16 Ibid. 3.

17 Stanton (n 15) 26. Also see ibid. 3.

initiatives are the implementation of environmental, social and economic improvements to an area of deprivation while ensuring such improvements are sustainable',[18] thus echoing the words of the three-pillar approach that has become central to local sustainability.[19] On this basis, the NDC supported plans that brought 'together local people, community and voluntary organisations, public agencies, local authorities and business in an intensive local focus to tackle problems such as: poor job prospects; high levels of crime; a rundown environment; and [the challenges posed by having] no one in charge of managing the neighbourhood and coordinating the public services that affect it'.[20]

Between 1999 and 2011, the intention was that the various NDC programmes would engage in partnership with other local bodies and organisations, such as local authorities and other public service providers, to achieve the objectives necessary in a given community.[21] The manner in which these particular objectives could differ from community to community, dependent on locally relevant issues, justified the local focus and meant that, in theory, the programme would be more responsive and efficient than one imposed by centralised authorities[22] that, on past experience, might have adopted more of a one-size-fits-all approach to local regeneration. Indeed, as *Bringing Britain Together* stated, 'the key to the New Deal for Communities is that it is . . . very local. [This] will allow communities to identify closely with the programme and be actively involved.'[23] This, as Stanton notes, 'helped to lay the foundations for what was intended to be a community-led, bottom-up regeneration programme. The rationale for the programme was that it would "empower local communities to shape a better future for themselves".'[24] At first glance, therefore, with its local focus, localised management of allocated funds and its community-led approach, the NDC programme was very much in tune with the justifications that go to the very core of local sustainability.

In terms of further explaining the nature of the NDC, however, it is necessary to explore a particular example of the programme. The EC1 NDC serves as such an example, and the chapter moves on now to consider the manner in which it worked in practice, so as to lay the foundations for later consideration of the extent to which it achieved accountability and encouraged citizen participation in the achievement of local sustainability. Regarded as one of the most successful examples of the programme,[25] the EC1 NDC partnership was set up in 2001 to

18 M Humphreys, 'Leaseholder Charges and Urban Regeneration' (2006) *Journal of Planning and Environmental Law* 1625 at 1626.

19 See Chapter 2.

20 *Bringing Britain Together* (n 6) para. 4.4, cited in Stanton (n 15) 27.

21 *An Early Progress Report on the New Deal for Communities Programme* (n 15) 3. These objectives might include: reducing the extent of crime, unemployment, poor health and low educational performance and improving the physical environment (3).

22 See Stanton (n 15) 27.

23 *Bringing Britain Together* (n 6) para. 4.9, cited in Stanton (n 15) 27.

24 Stanton (n 15) 27. He there cites: Tony Blair in *Bringing Britain Together* (n 6) foreword.

25 See 'Regeneration Consultancy of the Year: Renaisi' *Regeneration and Renewal*, 24 September 2009 <http://www.regen.net/news/940731/Regeneration-Consultancy-Year/?DCMP=ILC-SEARCH> accessed 10 November 2013.

tackle urban deprivation across parts of Clerkenwell and Finsbury in the London borough of Islington, doing so on the basis of a number of self-set targets aligned with broader objectives relating to sustainability.[26] The EC1 partnership was led by a Partnership Board on the basis that effective decisions should be made in a transparent and accountable way, and at the same time cognisant of the programme's objectives and the importance of upholding the community-led approach.[27]

As the strategic decision-making body responsible for establishing the direction and effective delivery of the programme,[28] the Partnership Board was one of the most important aspects of the NDC's governance structure. In all 39 of the NDC partnerships, the Boards were comprised 'of a combination of local residents and representatives of the main [local] service agencies',[29] who between them oversaw the operation and day-to-day delivery of the programme.[30] Headed by a chair,[31] the Boards had a number of core functions.[32] In the EC1 NDC, for example, these included the coordination and management of actions addressing deprivation across the respective community.[33] This involved identifying local needs, liaising with local service providers, developing and agreeing a long-term and annual development strategy with the regional Government Office, managing the delivery of local projects in line with the programme strategies, and managing and accounting for funds with the partnership's Accountable Body.[34] The Partnership Board, therefore, played a key day-to-day role in the NDC's pursuit of local

26 EC1 New Deal for Communities, *Governance Framework*, 17 July 2007, as amended on 16 April 2009 and 11 June 2009, para. 1.1 ('EC1 Governance Framework'). The Governance Framework noted these targets as stating that, by 2011, EC1 would be cleaner, greener, safer and a more attractive place to live, work, study, play, visit and do business in. The people in the EC1 area would be healthier and wealthier, with improved skills, qualifications and life opportunities. The community was to become stronger and more sustainable, with an improved sense of civic pride and social responsibility, and be more involved in shaping its own destiny (para. 1.1.1).

27 Ibid. para. 1.1.3.

28 Ibid. para. 1.1.3.

29 DCLG, *The New Deal for Communities Programme: Achieving a Neighbourhood Focus for Regeneration* (London: HMSO, 2010) para. 3.8 (a report written and compiled by CRESR).

30 DCLG, *Involving Local People in Regeneration: Evidence from the New Deal for Communities Programme* (London: HMSO, 2010) 6 (a report written and compiled by CRESR).

31 In the EC1 NDC, the chair was a local resident.

32 EC1 Governance Framework (n 26) para. 2.1.1. The Framework notes that these required it to: (a) Develop and promote strategies and oversee interventions to improve the physical aspects and quality of life of the area; improve the skills, confidence, health and aspirations of the people; improve their capacity to 'get involved'; create a more cohesive community; improve the local service infrastructure; improve local housing options; and facilitate ongoing community participation. (b) Ensure community involvement is central to all its strategies. (c) Develop plans to make best use of the allocated funding. (d) Scrutinise performance to ensure the various targets are met. (e) Act as 'champions' for the NDC programme. (f) Strengthen partnerships for the good of the community. (g) Consider all complaints and appeals (para. 2.1.1).

33 Ibid. para. 2.1.1.

34 *Achieving a Neighbourhood Focus for Regeneration* (n 29) para. 3.9. The Accountable Body was, in most cases, the respective local authority.

sustainability and, with the involvement of local people, was very much the driving force behind a partnership's tackling of local deprivation, as the chapter will go on to discuss.

Delivery of the NDC programme was, in each case, overseen by a Chief Executive, who was continually accountable to the Board,[35] and in the EC1 NDC delivery was also assisted by three external bodies: first, an EC1 Delivery Team, a locally based team responsible for coordinating and delivering the programme's day-to-day administration, programme management, coordination and delivery;[36] second, an Accountable Body, in the form of Islington Borough Council, responsible for the overall financial management of the NDC programme;[37] and finally, the Delivery Agents, which were a wide range of organisations and groups that delivered the approved NDC projects.[38]

National delivery of the NDC programme was overseen by the DCLG via the Neighbourhood Renewal Unit.[39] It worked with other government offices and neighbourhood renewal teams to support and oversee local partnerships in deprived communities across England, by responding to local circumstances rather than directing everything from Whitehall.[40] As part of this and in addition to its role in delivering the NDC programme, the NRU also had responsibility for the Neighbourhood Management programme, the Neighbourhood Warden scheme, Community Chest and the Neighbourhood Renewal Fund.

It was the purpose of the NRU to harness government money, spent on sustainability policies, and to monitor its ongoing spending by the NDC Partnership Boards.[41] Recalling that, in respect of the NDC, there was a need to depart from formerly top-down models of neighbourhood renewal, where centralised bodies had overseen the allocated funds, the NRU played a key role in ensuring that Whitehall was not being too prescriptive in the way in which local initiatives operated, protecting the community-led nature of the programmes. Indeed, in its own words, 'the Neighbourhood Renewal Unit [was] not about Whitehall telling local governments and communities how they should run things. [It was] about co-ordination, interaction and the exchange of ideas in the field of urban renewal . . . a continuous, two-way process.'[42] It provided a way in which Whitehall's policies could be negotiated with local communities, citizens and the regeneration programmes and ensured that communities had the opportunities to focus on local problems and lead the push for change on the basis of local interests. Indeed,

35 EC1 Governance Framework (n 26) para. 6.4.

36 Ibid. para. 1.3.5 (a).

37 Ibid. para. 1.3.5 (b).

38 Ibid. para. 1.3.5 (c).

39 Hereinafter NRU. Also see V Lowndes, and H Sullivan, 'How Low Can You Go? Rationales and Challenges for Neighbourhood Governance' (2008) 86(1) *Public Administration* 53 at 60.

40 See DCLG, *About the NRU* <http://collections.europarchive.org/tna/20090106142604/; http://www.neighbourhood.gov.uk/page.asp?id=3> accessed 10 November 2013.

41 Ibid.

42 Ibid.

Kearns highlights the community emphasis that the NRU was intended to encourage in noting that the NRU was given the 'task of making "community cohesion a central objective of all its programmes" and to promote cross-community . . . experience'.[43] The NRU, therefore, played an integral part in the process of local sustainability. Working closely both with central government and community-led regeneration initiatives, such as the NDC, it oversaw the operation and the funding of neighbourhood renewal and strived to maintain the community-led nature of the various programmes which were so central to Labour's strategy.

In addition to, and working alongside, the NRU, the nine Government Offices[44] around the country also played a part in overseeing local regeneration programmes.[45] Prior to their abolition in 2011,[46] the Government Offices represented central government departments and provided a means through which a wide range of government policies could be communicated to and delivered in the regions.[47] One aspect of this work was to take responsibility 'for a wide range of activities to improve and promote sustainable communities'.[48] This involved administering 40 spending programmes and projects across London, including the NDC programme, the Neighbourhood Renewal Fund and the Neighbourhood Management programme.[49]

In respect of these, the Government Office for London provided advice and support and worked to ensure that they ran smoothly.[50] Indeed, its role was 'to ensure that sustainable development [was] . . . embedded in all related policies and programmes developed by these groups'.[51] This involved emphasising the need for social progress; recognising the needs of everyone; effective protection of the environment; prudent use of natural resources; and maintenance of high and stable

43 A Kearns, 'Social Capital, Regeneration and Urban Policy' in R Imrie and M Raco (eds) *Urban Renaissance? New Labour, Community and Urban Policy* (Bristol: Policy Press, 2003) 37 at 51. He there cites: Home Office, *Building Cohesive Communities: A Report of the Ministerial Group on Public Order and Community Cohesion* (2001) 32 <http://resources.cohesioninstitute.org.uk/Publications/Documents/Document/DownloadDocumentsFile.aspx?recordId=94&file=PDFversion> accessed 10 November 2013.

44 See Government Offices for the English Regions, *About the Network* <http://webarchive.nationalarchives.gov.uk/20100528142817/; http://www.gos.gov.uk/aboutusnat/> accessed 10 November 2013.

45 See, for example, in respect of the EC1 NDC, EC1 Governance Framework (n 26) 47.

46 M Sandford, House of Commons Library, *The Abolition of Regional Government* (Standard Note SN/PC/05842, 27 March 2013) 8 and 9.

47 Government Offices for the English Regions, *About the Network* (n 44).

48 Government Office for London, *People and Sustainable Communities* <http://webarchive.nationalarchives.gov.uk/20100528142817/; http://www.gos.gov.uk/gol/People_sustain_comms/?a=42496> accessed 10 November 2013.

49 Government Offices for the English Regions, *Neighbourhood Renewal: The National Picture* <http://webarchive.nationalarchives.gov.uk/20100528142817/; http://www.gos.gov.uk/peoplesuscomms/neighbourrenewal/?a=42496> accessed 10 November 2013.

50 See EC1 Governance Framework (n 26) para. 7.7.1.

51 Government Office for London, *Sustainable Development* <http://webarchive.nationalarchives.gov.uk/20100528142817/; http://www.gos.gov.uk/gol/People_sustain_comms/355601/?a=42496> accessed 10 November 2013.

levels of economic growth and employment.[52] These objectives clearly link in with and mirror those that lie at the very heart of the sustainability principle.[53] Through this role, the Government Office for London was required to submit individual NDCs' Delivery Plans for government approval, and to approve subsequent changes and annual spending plans, constantly monitoring the delivery and outcome of the programmes.[54] The Government Offices, therefore, had a key role to play in assisting with the delivery of the NDC, working alongside the NRU in administering the scheme on behalf of central government. Whilst the NRU's task was primarily to harness and monitor government spending on the ground in the individual programmes, the Government Offices were concerned more widely with ensuring that sustainability was at the heart of the local initiatives and programmes.

This section has set out the way in which the NDC operated within the wider context of Labour's neighbourhood renewal strategy, amidst a plethora of bodies and roles that assisted with its delivery at the local level. It was a flagship policy in neighbourhood renewal and came to be a key driver in determining the regeneration of deprived areas across England. In order that the chapter might later explore, in more detail, the way in which the NDC worked towards local sustainability and, in particular, evaluate the extent to which this was achieved, in line with the hypothesis set out in Chapters 2 and 3, it is necessary now to examine more closely the workings of the programme and to consider the extent to which it can be said to have achieved accountability and encouraged citizen participation.

Accountability and citizen participation in the NDC

This section is structured first to consider the extent to which the operation of the NDC achieved accountability, later exploring the manner in which the programme sought to encourage citizen participation through its community-led approach, both in terms of the participatory opportunities that were provided and the degree to which these were taken up in practice. This discussion will enable later examination of the extent to which the NDC's achievement of local sustainability was enhanced on the basis of the conceptual hypothesis set out in Chapters 2 and 3.

Accountability

It is recalled that accountability entails 'being liable to be required to give an account or explanation of actions and . . . to suffer the consequences, take the blame or undertake to put matters right if . . . errors have been made'.[55] As explained in Chapter 3, fundamental to this is the idea that citizens and communities should be

52 Ibid.
53 See Chapter 2.
54 EC1 Governance Framework (n 26) 47.
55 D Oliver, *Constitutional Reform in the UK* (Oxford: OUP, 2003) 48.

able to see how and why decisions and policies are made; they should have opportunities to communicate with decision and policy-makers, and they should be afforded appropriate mechanisms through which their rights of accountability can be exercised. Where such transparency, communication and accountability mechanisms exist, citizens can have a degree of control over the system to ensure that decisions and policies are locally relevant and that they are consequently responsive to locally specific needs and problems. Bearing all this in mind, this section sets out to explore the manner in which these various aspects of accountability – including the way in which it relates to wider aspects of decision-making – are achieved in respect of the NDC programme.

One of the first issues to consider, particularly in respect of the network of institutions tasked with delivery of the NDC programme, is to determine the relationship between responsibility and accountability. Though local authorities work at a level clearly subordinate to central government and operate on the basis of relatively clear powers, the community initiatives operated within a complex network of organisations and authorities, at the sub-governmental level. Various responsibilities were shared in respect of the achievement of local sustainability.

It is recalled that the notion of responsibility relates to broader issues, and sometimes at a higher level, than accountability and that, as a result, there must be responsibility in a decision-making process before accountability can be said to arise out of that process.[56] This is evident in respect of the bodies and institutions that oversaw the delivery of the NDC. The NRU, for example, was part of the DCLG and oversaw funding of the countrywide programme. In this way, it can be said to have had responsibility over the NDC's delivery. Consequently, accountability for the specific tasks and projects with which each of the individual programmes was engaged fell to the NDC Partnership Boards. And this makes sense. Whilst it was the role of the NRU to supervise the broad delivery of the programme in terms of negotiating the government's regenerative policies with local communities and overseeing the funding of the NDC (hence its responsibility for them), it was perhaps not so acutely aware of particular issues, local problems and community-specific needs that were the focus of decisions and policies implemented by the particular programmes themselves. As such, the NDC Partnership Boards can be said to have been more appropriately accountable. Indeed, recalling that it was their role to establish the direction of their respective partnerships, liaising with members of the community and service providers as to local needs and interests and making decisions setting out the strategy for development, it fell to the Partnership Boards 'to give an account or explanation of actions . . . [or] suffer the consequences, take the blame or undertake to put matters right if . . . errors have been made' in respect of the decisions and policies relating to the regeneration of their particular area.[57] Through examination of the relationship between these institutions, therefore, it is clear to see who was accountable for the

56 See 'Accountability and responsibility' section, p. 36 above.
57 Oliver (n 55) 48.

achievement of local sustainability and who was merely responsible for the broad delivery of wider objectives aligned with that sustainability.

Similarly, on a more regional level, the relationship between individual Government Offices and local NDC partnerships also exemplifies the connection between accountability and responsibility. For instance, the Government Office for London administered the EC1 NDC on behalf of the DCLG and was, therefore, responsible for facilitating the delivery of the EC1 NDC partnership. This involved administering the initiative, providing advice and support to ensure that it ran smoothly, and constantly monitoring the achievement of local outcomes.[58] As a consequence, the EC1 NDC was accountable, answerable and potentially blameworthy for the actual decisions it made, the policies it sought to implement, and the way in which it sought to regenerate that particular neighbourhood.

Consideration of accountability and responsibility, therefore, provides understanding of the relationship between the NRU, the Government Offices and the NDC, and the nature of their specific roles. Whereas the higher bodies were responsible for the broad facilitation of the programme, the NDC itself and, in particular, its Partnership Board were accountable for the specific decisions and regenerative policies it sought to implement on the ground in local communities. These relationships, therefore, structured around this connection between accountability and responsibility, were key to the success of the NDC. They ensured a foundation for support and delivery of the programme and, as will be explored now, a potential basis for local accountability.

It is recalled that one of the most basic requirements for accountability is the existence of a clearly identifiable leader or decision-maker who, due to the transparency of their position, can be held easily to account for the decisions and policies that they make by individuals who can see how and by whom decisions are made and the process by which they are formulated. In the NDC, the Partnership Board, headed by a local chair and working alongside the Chief Executive, provided that clearly identifiable leadership. It was their role to make decisions in the pursuit of local regeneration and to oversee the working of the partnership.[59] Indeed, the EC1 NDC, for example, published on its website a Governance Framework which set out the structure within which the partnership operated, the roles and functions of the Board, and their decision-making responsibilities.[60] As a result, local citizens were aware of the way in which the process operated and were able to identify decision-makers and, as a result, exercise their rights of accountability more effectively.

In addition to the need for clearly identifiable leadership, however, it is also important that citizens and communities have appropriate mechanisms through which they can exercise their rights of accountability, as Chapter 3 explained. One such mechanism in respect of the NDC programme relates to the way in which

58 EC1 Governance Framework (n 26) 47.

59 *Involving Local People in Regeneration* (n 30) paras. 1.2 and 2.30.

60 See EC1 Governance Framework (n 26).

members were selected to join the Partnership Boards. Though in some instances Board Members were appointed, all of the 39 NDC partnerships employed a process of elections at some point during the programme's life.[61] The value of elections as a key mechanism for accountability has already been discussed,[62] though, in respect of the NDC, it is worth adding that the 'advantages of elections are straightforward, and include demonstrable accountability, a way of increasing Board Members' sense of legitimacy'.[63] Simply put, through the ballot box and in line with *ex-ante* accountability, individuals had the opportunity directly to select those representatives who might best understand and strive to meet their needs and interests, also giving the citizens greater legitimacy to exercise their rights of accountability to ensure that the Board was collectively blameworthy or praiseworthy in respect of its decisions and policies.[64] Indeed, as Shaw and Davidson note, these NDC elections served 'to legitimate the role of community representatives' and 'establish the credibility of a new approach to regeneration'.[65] In addition, and linked to this 'right of accountability', the NDC elections also inspired a sense of ownership over local issues and gave 'local people . . . the opportunity to reclaim from local agencies some of the decisions which affect their everyday lives'.[66]

Over and above the level of accountability potentially ensured through NDC elections, however, the avenues of communication and potential for dialogue between decision-makers and citizens also ensured accountability. Indeed, recalling the words of Mulgan who notes that accountability 'involves social interaction and exchange, in that one side, that calling for the account, seeks answers and rectification while the other side, that being held accountable, responds and accepts sanctions',[67] it was a fundamental part of the NDC's accountability that it interacted with the local community and communicated with local citizens as regards local issues and problems and took the necessary action to address them.

One way through which this was achieved in the EC1 NDC was by way of a neighbourhood scheme called EC1 Connect. This was a project, unique to the EC1 partnership, which operated across the local area and that involved advisers contacting local residents through systematic door knocking on all social housing

61 All NDC partnerships had board elections at some point. *Achieving a Neighbourhood Focus for Regeneration* (n 29) para. 3.16.

62 See 'Mechanisms for accountability' section, p. 33 above.

63 *Achieving a Neighbourhood Focus for Regeneration* (n 29) para. 3.17.

64 See JM Moncrieffe, 'Accountability: Idea, Ideals, Constraints' (2001) 8(3) *Democratization* 26 at 27 and Oliver (n 55) 48.

65 K Shaw and G Davidson, 'Community Elections for Regeneration Partnerships: A New Deal for Local Democracy?' (2002) 28(2) *Local Government Studies* 1 at 7.

66 Ibid. 7.

67 See R Mulgan, 'Accountability: An Ever-Expanding Concept' (2000) 78(3) *Public Administration* 555 at 555.

estates and at community events.[68] This enabled the issues and concerns of local citizens to be linked into local agencies and the NDC partnership, thereby allowing local experience and expert knowledge to inform and enhance the tackling of local problems and to support service provision across the area. As a consequence, local citizens not only had a direct input into the process, thus ensuring responsiveness of decision-making and service provision,[69] but also had a valuable opportunity to hold the partnership to account for issues affecting the local area. Through discussion with residents, those working on behalf of the partnership were able to explain and respond to questions relating to the operation of the EC1 NDC and to note input from residents, outlining local needs and interests, thereby fulfilling one of the crucial aspects of accountability.

In addition to EC1 Connect, the Complaints and Appeals procedure provided by the EC1 NDC partnership also encouraged citizens to come forward and talk about their issues and concerns with those leading the partnership.[70] This provided an avenue expressly for the purpose of inputting needs and issues into the process and ensured that citizens had the means through which they could question and scrutinise decision-makers, apportion blame where necessary and hold the process adequately to account. Through the EC1 Connect project and the Complaints and Appeals procedure, therefore, the EC1 NDC ensured that there were appropriate avenues of communication and dialogue through which citizens could question and scrutinise as well as voice their concerns and input issues and needs into the process. This satisfies the dialectical nature of the principle and demonstrates a further way through which the programme worked to ensure appropriate accountability to local people.

The achievement of accountability, therefore, was central to the NDC programme. Numerous mechanisms, in particular those facilitating and encouraging communication and dialogue between citizens and those working as part of the programme, ensured that there could be ample opportunity for explanation and scrutiny as well as ways through which citizens could input their needs and concerns into the process.

As a consequence of this, and recalling that accountability can be a mechanism for control,[71] it provides a way through which citizens are able to direct, to a degree, a decision-making process that affects them. Where that process is a local one, citizens can more easily hold decision-makers to account and exercise control over their decisions.[72] This is demonstrated by the example of the EC1 NDC

68 See foreword to Help on Your Doorstep, *Connecting People: Improving Lives* <http://www.helponyourdoorstep.com/SummaryReport.pdf> accessed 10 November 2013. Help on Your Doorstep was the successor to EC1 Connect and worked within the same model. It provides a suitable example, therefore, of the way in which the former scheme operated. Also see Stanton (n 15) 33.

69 See Stanton (n 15) 33.

70 EC1 Governance Framework (n 26) Appendix 7, 54–6.

71 See 'Accountability as a mechanism for control and responsiveness' section, p. 35 above.

72 It was noted, in Chapter 4, that 'decentralization makes government most responsive to local needs'. J-P Fauget, 'Does Decentralization Increase Government Responsiveness to Local Needs?' (2004) 88 *Journal of Public Economics* 867 at 867.

programme. With its decisions being made at the local level and with the input of local people through the EC1 Connect scheme and residents' involvement on the Partnership Board, people across the area were able to exercise a degree of control over the way in which the partnership operated and the decisions affecting the regeneration of their local community.

In addition to this, accountability can also be a mechanism for responsiveness. By way of the aforementioned EC1 Connect scheme and the EC1 NDC Complaints and Appeals procedure,[73] for example, local citizens also had the opportunity to air their grievances, to voice their issues and concerns, and to alert decision-makers to problems and issues troubling the local area. The input of local knowledge and expertise in this way gave the NDC Partnership Board the opportunity to take appropriate action and make relevant and responsive decisions, acting in a way best for the local community.[74] Indeed, in Chapter 3 it was noted that, 'in order to act . . . in the citizen's interests, representatives must . . . know what these interests are; allow for deliberation and consultation so that policies may be corrected where appropriate . . . [and] provide . . . opportunities for public response'.[75] Through a complaints procedure and the EC1 Connect scheme, therefore, the EC1 NDC partnership worked to understand local issues and problems and provide avenues for deliberation and consultation; consequently, it was well placed to provide relevant and responsive decision-making on the basis of local concerns.

Accountability, therefore, was a crucial part of the NDC programme's decision-making process. The various mechanisms not only gave citizens the opportunity to seek answers and explanations in respect of decisions, but they also, due to the decentralisation that was fundamental to the operation of the programme and its community-led nature, meant that citizens could exercise a degree of control over the process and ensure that resultant decisions were responsive to local needs and problems.

Another key aspect of the programme's community-led approach, however, was its potential for citizens' involvement in local decision-making. This chapter now considers the extent to which the NDC encouraged citizen participation and the potential impact that this had on the programme, before later discussing the wider reality of the NDC's potential to achieve accountability and encourage citizen participation.

Citizen participation

Citizen participation is fundamental to local sustainability, not only in terms of the democratic benefits that can come from drawing on local experience, knowledge

73 EC1 Governance Framework (n 26) Appendix 7, 54–6.
74 Ibid. Appendix 7, 54–6.
75 Moncrieffe (n 64) 27.

and possibility, but also in terms of public participation being a key principle of sustainability and environmental decision-making more widely.[76] This section, therefore, is structured to explore the community-led nature of the programme, to evaluate the extent to which it can be said truly to have encouraged citizen participation and, in line with conclusions set out in Chapter 3, to consider the way in which the relationship between accountability and citizen participation is linked to the way the NDC programme operated.

It was noted above that the NDC was community-led. As a result, a desire and need to involve members of the community was embedded in the very nature of the programme from the outset. Indeed, as Dinham notes, 'in community development, local participation is regarded as axiomatic, both to the success of any local initiative, which requires "insider knowledge" and expertise in order to make appropriate and sustainable interventions and in terms of the fundamental values of empowerment, partnership and involvement which underpin it'.[77] As a result of the NDC's community-led nature, therefore, citizens enjoyed a range of opportunities to input their 'insider knowledge' and local expertise into the process, thus ensuring a platform upon which they could drive forward the push for change and community regeneration on the basis of their own participation.

This was a key characteristic of the NDC, as Foley and Martin observe in noting that many past regeneration projects and initiatives had predominantly existed within 'top down' structures, with the motivation coming from bureaucrats and businessmen rather than the people within the communities themselves.[78] Consequently, local communities and citizens had little influence over the plans to revitalise their local areas and little or no say in the design or delivery of the services.[79] In view of past experiences, therefore, 'it has become conventional wisdom that communities need to be involved both in designing what is to be done and in implementing it',[80] something that was reflected in the community-led nature of the NDC. In the EC1 NDC, for instance, local citizens were heavily involved in regenerating changes that were made to Spa Fields, an open space in

76 See, as discussed in Chapter 3, UN, *Rio Declaration on Environment and Development*, Annex 1 to the *Report of the United Nations Conference on Environment and Development*, Rio de Janeiro, 3–14 June 1992, A/CONF.151/26, Vol. I, New York: UN, Principle 10, and UNECE, *Convention on Access to Information, Public Participation in Decision-Making and Access to Justice in Environmental Matters*, 25 June 1998, Aarhus, Denmark, Article 1 ('Aarhus Convention').

77 A Dinham, 'Empowered or Over-Powered? The Real Experience of Local Participation in the UK's New Deal for Communities' (2005) 40(3) *Community Development Journal* 301 at 303. He there cites: A Twelvetrees, *Community Work* (3rd edn, Basingstoke: BASW/Macmillan, 2001); D Finneron, *Faith in Community Development: Case Studies of Church Based Community Development Projects in Urban Priority Areas* (Manchester: Manchester Monographs, 1993); S Jacobs and K Popple, *Community Work in the 1990s* (Nottingham: Spokesman, 1994); K Popple, *Analysing Community Work: Its Theory and Practice* (Maidenhead: Open University Press, 1995); A Dinham and D Finneron, *Building on Faith: Faith Buildings in Neighbourhood Renewal* (London: Church Urban Fund, 2002).

78 Foley and Martin (n 1) 480.

79 Ibid. 479.

80 *Bringing Britain Together* (n 6) para. 2.3, cited in Dinham (n 77) 302.

the south-west corner of Islington, and the promenade area of Old Street, close to the London underground station of the same name,[81] and also in the delivery of the aforementioned EC1 Connect scheme.[82]

At Spa Fields, formerly a run-down playground that attracted antisocial behaviour, some of the young people who had 'previously made the park feel . . . quite . . . threatening . . . were deliberately involved in the design and implementation process' and were given the opportunity to undertake training and work experience as part of the project, three of them thereafter being offered full-time work by the contractor.[83] The result, as a consequence of such involvement, is a completely redesigned park, better suited to broader local needs, attracting residents and workers alike and with far fewer problems than were previously experienced.[84] This illustrates the value of citizen participation and demonstrates the extent to which local input was able to lead to key improvements and developments that were responsive to the needs of the local community. Similarly, the previously 'gloomy and . . . unsafe' promenade on Old Street, the deprivation of which had attracted many 'street drinkers and drug addicts', was transformed as a result of public consultation during which many local people urged the NDC to create a greener area, with more planting.[85] Consequently, 'there is now new seating, paving, flower beds and [a] promenade of trees and lights', causing the area to feel safer and be much enjoyed by local citizens.[86]

Finally, recalling that the EC1 Connect scheme involved advisers contacting local residents to identify the issues affecting the area and linking them to agencies that could provide support, the project was citizen-led and brought residents and service providers together to combine local experience and expert knowledge to tackle key local problems.[87] The manner in which residents were able to have their issues heard and dealt with by those individuals who were working as part of the EC1 Connect scheme exemplifies further the way in which citizen participation could be used to gauge the needs of the people and form a key part of the NDC's regeneration of the EC1 area. Indeed, this is reflected in Stanton's consideration that EC1 Connect serves as an example of the NDC actively seeking to engage members of a community through teams dedicated to promoting engagement and involvement.[88]

These three examples demonstrate that, through the community-led nature of the EC1 NDC programme, citizens were involved in the day-to-day work of the programme and had opportunities to play an active role and to input their experi-

81 L Kessler, 'EC1 New Deal for Communities – before and after Transformations' *Horticulture Week*, 13 August 2010 <http://www.hortweek.com/news/1021460/> accessed 10 November 2013.

82 See *Connecting People: Improving Lives* (n 68) above.

83 Kessler (n 81).

84 Ibid.

85 Ibid.

86 Ibid.

87 Stanton (n 15) 33.

88 Ibid. 33. He there cites: *Involving Local People in Regeneration* (n 30) figure 4.5.

ences and knowledge into the system to ensure that regeneration could be achieved in line with local needs and interests.

Over and above the day-to-day opportunities that citizens had to participate in the programme, however, one of the most significant ways through which the NDC facilitated the involvement of local citizens was through the appointment or election of residents to the Partnership Boards. Though the role that these Boards fulfilled has already been noted, the manner in which they included local residents served to ensure that citizens could directly participate in decisions, policies and the general day-to-day running of the partnership, playing a key part in the sustainable development of their local community. Indeed, as Robinson *et al.* note, citizen involvement in this way was 'a key feature of the NDC programme . . . [aiming as it was] to develop and pursue regeneration that [was] . . . "resident-led"'.[89] Their role was an important one as they provided a link between the Board and their fellow residents, inputting key information and advice on the day-to-day quality of life in the neighbourhood, ensuring local concerns were raised and could be addressed by the Board, thus influencing key decisions.[90]

The number of local citizens having the opportunity to participate on the Partnership Boards varied from scheme to scheme, though 'in 2008, [a survey noted that] community residents made up at least 50 per cent of the membership of 31 partnership boards'.[91] In the EC1 NDC, for example, the 18-strong Partnership Board was made up of eight local residents, one of whom, as Chair, had a casting vote when decisions came to be made.[92] The Partnership Boards, therefore, demonstrate a key way through which local citizens were encouraged to engage with the programme, whilst these statistics serve to illustrate the extent to which this involvement was taken up and the value with which it was regarded.

With all this discussion about the opportunities for citizen participation in the NDC programme, however, it is important to consider the manner in which this fits with discussions in Chapter 3 relating to the need to ensure a minimal degree of representation. In terms of ensuring an organised and effective process of decision-making in the face of potentially widespread citizen participation, it is important that some degree of representation be upheld so as to accord elected decision-makers the final say at the same time as affording local citizens appropriate opportunities to get involved. This, it was suggested, accords with the levels of placation and partnership on Arnstein's 'ladder of citizen participation'.[93]

89 F Robinson, K Shaw and G Davidson, '"On the Side of the Angels": Community Involvement in the Governance of Neighbourhood Renewal' (2005) 20(1) *Local Economy* 13 at 15.

90 EC1 Governance Framework (n 26) para. 2.3.5 (a).

91 DCLG, *The New Deal for Communities Experience: A Final Assessment* (London: HMSO, 2010) para. 2.5 (a report written and compiled by CRESR).

92 EC1 Governance Framework (n 26) para. 2.2.2 (a) and (b).

93 S Arnstein, 'A Ladder of Citizen Participation' (1967) 35(4) *Journal of American Institute of Planners* 216.

Applying this view here, the elections that were held in places to select members of NDC Partnership Boards, taken in the context of the wider participatory opportunities that were available to local citizens, serve to exemplify this balance between the 'minimal degree of representation' and appropriate citizen participation. On the one hand, citizens were able to participate in a range of NDC decisions and activities not only through the election of Board Members, but also through wider opportunities to get involved in specific projects and schemes. On the other hand, however, the elections themselves and the work of the Partnership Board meant that there was a degree of representation overseeing the delivery of an NDC partnership and ensuring that decisions could be made in an organised, legitimate and effective fashion. Whilst it has been argued that electing residents to the Partnership Board might have served to create something of a citizen hierarchy, with those sitting on the Boards perhaps being viewed as more valuable to the process than other residents,[94] the elections, alongside the community-led, participation-driven NDC, ensured that a minimal degree of representation could be maintained, thus protecting the effectiveness of the programme.

The NDC Partnership Boards, therefore, were at the very heart of the programme's community-led approach and served to ensure that citizens could be at the centre of decision-making in respect of local regeneration. Together with further examples, such as the EC1 Connect scheme and specific localised projects, this demonstrates the extent to which citizen participation was a central part of the NDC. It brought notable benefits in terms of the programme's community-led approach and ensured that decisions could be made with the involvement of local people and on the basis of their valuable input and expertise. In addition, and tying in with discussions in the previous section, this community-led approach and encouragement of citizen participation also served to enhance the achievement of accountability.

Indeed, recalling that 'where there is a strong culture of participation, then accountability will occur naturally . . . in that those most affected by the decision have been a part of making it, and will be immediately aware of its implementation',[95] through sitting on Partnership Boards, volunteering for and engaging with schemes and involving themselves in specific projects, local citizens were able to hold decision-makers to account with greater ease due to the manner in which they were a part of the process itself. Indeed, as Foley and Martin note, 'an enhanced role for local people will increase accountability and improve service standards'.[96] Consequently, as a result of both the improved accountability and the encouragement of participation, and in light of discussions throughout this chapter thus far, citizens were able to ensure that resultant decisions were potentially more responsive to local needs and interests.

94 Wright *et al.* argue that it brings with it feelings of inferiority and helplessness for the indirect participants: JSF Wright, J Parry, J Mathers, S Jones and J Orford, 'Assessing the Participatory Potential of Britain's New Deal for Communities' (2006) 27(4) *Policy Studies* 347 at 356.

95 J Onyx and B Dalton, 'Accountability and Advocacy' (2006) 12(1) *Third Sector Review* 7 at 15.

96 Foley and Martin (n 1) 480.

As these two sections have demonstrated, therefore, the achievement of accountability and encouragement of citizen participation were, on the face of it, central to the NDC programme and its community-led approach. Localised decision-making meant that citizens could more easily exercise their rights of accountability and influence the course of activity affecting the regeneration of their local areas, whilst a range of participatory opportunities meant that they could potentially be actively involved in local decision-making and activity, ensuring that the work of the NDC was both democratic and appropriate to the needs and interests of a particular community. Before considering the impact that this had on the NDC's pursuit of local sustainability, however, it is necessary now to consider the way in which this potential for accountability and citizen participation was achieved in practice.

Citizen participation and accountability in the NDC: the reality

Despite clear intentions that the NDC's approach would be instrumental to its success and to the achievement of local regeneration, there were doubts in its early stages as to whether the government could sustain and work with the bottom-up approach, with, as Foley and Martin note, past experiences and central government's strong centralising instinct potentially hindering the success of the initiative.[97] In addition, though the framework for citizen participation and a community-led approach was evidently put in place, its success was also dependent on the inclination of local people to take up available opportunities and to involve themselves in NDC decision-making and activity. This section considers these issues, first exploring evidence demonstrating the extent to which citizens were involved in the programme, before then discussing the success with which central government entertained the community-led approach.

Statistics published towards the end of the NDC show that in 2008, across the whole of the programme, not even a quarter of all those who were aware of their local NDC partnership were involved in NDC-organised activities.[98] Though this had increased from 16 per cent in 2002,[99] it speaks volumes in terms of the realisation of widespread community involvement that was perhaps envisaged at the programme's outset. Furthermore, though various statistics point favourably towards relative success in terms of personal development and community cohesion in NDC areas,[100] the fact remains that barely one in five citizens who were aware of the programme involved themselves in its projects and activities.

97 Ibid. 480.

98 The report (*Involving Local People in Regeneration* (n 30) para. 2.26) notes that 22 per cent of those who were aware of their local NDC partnership were involved in some way. Also see P Lawless, M Foden, I Wilson and C Beatty, 'Understanding Area-Based Regeneration: The New Deal for Communities Programme in England' (2009) 47(2) *Urban Studies* 257 at 269.

99 Lawless *et al.* (n 98) 269.

100 A 2008 Ipsos MORI Household Survey reports that more than half of all NDC residents who were not involved in NDC-related activities felt that the community-led NDC programme had improved

Of course, it is important not to lose sight of the clear evidence that where citizens did participate, they did so generally with positive effects; however, engagement and motivation to participate on the part of an empowered few were surpassed by wider apathy and disengagement across NDC communities. Indeed, as Wright *et al.* note, 'partnerships [relied] on a relatively small number of community participants . . . [there was] a general sense of apathy within communities towards the programme . . . [with] 75 per cent of residents not [having] heard of the NDC'.[101] This is demonstrated by the fact that, on the one hand, 'the proportion of NDC Board Members living within their NDC area [was as high as] . . . 83 per cent' in some neighbourhoods.[102] There was evidently a core group of citizens keen to play an active role on the Partnership Boards. On the other hand, however, wider apathy and disinterest amongst non-participants is evident upon consideration of the fact that, 'across the programme as a whole, turnout in [NDC Board] elections . . . averaged 23 per cent, [ranging] . . . from 4 per cent to 54 per cent'.[103] It is perhaps for this reason, amongst others, that some partnerships sought to shift from an elected Board to an appointed one.

It is clear, therefore, that, despite the dedication of a core group of individuals who took up opportunities to participate in their local NDCs, the full vision of widespread participation and an inherently community-driven pursuit of local regeneration was perhaps not fully realised. The impact that this had on the NDC's achievement of local sustainability is explored below, but at this point it is important to consider why it is that more people did not get involved in the NDC programme. Whilst it is not the purpose of this chapter to entertain sociological discussions around human behaviour in such circumstances, it is suggested here that there was perhaps a link between central government's supervision of the NDC programme and the apparent reluctance on the part of citizens fully to get involved.

Central government played a crucial part in the initial development and continued operation of the NDC programme. Indeed, as Lawless illustrates, 'the centre devised, funded and oversaw the Programme'.[104] Recalling, however, that there were concerns as to whether Labour could maintain the bottom-up approach, some doubted 'the government's willingness to trust local communities

their local areas, whilst 74 per cent of those involved in NDC activities were of the same opinion. B Duffy, J Vince and L Page, *Searching for the Impact of Empowerment* (2008) Ipsos MORI, Social Research Institute <http://www.ipsos-mori.com/DownloadPublication/1227_sri_local govt_searching_for_the_impact_of_empowerment_072008.pdf> accessed 10 November 2013. Figure 4.5 in *Involving Local People in Regeneration* (n 30) also shows that 89 per cent of those involved in NDC activities felt that people across the local area were very friendly, 65 per cent felt a part of the community and 58 per cent thought they knew most of the people in the local area.

101 Wright *et al.* (n 94) 347.

102 *Involving Local People in Regeneration* (n 30) para. 2.30; it was as low as 36 per cent in other areas.

103 *Achieving a Neighbourhood Focus for Regeneration* (n 29) para. 3.16.

104 P Lawless, 'Can Area-Based Regeneration Programmes Ever Work? Evidence from England's New Deal for Communities' (2012) 33(4) *Policy Studies* 313 at 321.

. . . with policy space, resources and autonomy' in the way set out in the NDC programme.[105] Indeed, to a degree, these fears were justified as, across the programme, central government monitored and scrutinised how the NDC's funds were spent. There was, for instance, considerable central instruction on the prioritisation of 'spending . . . annual financial allocations',[106] which meant that individual NDC partnerships came 'to place too much of an emphasis on annual spending plans, and not enough on devising evidence-based programmes to meet the particular needs of . . . localities'.[107] Indeed, whilst 'community representatives were told initially that NDC programme funding was "their" money, and it was for them to decide how it should be spent',[108] the reality was that communities' freedom became severely limited by constant appraisals, monitoring and reporting in respect of that money.[109] The trend was for NDC partnerships to work to meet objectives and targets set by the centralised executive rather than to strive to attain the primary goals of local development specific to their respective communities and with full control of available resources, therefore adding an unnecessary level of bureaucracy to what should have been a locally focused programme. Indeed, this is true not only in respect of NDC funds; it is also reflected in the way in which central government was keen to instruct communities as to the most effective manner of operation and the fact that it 'laid down a broad framework through which the Programme was to be implemented'.[110] Its approval was necessary both for Partnerships' succession strategies and for annual delivery plans,[111] and it provided constant support and advice, with the DCLG contributing to the training of NDC Board Members.[112]

It is evident, therefore, that there was a degree of reluctance on the part of central government to 'let go' of the power it was seemingly giving to communities to lead local regeneration, and to allow NDC partnerships to decide for themselves how local problems should be tackled and the most effective way of meeting a community's needs and interests. Despite the ostensible decentralisation of power, the government, it seems, retained a central grasp on the use of NDC funds and the manner of the programme's delivery. It was perhaps an example of Perrons and Skyers' view that, 'in the urban sphere in the UK, the formal devolution of responsibility to the local community often occurs in parallel with a centralization of effective control'.[113] This meant that in reality, as Wright *et al.* note, if the NDC was a bottom-up, community-led programme, then it was

105 Wright *et al.* (n 94) 348.
106 Lawless (n 104) 321.
107 Ibid. 321.
108 *Achieving a Neighbourhood Focus for Regeneration* (n 29) 9.
109 Ibid. 9. Also see Wright *et al.* (n 94) 357.
110 *The New Deal for Communities Experience: A Final Assessment* (n 91) para. 1.7.
111 *Achieving a Neighbourhood Focus for Regeneration* (n 29) paras. 6.8 and 7.7.
112 Ibid. para. 3.14.
113 D Perrons and S Skyers, 'Empowerment through Participation? Conceptual Explorations and a Case Study' (2003) 27(2) *International Journal of Urban and Regional Research* 265 at 265.

community-led in the sense that the government decided how the community would be involved, why they would be involved, what they could do and how they could do it.[114]

This section has explored in detail the manner of the NDC's encouragement of citizen participation and the impact of its relationship with central government. As the chapter has demonstrated, the community-led nature of the programme was one of its most defining characteristics. This gave rise to numerous mechanisms through which citizens could exercise accountability in respect of the NDC's decisions and actions, as well as a range of participatory opportunities through which local people could get involved in the programme. In this regard, the NDC can be said to have been relatively successful; where local people did participate, their communities benefited from that involvement and were improved as a result.[115]

There were issues, however. The levels of citizen participation were not as high as was perhaps envisaged at the outset, with less than a quarter of citizens who were aware of the NDC involving themselves in the programme's activities, whilst, more widely, there was something of a reluctance on the part of central government really to 'let go' and allow the individual partnerships to oversee a purely local focus on regeneration. The ways in which these two key issues might be addressed in terms of future efforts sustainably to develop local communities are considered further in Chapter 6. For now, however, it is necessary to explore the impact of the participation that was, to a degree, achieved by the NDC and the mechanisms for accountability that were evidently provided by the programme, and to consider the extent to which these can be said to have enhanced its achievement of local sustainability.

Accountability, citizen participation and sustainability in the NDC

This section seeks to apply the 'model of local sustainability' as set out in Chapter 2 to the NDC programme. In doing this, it is structured to address the five aspects of sustainability in turn, considering in respect of each the extent to which accountability and citizen participation can be said to have enhanced their achievement.

The role that the NDC played in achieving local sustainability went very much to the heart of its *raison d'être*. Whilst Chapter 2 noted the extent to which 'local decision-makers should "shape the place" because they "know best"',[116] above has been set out the manner in which the NDC programme was an experiment in community-led neighbourhood renewal, ensuring that local people could influence

114 Wright *et al.* (n 94) 349.

115 See, for example, the developments within the EC1 NDC that took place at Spa Fields and on Old Street (Kessler (n 81)).

116 Layard (n 3) 552.

the tackling of local deprivation.[117] Indeed, as Humphreys has already been quoted as saying, regeneration initiatives such as the NDC involve the 'implementation of environmental, social and economic improvements to an area of deprivation while ensuring such improvements are sustainable',[118] thus echoing the wording of the three-pillar approach and mirroring key aspects of the 'model of local sustainability'. The role that the NDC could play in terms of achieving local sustainability, therefore, was a key one, and it is on this basis that this section seeks to evaluate the extent to which accountability and citizen participation enhanced this role.

Needs of the people

The first aspect of the 'model of local sustainability' relates to the importance of meeting citizens' needs, something that is central to the principle, as the Brundtland Commission's definition serves to demonstrate.[119] The important role that accountability and citizen participation can play here relates to the manner in which they harbour the potential for responsive decision-making and the opportunity for citizens to have their say and to input into local processes.

Indeed, recalling the importance of the dialectical nature of accountability, the manner in which local citizens were able to engage and communicate with their NDC partnerships meant that they were able not only to scrutinise and demand answers and explanations in respect of the process, but also to ensure that their local needs and interests were acknowledged and taken into account. With regard to the EC1 Connect scheme, for example, the fact that NDC advisers sought to contact local residents through systematic door knocking meant that their local issues and concerns could be heard and taken into consideration.[120] On this basis, and with the input of local experience and expert knowledge, the partnership's decisions could be more responsive to local issues and problems, thus more effectively meeting citizens' needs. Furthermore, in those instances where the partnership had perhaps fallen short of meeting local needs, through the EC1 Connect scheme again, as well as further avenues of communication,[121] the dialectical nature of accountability served to provide local people with the opportunity to question and scrutinise decision-makers, holding them to account in respect of local needs and interests. The way in which the NDC programme

117 *An Early Progress Report on the New Deal for Communities Programme* (n 15) 3. Also see Stanton (n 15) 26–7.

118 Humphreys (n 18) 1626.

119 See World Commission on Environment and Development, *Our Common Future* (Oxford: OUP, 1987) ('Brundtland Report'), which defines sustainable development as 'development that meets the needs of the present without compromising the ability of future generations to meet their own needs' (43).

120 See Stanton (n 15) 33.

121 Such as the EC1 Complaints and Appeals process: EC1 Governance Framework (n 26) Appendix 7, 54–6.

provided mechanisms for accountability, therefore, ensured that decision-makers could take into consideration local needs and issues and provide responsive decision-making as a result. In addition, it meant that citizens were afforded valuable opportunities to seek explanations in the event of their needs not being sufficiently met. Thus the manner in which the NDC programme sought to achieve accountability enhanced the way in which it met local needs and interests, to the benefit of local sustainability.

In addition to the benefits of accountability, however, the responsiveness of the NDC decision-making process and the understanding and addressing of local needs also resulted from the participatory opportunities afforded to local people. Through facilitating the involvement of local residents and encouraging individuals to engage and get involved in the day-to-day operation of the programme, the NDC ensured that citizens who had first-hand experience of life in their local neighbourhood could input their needs, desires and issues directly into the decision-making process. Consequently, the resultant decisions were more responsive to local problems and able to satisfy the needs and desires of local people. In respect of the Partnership Boards, for instance, having local people elected to play a part in NDC decision-making meant that local knowledge and expertise and an understanding of issues and concerns could directly influence the resultant decisions and make the process potentially more responsive and more effective at meeting citizens' needs and improving the local area. Indeed, 83 per cent of resident Board Members felt that, through their involvement, they had made a difference to their local areas.[122] In addition to this though, citizen participation arising out of the community-led nature of the NDC also improved the extent to which the programme could meet the needs of local people. Through encouraging involvement in specific initiatives, such as those at Spa Fields and on Old Street in the EC1 NDC,[123] direct consultation and citizen participation served to ensure that local changes and developments were responsive and appropriate to a local area and its issues. The mechanisms for accountability set out by the NDC programme, as well as the opportunities it provided for citizen participation, therefore, ensured that local needs and interests were central to the programme and that it was well placed to work to ensure that they were met, thus demonstrating satisfaction of a key aspect of sustainability.

Sustainability

The second aspect of the model relates to sustainability. Its importance is justified on the basis that, consistent with the Brundtland Commission's definition of the principle,[124] developments made now must not only meet the needs of existing generations, but also provide a foundation for the needs of future generations. At

122 *Involving Local People in Regeneration* (n 30) para. 4.6 and figure 4.1.
123 See Kessler (n 81).
124 Brundtland Report (n 119) 43.

the local level, sustainability can be ensured through an ongoing commitment by communities and local people working to ensure that standards and achievements attained by developments are maintained into the future. As noted above, one way in which this can be fulfilled is through citizen participation in the constant maintenance and development of a local area.

In relation to the NDC programme, this ongoing commitment to sustainability could be ensured through the constantly community-led, bottom-up nature of the programme and the way in which decisions were made at a level close to citizens and, in many respects, with the benefit of their input and involvement. This is best exemplified by the aforementioned EC1 Connect scheme. During the life of the partnership, the scheme, which was resident-led, sought to draw from a wealth of local knowledge and experience as to the ways through which local services could be improved and community issues addressed. Upon the expiration of the NDC, local people worked to ensure that the work of EC1 Connect could continue into the future by setting up Help on Your Doorstep. This is a local charity that operates more widely throughout the London borough of Islington and that is led and overseen by local people.[125] Established in 2009 and based on the model of EC1 Connect, it seeks 'to improve the health and wellbeing of isolated and vulnerable Islington residents in areas with high levels of deprivation. By providing information and guidance, and through partnerships with local service providers, it aims to empower individuals to overcome barriers they face and improve their lives.'[126] Much like the EC1 Connect scheme before it, therefore, Help on Your Doorstep works to identify important local issues, promote local services and improve their reach, empowering local citizens to become involved, and to learn from their expertise and experience as to what the issues are across a local area.[127] In this way, it provides an example of the way in which local people were engaged and involved in efforts to ensure that improving developments, set up as part of the NDC programme, could be sustained into the future.

This commitment to the sustainability of local changes, however, runs deeper than the establishment of further projects designed to steer continuing developments and can also relate, it is suggested, to the local, personal interest that participating citizens might have as regards the state of their local area. To explain, if changes are being made which rectify local problems, improve quality of life and meet the needs of a community, then local people are likely to be more inclined to ensure that these changes are lasting as they affect their lives directly. For example, resident Board Members played a key participative role in NDC decision-making and ensured that local needs and interests could be appropriately represented on the Board. Though their decision-making responsibilities effectively ceased upon the expiration of the programme, as local residents they would

125 See Help on Your Doorstep, *About Us* <http://www.helponyourdoorstep.com/aboutus.asp?shead=whatwedo> accessed 10 November 2013.

126 *Connecting People: Improving Lives* (n 68) 3.

127 Help on Your Doorstep, *About Us* (n 125).

continue to benefit from their effects or, indeed, suffer if the consequent developments were not sustained into the future, giving rise to increased levels of deprivation. Consequently, it can be said that, as residents, they perhaps had a vested interest in ensuring that the improvements made by the programme could be sustained for their own future benefit. Indeed, from the programme's outset, it was 'anticipated that by involving local residents in decision making, NDC partnerships would help to ensure the sustainability of benefits and interventions once Programme funding came to an end'.[128]

It is perhaps as a result of this local interest that succession plans, which set out the way in which changes introduced as part of the NDC would be sustained beyond the life of the programme, were drawn up with the input of local people. In the EC1 NDC, for instance, the partnership, in consultation with local residents, set out key objectives for succession, suggesting ways in which they could be achieved and taking into account future risks and issues that might arise, all the while remaining keen to ensure that the needs of future generations could be met.[129]

Though, as this chapter earlier noted, there was perhaps a lack of widespread citizen participation across the NDC programme as a whole, where there was such participation, involved citizens had the opportunity to work to ensure the sustainability of changes and developments. Engagement with the EC1 Connect scheme and its successor, Help on Your Doorstep, for example, as well as involvement on the Partnership Boards and consultation as regards succession plans, display the sort of commitments that local people were able to display with regard to ensuring sustainable development into the future.

Three pillars of sustainability and the NDC

Having explored the manner in which accountability and citizen participation enhanced the NDC's work towards meeting the needs of local people and ensuring the sustainability of developments introduced as part of the programme, it is necessary now to consider the more substantive aspects of the 'model of local sustainability' that are reflected in the three pillars of the principle. In doing this, this section explores particular examples of the NDC programme and considers the extent to which it worked towards and achieved certain objectives aligned with each of the three pillars. Though it does not primarily or comprehensively seek to examine the success of the programme *per se*, it analyses its success in respect of certain objectives in order that the chapter might then proceed to evaluate the extent to which accountability and citizen participation enhanced its role in their regard.

The three pillars of sustainability were very much at the heart of the NDC programme, being an example of a local regeneration initiative that involved 'the

128 *Involving Local People in Regeneration* (n 30) para. 1.13.

129 See EC1 New Deal for Communities, *EC1 Beyond 2011* <http://www.renaisi.com/2011/wp-content/uploads/2011/05/EC1_Beyond_2011.pdf> accessed 10 November 2013.

implementation of environmental, social and economic improvements to an area of deprivation'.[130] Indeed, it is easy to identify key objectives of the NDC programme as falling under each of these aspects of sustainability. In respect of the EC1 NDC, for example, the aim was that, by 2011, the EC1 area would be:

> [C]leaner, greener, safer and [a] more attractive place to live, work, study, play, visit and do business . . . [with local people] healthier and wealthier, with improved skills, qualifications and life opportunities . . . [and the community] stronger and more sustainable, with an improved sense of civic pride and social responsibility . . . more involved in shaping its own destiny.[131]

Such objectives were set out on the basis that the NDC programme was 'aimed at addressing the problems associated with deprivation . . . carrying out 10 year strategic programmes designed to transform these deprived neighbourhoods and to improve the lives of those living within them'.[132] In this regard, from the government's perspective, the NDC enjoyed relative success, with a 2008 report noting that the NDC 'is delivering real improvements to people's lives, raising satisfaction, and bridging the gap between some of our most deprived neighbourhoods and the rest of England'.[133] Indeed, Hazel Blears, the then Secretary of State for Communities and Local Government, added in 2008 that 'NDC projects are transforming areas that for too long have been blighted by the cycle of deprivation. For some people NDCs have helped, it is the first time that they have felt proud of where they live, getting involved with and feeling part of their local communities.'[134]

With objectives very much aligned with the three pillars of sustainability, therefore, the NDC had a key role to play in tackling local deprivation and turning around local communities. With this in mind, and on this basis, it is important now to consider the extent to which accountability and citizen participation served to enhance the work of the programme. In doing so, this section is structured first to explore in detail the manner of the NDC's work in line with the three pillars of sustainability, before then considering the way in which accountability and citizen participation served to enhance this role.

It is recalled that environmental improvements generally relate to the physical aspects of a local area; with regard to the NDC, this could include the development and maintenance of local spatial areas and ensuring that the local physical environment is a pleasant place in which to live and work. As Stanton notes:

130 Humphreys (n 18) 1626.

131 EC1 Governance Framework (n 26) para. 1.1.1.

132 DCLG, *Transformational Change? A Synthesis of New Evidence 2008–2009* (London: HMSO, 2009) paras. 1.1–1.2.

133 DCLG, *New Deal for Communities Is Turning around England's Most Deprived Areas*, 11 February 2008 <http://www.gov-news.org/gov/uk/news/new_deal_communities_turning_around_england39s/88935.html > accessed 10 November 2013. Made available by Government News <http://www.gov-news.org/>.

134 See ibid.

> [I]improving the physical environment of . . . communit[ies was] . . . at the heart of the NDC . . . The scheme adopted a wide range of initiatives to improve and develop the physical environment which included, *inter alia*, supporting the modernisation of social housing and improving the residential environment, including cleaning up public spaces, remodelling residential environments in a bid to design out crime, and introducing more green spaces, improving gardens and alleyways.[135]

In the EC1 NDC, for example, the programme worked to revitalise and landscape residential estates, parks and gardens, providing new facilities and allotments and reducing vehicular traffic.[136] It also regenerated street markets and added more greenery, making parts of the area generally more desirable.[137] Areas at Spa Fields and on Old Street, for example, as discussed above, demonstrate the way in which the programme worked to develop the physical environment within the EC1 area – regenerating a formerly run-down playground into an attractive and often used park, and transforming a previously 'gloomy and . . . unsafe' promenade into a greener, safer and more pleasant street.[138]

The second of the three pillars, social development, is associated with objectives seeking to ensure that a neighbourhood is a healthy and safe place in which to live and work, as well as with a community's vibrancy and cohesiveness. In this regard, across the programme, local residents generally felt that the NDC had improved their local areas, with statistics showing a reduction in total crime rates and fear of crime, an improvement in GCSE results, increased satisfaction with NDC areas as places to live and a large number of people feeling that the NDC scheme had improved their area.[139] Indeed, with a specific focus on the EC1 NDC, changes to housing estates and local parks resulted in the area being safer, whilst improvements to local facilities meant that they could be more integrated into community life and attract more people.[140] Consequently, the area was one which local people could enjoy to a greater extent. More people now use the parks and open spaces, and local residents have commented that the area now 'feels more alive', with an increased sense of neighbourliness.[141] In respect of the aforementioned developments at Spa Fields, for example, following the transformation from a run-down playground, the new park is now used much more frequently by those living and working in the area, and the space is much safer and more enjoyable than it was previously.[142]

135 Stanton (n 15) 37. He there cites: DCLG, *Making Deprived Areas Better Places to Live: Evidence from the New Deal for Communities Programme* (London: HMSO, 2010) para. 2.41 (a report written and compiled by CRESR).

136 Kessler (n 81).

137 Ibid.

138 Ibid.

139 See DCLG, *New Deal for Communities: A Synthesis of New Programme Wide Evidence: 2006–07* (London: HMSO, 2008) Table 2.1 (a report written and compiled by CRESR).

140 Kessler (n 81).

141 Ibid.

142 Ibid.

In addition, and over and above the effects of specific, localised projects, the EC1 Connect scheme also contributed to the social development of the NDC area. Through knocking on residents' doors and determining community issues that were affecting them, the partnership worked to bring local people together and to inspire a greater sense of cohesion. Indeed, in respect of Help on Your Doorstep, which succeeded EC1 Connect, a recent evaluation notes the manner in which the scheme worked to improve local well-being, assisting citizens in accessing support and advice on key social issues – unemployment, housing and health, to name just three.[143]

The NDC programme, therefore, and the particular examples cited here in respect of the EC1 NDC, demonstrate that, through a range of developments and improvements, local areas could become more socially vibrant with safer and more cohesive communities, thus satisfying the second of the three pillars of sustainability.

In respect of the third and final pillar, economic development, the NDC worked to improve the health of community economies, focusing, in particular, on the reduction of worklessness and improvement of the quality of local services. For instance, in the EC1 area, the NDC helped to regenerate Whitecross Street market. Prior to the programme, 40 per cent of the shops there had been empty and the market itself had been reduced to a mere five traders.[144] The partnership, however, worked to create a new trading strip that now includes 50 market stalls, some of which are run by unemployed local residents,[145] offering an example of the way in which the NDC encouraged the strengthening of the local economy.[146] Furthermore, through not only facilitating the regeneration of Whitecross Street market but also inviting local people to train and work as part of the aforementioned Spa Fields development, the EC1 NDC provided employment opportunities for people across the area, demonstrating a further way in which the partnership worked to reduce worklessness.[147] Indeed, in respect of the EC1 NDC partnership more widely, statistics suggest that between 2002 and 2008 the unemployment rate fell by 1.6 per cent, the number of households with an income of less than £200 per week fell by 6.9 per cent, and the number of workless households dropped by 3 per cent.[148] The various projects and initiatives aimed at tackling worklessness and local financial deprivation, therefore, ensured that the partnership could strive to work towards objectives aligned with economic development and that it did so to some effect.

This section has demonstrated the manner in which the NDC programme and, in particular, examples provided by the EC1 partnership set out and worked

143 *Connecting People: Improving Lives* (n 68) 1.
144 Kessler (n 81).
145 Ibid.
146 See Stanton (n 15) 40.
147 Kessler (n 81).
148 The statistics are available here: CRESR, *NDC Secondary and Administrative Data* <http://extra.shu.ac.uk/ndc/ndc_data.htm> accessed 10 November 2013.

towards achievements aligned with the three pillars of sustainability. In doing this, it has shown that aspects of the EC1 area were improved as a result of the programme's work. Environmental changes, such as those at Spa Fields and on Old Street, meant that the local area could be enjoyed by a greater number of people. Social improvement projects, such as EC1 Connect, meant that the community was more cohesive, whilst efforts to tackle economic deprivation resulted in healthier unemployment figures. Recalling, however, that it is the thesis of this book to consider the extent to which accountability and citizen participation enhance the achievement of local sustainability, it is important now to assess to what degree the NDC's decision-making and its encouragement of local involvement played a part in the work that it did.

Citizen participation, accountability and the three pillars in the NDC

This section is structured to consider citizen participation and accountability in turn, exploring the extent to which they served to enhance the work of the NDC in pursuit of the three pillars of sustainability.

As noted above, the NDC's objectives were, from the outset, reflective of the three pillars of sustainability. Keeping this in mind, it can be argued that, even on the most basic level, use of the community-led approach in meeting these objectives demonstrated the importance of citizen participation in their achievement. Through inviting and encouraging resident involvement on the Partnership Boards, for instance, their local knowledge and expertise could input into decisions and policies striving to create a local community that could be 'cleaner, greener, safer and [a] more attractive place . . . [with local people] healthier and wealthier . . . [and the community] stronger and more sustainable, with an improved sense of civic pride and social responsibility'.[149]

The focus here will be on specific aspects of the three pillars. In terms of environmental development, citizen participation played a key role in ensuring that decision-makers could understand the needs and desires of local people and provide avenues through which citizens themselves could play a part in and influence decisions and actions setting out improvements to the local physical area. In respect of the EC1, for instance, citizens were consulted and played an active role in developing and improving the formerly run-down playground at Spa Fields and the previously dimly lit and gloomy promenade on Old Street,[150] inputting their views and working with the partnership to ensure that the areas were developed in ways that were appropriate for the local area and consistent with wider community needs and desires. This meant that the development of the local physical environment could be enhanced by the participation of local people.

Citizen participation also played a key role in shaping the NDC's achievement of social development, both in terms of specific projects aimed at improving local

149 EC1 Governance Framework (n 26) para. 1.1.1.
150 See Kessler (n 81).

cohesiveness and through involvement in wider developments as well. In respect of the EC1 Connect scheme, for instance, were it not for local people taking the time to engage with residents and to determine and understand their local issues, concerns and problems, the partnership would not have been able to work to tackle those issues – the consequence would have been changes that were not so in tune with citizens' needs and interests. Indeed, the value of the EC1 Connect scheme and its work in line with the social pillar of sustainability are highlighted by Stanton, who notes that it enabled the local community to come together and ensured local people could benefit from the partnership's advice, care and promotion of safety and inclusiveness.[151]

In addition, however, through involvement in wider developments and projects, and as a result of the community-led nature of the programme, local people had the opportunity to improve the sense of community, the quality of life and the cohesiveness of their neighbourhood. For example, in respect of both the Spa Fields and Old Street developments, citizens' involvement and input had helped establish areas that attracted a higher number of local people, were safer and experienced far fewer problems than previously encountered.[152] In this way, local citizens had the opportunity to play a fundamental part in improving the social aspects of their local community. Indeed, as Hazel Blears noted, '[f]or some people NDCs have helped, it is the first time that they have felt proud of where they live, getting involved with and feeling part of their local communities'.[153] Citizen participation, therefore, was crucial not only to specific projects that worked to improve the social aspects of the area, but also in respect of ensuring that wider projects were locally relevant and improved the quality of life in and the cohesiveness of a community.

Finally, the involvement of local people also played a small though key role in local economic development. Through citizens setting up stalls in EC1's Whitecross Street market, for example, the residents themselves were taking active steps towards reducing local unemployment. In addition, by buying in the local area and choosing to invest in and trade with local businesses and markets rather than established corporate chains,[154] citizens who used the market contributed to the health of the local economy by ensuring that their money was going back into local services and businesses.[155]

Citizen participation, therefore, played a crucial part in the NDC's pursuit of the three pillars of sustainability. Through local peoples' involvement, environmental development could occur on the basis of local needs and interests, whilst engagement with efforts to improve social aspects of community life increased local cohesiveness and helped to create a safer, more vibrant neighbourhood. Finally, through assuming an active role in local businesses and seeking actively to tackle

151 Stanton (n 15) 33.

152 See Kessler (n 81).

153 *New Deal for Communities Is Turning around England's Most Deprived Areas* (n 132).

154 Stanton (n 15) 40.

155 Ibid. 40.

unemployment, citizens helped to ensure that economic development could progress.

Alongside this, however, accountability in decision-making also had a key part to play in respect of the NDC's pursuit of the three pillars of sustainability. The manner in which the programme facilitated dialectical engagement and provided opportunities for communication between decision-makers and local citizens served to ensure that local people had the mechanisms through which to hold partnerships to account in respect of decisions and, importantly, that those making the decisions and setting out the policies were aware of and acknowledged local needs and interests. With regard to the aforementioned EC1 Connect scheme, for example, citizens had a valuable medium through which they could discuss and communicate with those working on behalf of the partnership as regards local issues and concerns; in addition, it ensured that they had opportunity to input their views and suggestions into the process as regards the manner in which the environmental, social and economic aspects of their community might be improved.

Furthermore, recalling that accountability can be a mechanism for responsiveness and control, through engaging with their local NDC partnerships and inputting their views and scrutinising decisions and actions, citizens were able to exercise a degree of control over the decision-making process and had the opportunity to ensure that decisions were responsive to local needs in respect of the environmental, social and economic aspects of their communities. For example, it has already been noted that, in seeking to develop the Old Street area of Islington, the EC1 NDC partnership engaged in consultation with local people, during which they urged the programme to create a greener area with more planting.[156] This was acknowledged by the partnership, and the improved area now includes 'new seating, paving, flower beds and [a] promenade of trees and lights', causing the area to feel safer and be much enjoyed by local citizens.[157] Through such dialogue, therefore, citizens were able to input their views and to steer the developments in a way that ensured they could be responsive to local needs and desires. Through the dialectical nature of accountability, therefore, local people were able to input their needs and interests into the process and to question and scrutinise their NDC partnership's decisions and actions. In this way, they could work to control the course of local development and ensure that resultant decisions and actions were responsive to the environmental, social and economic concerns of the local community.

This section has applied the 'model of local sustainability' to the NDC programme and provided an opportunity for evaluation of the extent to which citizen participation and accountability can be said to have enhanced the programme's achievement of local sustainability. It has shown that, through the involvement of local people and the accountability and responsiveness of decision-making, the needs and desires of communities can be met, developments can be sustained

156 Kessler (n 81).
157 Ibid.

through an ongoing commitment to improve local areas, and environmental, social and economic development can take place on the basis of local knowledge and expertise and with the involvement of and accountability to local people. Whilst there were issues as regards the widespread involvement of local people in the NDC and issues regarding decentralisation, as highlighted above and to be discussed further in Chapter 6, where citizens did participate and engage, they were able to bring change to their local areas and ensure the effectiveness and relevance of local decision-making. In conclusion, therefore, though wider issues mean that the NDC did not perhaps meet its full potential in terms of empowering citizens to get involved or in respect of the decentralisation of power, analysis of a range of examples – particularly the EC1 NDC – shows that, as an example of community-led regeneration under the 1997–2010 Labour government, the programme demonstrated the extent to which accountability and participation can enhance the achievement of local sustainability.

Sustainability in local communities: the Coalition and the Big Society

Following the General Election in May 2010, the Labour government was replaced by a Conservative–Liberal Democrat Coalition. Coupled with the planned expiration of the NDC programme in March 2011, this inevitably brought the potential for a change in approach and a fresh range of policies aimed at local democratic reinvigoration and the development of deprived communities. In view of this, it is the purpose of this section to explore some of the policies that the Coalition government has implemented over the past couple of years and to consider their potential successfully to regenerate deprived areas through citizen participation and local accountability. Though it is too soon to consider an in-depth analysis akin to that carried out in respect of the NDC programme above, the section at least sets out the nature of the Coalition's approach and considers its potential to demonstrate the enhancement of local sustainability through accountability and citizen participation. In doing this, it first outlines the relevant aspects of the Big Society policy and identifies the pertinent provisions of the Localism Act, before then considering the work of Locality, a charity set up in 2011 'to inspire local communities to change and improve'.[158]

The Big Society and community rights

The Big Society is one of the major policies of the Coalition government, having been one of the key drivers in the Conservatives' manifesto in the run-up to the 2010 election. Aimed at giving citizens, communities and local government greater power to come together, tackle local problems and 'build the Britain they want', the Big Society sets out a range of policies and promises which explore the

158 Locality, *About Us* <http://locality.org.uk/about/> accessed 10 November 2013.

strengthening of local society and the decentralisation of power and responsibility.[159] As part of this, the government promised, *inter alia*, to give communities more powers, to encourage local people to take up active roles in their neighbourhoods and to transfer power from central to local government.[160] These promises have evolved into a range of key policies and reforms, some of which were discussed in Chapter 4; this section, however, seeks to consider the Coalition's focus on local democratic reinvigoration, particularly in the context of community-led sustainability. In doing this, it is chiefly concerned with policies and reforms that have come out of the government's promise to give communities more power.

As this chapter has thus far explored, the previous Labour government's attitude towards community-led regeneration was based on the introduction of a range of broad programmes, such as the NDC, the Neighbourhood Management programme and the Neighbourhood Warden scheme, which were designed to deliver centrally prescribed objectives and visions for local sustainability. By contrast, the Coalition government's approach centres more on the implementation of specific policies, focusing on particular themes, such as local empowerment and the development of community rights. Indeed, and for example, in terms of empowering local people generally, the DCLG has recently published policies and instigated discussions designed to bring people together in strong united communities,[161] and promoting social action through encouraging and enabling people to play a more active part in society.[162] With a specific focus on local community development, however, the Coalition's most notable introduction relates to new neighbourhood planning measures and the 'community right to build', contained in the Localism Act. These provide a foundation for giving local people more power, particularly with regard to improving local communities and tackling deprivation,[163] and it is these with which this final part of the chapter is chiefly concerned.

In respect of new neighbourhood planning measures, s 116 and schedule 9 of the Localism Act amend the Town and Country Planning Act 1990 and provide that a parish council or neighbourhood forum can initiate a process for the

159 Cabinet Office, *Building the Big Society*, 18 May 2010, 1 <https://www.gov.uk/government/uploads/system/uploads/attachment_data/file/78979/building-big-society_0.pdf> accessed 10 November 2013.

160 Ibid. generally.

161 See DCLG, *Bringing People Together in Strong United Communities* (2013) <https://www.gov.uk/government/policies/bringing-people-together-in-strong-united-communities> accessed 10 November 2013.

162 See DCLG, *Promoting Social Action: Encouraging and Enabling People to Play a More Active Part in Society* (2013) <https://www.gov.uk/government/policies/promoting-social-action-encouraging-and-enabling-people-to-play-a-more-active-part-in-society> accessed 10 November 2013.

163 See DCLG, *Giving People More Power over What Happens in Their Neighbourhood* (2013) <https://www.gov.uk/government/policies/giving-people-more-power-over-what-happens-in-their-neighbourhood#bills-and-legislation> accessed 10 November 2013.

purposes of developing a particular neighbourhood area. As Layard notes, this empowers 'communities to make neighbourhood plans and neighbourhood developments orders'[164] and makes provision for community organisations to bring forward development proposals, supported by local referenda, without going through separate planning application processes.[165] This essentially 'allows local areas to come together to establish general planning policies for development and use of land in their neighbourhood, which then becomes part of the local plan'.[166] These are powers that have already been used in communities across England and Wales,[167] as the DCLG itself reports.[168] Linked to this new neighbourhood planning provision, however, is the 'community right to build'. This 'allows a community to draw up a Community Right to Build Order which, if supported in a local referendum, enables small local development[s] to go ahead without going through the normal planning application process'.[169] It means that local people will have the power to drive forward local development without being constrained by centralised restrictions and powers.[170]

Through these provisions, therefore, the Localism Act 2011 appears to give important powers to local people and local bodies to improve and develop their areas, though the extent to which they are attuned with the principle of accountability and the encouragement of citizen participation is explored below. On the face of it, the provisions appear to encourage local innovation, enabling communities to decide for themselves the issues in need of attention and ways through which they might be tackled. Indeed, as Layard notes: 'Where neighbourhood plans are prepared under the [Localism] Act, these initiatives are to empower local communities . . . rather than leaving their "place shaping" choices subject to the approval of the local authority.'[171] Indeed, she quotes Greg Clark MP as emphasising that the government intends that neighbourhoods should be able to 'to exert more influence in the planning system . . . We aim to create a means for people to formulate their own plans about what their area should look like in five, ten, twenty years' time.'[172]

164 Layard (n 3) 557.

165 DCLG, *A Plain English Guide to the Localism Act*, 15 November 2011, London: DCLG <https://www.gov.uk/government/uploads/system/uploads/attachment_data/file/5959/1896534.pdf> accessed 10 November 2013.

166 Locality, *Community Right to Build: Understanding the Community Right to Build*, 2 <http://mycommunityrights.org.uk/wp-content/uploads/2012/04/LOCALITY-BUILD_UNDERSTANDING.pdf> accessed 10 November 2013.

167 Localism Act 2011, s 239, notes that the Act applies only to England and Wales.

168 DCLG, *Historic First as Neighbourhood Plan Is Voted in by Community*, 8 March 2013 <https://www.gov.uk/government/news/historic-first-as-neighbourhood-plan-is-voted-in-by-community> accessed 12 November 2013.

169 *Community Right to Build* (n 166) 2.

170 *A Plain English Guide to the Localism Act* (n 165) 12.

171 Layard (n 3) 557.

172 Rt. Hon. Greg Clark MP, 'Better Planning: From Principle, to Practice', speech given 18 November 2010, cited in ibid. 557 <https://www.gov.uk/government/speeches/better-planning-from-principle-to-practice> accessed 10 November 2013.

In terms of ensuring that this can become a reality and that local people and bodies can use these community powers to best effect, Locality, a charity set up in April 2011, works across the UK 'to inspire local communities to change and improve' and provides information, advice and support in respect of community rights.[173] Made up of a network of community-led organisations across the UK that work to support locally owned and led organisations to encourage change and development across local communities, Locality also seeks to focus on a range of particular projects which aim to empower local people and improve local communities.[174] One such project is the Community Organisers project. As part of this, Locality trains community organisers to listen to local residents and citizens to encourage and help them to take action on their own behalf, to tackle local problems and issues and to make the most of the community rights provided in the Localism Act 2011.[175] Finally, through its neighbourhood planning role, Locality provides guidance to local communities on the way in which they can produce a Neighbourhood Plan.[176] Locality, therefore, supplements much of what the government has sought to do in this area and provides support and advice for local communities seeking to become more empowered and to play a greater role in the development of their areas.

The Coalition government, therefore, takes a markedly different approach to local regeneration and renewal from that of its Labour predecessor. The NDC programme, for instance, operated within a structure that saw decisions and policies made by a Partnership Board, involving local residents, within a broader framework that the DCLG was able to oversee. By contrast, initiatives under the Big Society seem focused more on general policies aimed at empowering citizens and encouraging community-led regeneration more generally. Indeed, as this section has explored, the Localism Act sets out provisions seeking to encourage communities themselves to instigate the process of development and to set out its form, with the aid of guidance provided through advice and support from an independent charity rather than through governmental structures as was previously the case. The passage of time will reveal the extent to which these provisions will lead to success as regards local community development; this next section, however, considers their potential in the context of accountability and citizen participation.

Citizen participation, accountability and sustainability under the Coalition government and the Big Society

The neighbourhood planning provisions contained within the Localism Act 2011, alongside the 'community right to build' and the work that Locality does, provide

173 Locality, *About Us* (n 158).

174 See ibid.

175 Locality, *Community Organisers* <http://locality.org.uk/projects/community-organisers/> accessed 10 November 2013.

176 Locality, *Neighbourhood Planning Roadmap Guide* <http://locality.org.uk/resources/neighbourhood-planning-roadmap-guide/> accessed 10 November 2013.

potential examples of the citizen empowerment that can and is intended to flow from the decentralisation of power. Indeed, recalling that where there is a decentralisation of power it is easier for local people to participate and involve themselves in the process as that power is more accessible, it follows that through encouraging local communities to set out their own neighbourhood development orders local people could become directly involved in the continuing development and improvement of their local areas, cutting out the previously strong governmental influence that had perhaps hindered, in some respects, the success of the NDC programme. As Leyland notes: 'By preparing development plans and orders local councils and local people are intended to have a much greater input in guiding development in their immediate locality.'[177]

Going further, however, the provisions in the Localism Act are even more notable in that they not only give citizens a direct role in shaping local areas by affording them the opportunity to decide, through their local knowledge and expertise, how a local area should be developed, but also ensure that, on the basis of local referenda, they have the power to instigate that development and to drive it forward. This can happen with the consensus of those within the wider local area, and without prescription from centralised authorities. As Locality notes, provisions relating to neighbourhood planning and the 'community right to build' were introduced 'to decentralise power over planning directly into the hands of local communities and cut red tape for areas that wish to encourage local development'.[178]

The decentralisation of power and the empowerment of local communities in the way set out in the Big Society policy and the Localism Act could also potentially impact on the accountability of the local bodies leading the neighbourhood development. On the one hand, through facilitating the potential for citizens' involvement in the way outlined above, the reforms could demonstrate that 'where there is a strong culture of participation, then accountability will occur naturally . . . in that those most affected by the decision have been a part of making it, and will be immediately aware of its implementation'.[179] In addition to this, however, it is argued that, through having the power exercised at a local level, citizens can more easily hold those wielding such power – parish councils and neighbourhood fora – to account and will be able to scrutinise and question the way in which decisions are made and policies implemented in respect of local community development. As Farag was quoted as noting in Chapter 3, 'in principle, decentralisation can increase . . . access to decision-making by otherwise excluded groups, as well as increasing accountability, through proximity of decision-makers to citizens'.[180]

177 P Leyland, 'The Localism Act 2011: Local Government Encounters the "Big Society"' (2012) 4 *Istituzioni del Federalismo* 767 at 776.

178 *Community Right to Build* (n 166) 2.

179 Onyx and Dalton (n 95) 15.

180 AS Farag, 'Decentralization: Objectives, Forms and Implementation of Decentralized Governance' (2013) 11(1) *International Journal of Social Sciences* 138 at 139.

New powers and policies set out by the Coalition government as part of the Big Society, therefore, are potentially notable. Not only do they set out ways in which local citizens can be empowered and get involved 'to deliver the development that their local communit[ies] want',[181] but they also lay the foundations for the promotion of local accountability, ensuring local people have adequate means through which to input their needs and desires and to question and scrutinise decisions in respect of neighbourhood development. These provisions are, as Layard notes, one of the most innovative introductions in the Localism Act.[182] That being true, however, there are wider concerns as regards their potential to encourage citizen participation to the extent envisaged and to ensure local accountability. Indeed, as Layard continues: 'While participation in these forums is open to all, they lack democratic accountability and there is a real concern that these new institutions of local governance will be dominated by the "usual suspects" and may not develop at all in more disadvantaged communities.'[183] This echoes problems that have already been identified in respect of the NDC programme above and is perhaps reflective of wider concerns with regard to the encouragement of citizen participation in local affairs. Indeed, this is a view shared by Buser, who comments that the community-led approach, exemplified by neighbourhood development orders, raises a number of concerns, including 'issues of capacity, ability and willingness of individuals and groups to participate in neighbourhood planning processes', and later goes on to question whether the powers will give neighbourhoods and citizens 'enough freedom and authority within neighbourhood planning to make it a useful tool for civic engagement and local decision-making'.[184]

There are genuine concerns, therefore, as to whether the Coalition's community-led approach has succeeded in breaking free from the problems of citizen and community engagement that have perhaps plagued previous attempts at local development. Whilst the fullness of time will reveal further the validity of these concerns, for now it suffices to conclude that the Coalition's policies and reforms seem at least to offer the potential for empowerment and decentralisation, free from overly bureaucratic centralised supervision, and with greater citizen participation and local accountability.

Concluding remarks

This chapter has explored the nature of community-led regeneration under both the 1997–2010 Labour government and the Coalition government that succeeded it.

181 *A Plain English Guide to the Localism Act* (n 165) 12.

182 Layard (n 3) 557.

183 Ibid. 557.

184 M Buser, 'Tracing the Democratic Narrative: Big Society, Localism and Civic Engagement' (2013) 39(1) *Local Government Studies* 3 at 13.

Using the NDC programme as an example of Labour's work towards local sustainability, the chapter has demonstrated the extent to which neighbourhoods and citizens were encouraged to play an integral part in developing and improving local areas. Whilst there were issues relating to the extent of widespread involvement and the appropriate decentralisation of power, the chapter demonstrated that where local people did participate and where there were mechanisms for accountability, communities' and citizens' needs and interests could input into the system, sustainability could be achieved and environmental, social and economic changes could be made to a local area. In short, it demonstrated that, through encouraging citizen participation and local accountability, the NDC's achievement of local sustainability was enhanced.

Following on from the NDC, the Coalition government appears to have continued the focus on community-led efforts to develop local areas, setting out policies and reforms that seek to empower local neighbourhoods and decentralise authority to facilitate the creation of neighbourhood development orders and use of the 'community right to build'. Whilst similar concerns relating to citizen participation are echoed here, early signals suggest that, on paper, the reforms display the potential to ensure a community-focused approach to regeneration, free from too much central control.

This evaluation demonstrates, therefore, that, despite certain issues, the extent to which accountability and citizen participation can enhance the achievement of local sustainability is clearly evident. Through ensuring that local citizens can input local needs and desires into a process and can question and scrutinise decisions, local accountability can provide a platform for responsiveness and citizen control of locally relevant decisions and actions. In addition, by providing a range of opportunities through which local citizens can bring their local knowledge and experience to a process focused on objectives aligned with sustainability, the results can be more in line with local needs and can ensure that relevant and appropriate environmental, social and economic changes are made to local communities. Whilst Chapter 6 will explore the way in which lessons can be learned from conclusions and issues identified in this chapter, and applied in respect of local sustainability in the future and throughout the wider world, discussions and evaluations considered here show the extent to which accountability and citizen participation, at a community level, really can enhance the achievement of local sustainability.

Bibliography

Arnstein, S, 'A Ladder of Citizen Participation' (1967) 35(4) *Journal of American Institute of Planners* 216.

Buser, M, 'Tracing the Democratic Narrative: Big Society, Localism and Civic Engagement' (2013) 39(1) *Local Government Studies* 3.

Cabinet Office, *Building the Big Society*, 18 May 2010 <https://www.gov.uk/government/uploads/system/uploads/attachment_data/file/78979/building-big-society_0.pdf> accessed 10 November 2013.

Clark, G, Rt. Hon. MP 'Better Planning: From Principle, to Practice', speech given on 18 November 2010 <https://www.gov.uk/government/speeches/better-planning-from-principle-to-practice> accessed 10 November 2013.

Committee of Public Accounts, *An Early Progress Report on the New Deal for Communities Programme* (HC 2003–04, 492).

CRESR, *NDC Secondary and Administrative Data* <http://extra.shu.ac.uk/ndc/ndc_data.htm> accessed 10 November 2013.

DCLG, *About the NRU* <http://collections.europarchive.org/tna/20090106142604/; http://www.neighbourhood.gov.uk/page.asp?id=3> accessed 10 November 2013.

DCLG, *New Deal for Communities Is Turning around England's Most Deprived Areas*, 11 February 2008 <http://www.gov-news.org/gov/uk/news/new_deal_communities_turning_around_england39s/88935.html> accessed 10 November 2013. Made available by Government News <http://www.gov-news.org/>.

DCLG, *Transformational Change? A Synthesis of New Evidence 2008–2009* (London: HMSO, 2009).

DCLG, *Involving Local People in Regeneration: Evidence from the New Deal for Communities Programme* (London: HMSO, 2010) 6 (a report written and compiled by CRESR).

DCLG, *Making Deprived Areas Better Places to Live: Evidence from the New Deal for Communities Programme* (London: HMSO, 2010).

DCLG, *The New Deal for Communities Experience: A Final Assessment* (London: HMSO, 2010).

DCLG, *The New Deal for Communities Programme: Achieving a Neighbourhood Focus for Regeneration* (London: HMSO, 2010).

DCLG, *New Deal for Communities: A Synthesis of New Programme Wide Evidence* (London: HMSO, 2010).

DCLG, *A Plain English Guide to the Localism Act*, 15 November 2011, London: DCLG <https://www.gov.uk/government/uploads/system/uploads/attachment_data/file/5959/1896534.pdf> accessed 10 November 2013.

DCLG, *Bringing People Together in Strong United Communities* (2013) <https://www.gov.uk/government/policies/bringing-people-together-in-strong-united-communities> accessed 10 November 2013.

DCLG, *Giving People More Power over What Happens in Their Neighbourhood* (2013) <https://www.gov.uk/government/policies/giving-people-more-power-over-what-happens-in-their-neighbourhood#bills-and-legislation> accessed 10 November 2013.

DCLG, *Historic First as Neighbourhood Plan Is Voted in by Community* (8 March 2013) <https://www.gov.uk/government/news/historic-first-as-neighbourhood-plan-is-voted-in-by-community> accessed 12 November 2013.

DCLG, *Promoting Social Action: Encouraging and Enabling People to Play a More Active Part in Society* (2013) <https://www.gov.uk/government/policies/promoting-social-action-encouraging-and-enabling-people-to-play-a-more-active-part-in-society> accessed 10 November 2013.

Dinham, A, 'Empowered or Over-Powered? The Real Experience of Local Participation in the UK's New Deal for Communities' (2005) 40(3) *Community Development Journal* 301.

Dinham, A and Finneron, D, *Building on Faith: Faith Buildings in Neighbourhood Renewal* (London: Church Urban Fund, 2002).

Duffy, B, Vince, J and Page, L, *Searching for the Impact of Empowerment* (2008) Ipsos MORI, Social Research Institute <http://www.ipsos-mori.com/DownloadPublication/1227_sri_localgovt_searching_for_the_impact_of_empowerment_072008.pdf> accessed 10 November 2013.

EC1 New Deal for Communities, *Governance Framework* (17 July 2007, as amended on 16 April 2009 and 11 June 2009).

EC1 New Deal for Communities, *EC1 Beyond 2011* <http://www.renaisi.com/2011/wp-content/uploads/2011/05/EC1_Beyond_2011.pdf> accessed 10 November 2013.

Farag, AS, 'Decentralization: Objectives, Forms and Implementation of Decentralized Governance' (2013) 11(1) *International Journal of Social Sciences* 138.

Fauget, J-P, 'Does Decentralization Increase Government Responsiveness to Local Needs?' (2004) 88 *Journal of Public Economics* 867.

Finneron, D, *Faith in Community Development: Case Studies of Church Based Community Development Projects in Urban Priority Areas* (Manchester: Manchester Monographs, 1993).

Foley, P and Martin, S, 'A New Deal for the Community? Public Participation in Regeneration and Local Service Delivery' (2000) 28(4) *Policy & Politics* 479.

Government Office for London, *People and Sustainable Communities* <http://webarchive.nationalarchives.gov.uk/20100528142817/; http://www.gos.gov.uk/gol/People_sustain_comms/?a=42496> accessed 10 November 2013.

Government Office for London, *Sustainable Development* <http://webarchive.nationalarchives.gov.uk/20100528142817/; http://www.gos.gov.uk/gol/People_sustain_comms/355601/?a=42496> accessed 10 November 2013.

Government Offices for the English Regions, *Neighbourhood Renewal: The National Picture* <http://webarchive.nationalarchives.gov.uk/20100528142817/; http://www.gos.gov.uk/peoplesuscomms/neighbourrenewal/?a=42496> accessed 10 November 2013.

Help on Your Doorstep, *About Us* <http://www.helponyourdoorstep.com/aboutus.asp?shead=whatwedo> accessed 10 November 2013.

Help on Your Doorstep, *Connecting People: Improving Lives* <http://www.helponyourdoorstep.com/SummaryReport.pdf> accessed 10 November 2013.

Home Office, *Building Cohesive Communities: A Report of the Ministerial Group on Public Order and Community Cohesion* (2001) <http://resources.cohesioninstitute.org.uk/Publications/Documents/Document/DownloadDocumentsFile.aspx?recordId=94&file=PDFversion> accessed 10 November 2013.

Humphreys, M, 'Leaseholder Charges and Urban Regeneration' (2006) *Journal of Planning and Environmental Law* 1625.

Jacobs, S and Popple, K, *Community Work in the 1990s* (Nottingham: Spokesman, 1994).

Kearns, A, 'Social Capital, Regeneration and Urban Policy' in Imrie, R and Raco, M (eds), *Urban Renaissance? New Labour, Community and Urban Policy* (Bristol: Policy Press, 2003) 37.

Kessler, L, 'EC1 New Deal for Communities – before and after Transformations', *Horticulture Week*, 13 August 2010 <http://www.hortweek.com/news/1021460/> accessed 10 November 2013.

Lawless, P, 'Can Area-Based Regeneration Programmes Ever Work? Evidence from England's New Deal for Communities' (2012) 33(4) *Policy Studies* 313.

Lawless, P, Foden, M, Wilson, I and Beatty, C, 'Understanding Area-Based Regeneration: The New Deal for Communities Programme in England' (2009) 47(2) *Urban Studies* 257.

Layard, A, 'Law and Localism: The Case of Multiple Occupancy Housing' (2012) 32(4) *Legal Studies* 551.

Leyland, P, 'The Localism Act 2011: Local Government Encounters the "Big Society"' (2012) 4 *Istituzioni del Federalismo* 767.

Locality, *Community Organisers* <http://locality.org.uk/projects/community-organisers/> accessed 10 November 2013.

Locality, 'Community Right to Build: Understanding the Community Right to Build' <http://mycommunityrights.org.uk/wp-content/uploads/2012/04/LOCALITY-BUILD_UNDERSTANDING.pdf> accessed 10 November 2013.

Locality, *Neighbourhood Planning Roadmap Guide* <http://locality.org.uk/resources/neighbourhood-planning-roadmap-guide/> accessed 10 November 2013.

Lowndes, V and Sullivan, H, 'How Low Can You Go? Rationales and Challenges for Neighbourhood Governance' (2008) 86(1) *Public Administration* 53.

Moncrieffe, JM, 'Accountability: Idea, Ideals, Constraints' (2001) 8(3) *Democratization* 26.

Mulgan, R, 'Accountability: An Ever-Expanding Concept' (2000) 78(3) *Public Administration* 555.

Oliver, D, *Constitutional Reform in the UK* (Oxford: OUP, 2003).

Onyx, J and Dalton, B, 'Accountability and Advocacy' (2006) 12(1) *Third Sector Review* 7.

Perrons, D and Skyers, S, 'Empowerment through Participation? Conceptual Explorations and a Case Study' (2003) 27(2) *International Journal of Urban and Regional Research* 265.

Popple, K, *Analysing Community Work: Its Theory and Practice* (Maidenhead: Open University Press, 1995).

'Regeneration Consultancy of the Year: Renaisi', *Regeneration and Renewal*, 24 September 2009 <http://www.regen.net/news/940731/Regeneration-Consultancy-Year/?DCMP=ILC-SEARCH> accessed 10 November 2013.

Robinson, F, Shaw, K and Davidson, G, '"On the Side of the Angels": Community Involvement in the Governance of Neighbourhood Renewal' (2005) 20(1) *Local Economy* 13.

Sandford, M, House of Commons Library, *The Abolition of Regional Government* (Standard Note SN/PC/05842, 27 March 2013).

Shaw, K and Davidson, G, 'Community Elections for Regeneration Partnerships: A New Deal for Local Democracy?' (2002) 28(2) *Local Government Studies* 1.

Social Exclusion Unit, *Bringing Britain Together*, Cm 4045 (London: HMSO, 1998) © Crown Copyright, contains public sector information licensed under the Open Government Licence v2.0 <http://www.nationalarchives.gov.uk/doc/open-government-licence/version/2/>.

Social Exclusion Unit, *A New Commitment to Neighbourhood Renewal* (London: Cabinet Office, 2001).

Stanton, J, 'Local Sustainable Development: Lessons Learned from the New Deal for Communities' (2012) 14(1) *Environmental Law Review* 26.

Twelvetrees, A, *Community Work* (3rd edn, Basingstoke: BASW/Macmillan, 2001).

UN, *Rio Declaration on Environment and Development*, Annex 1 to the *Report of the United Nations Conference on Environment and Development*, Rio de Janeiro, 3–14 June 1992, A/CONF.151/26, Vol. I, New York: UN.

UNECE, *Convention on Access to Information, Public Participation in Decision-Making and Access to Justice in Environmental Matters*, 25 June 1998, Aarhus, Denmark.

World Commission on Environment and Development, *Our Common Future* (Oxford: OUP, 1987).

Wright, JSF, Parry, J, Mathers, J, Jones, S and Orford, J, 'Assessing the Participatory Potential of Britain's New Deal for Communities' (2006) 27(4) *Policy Studies* 347.

6 Democracy in sustainability

The wider world and lessons for the future

Introduction

This book has demonstrated the extent to which the principles of accountability and citizen participation can be said to enhance the achievement of local sustainability in the UK, with evaluation of the NDC programme, the Big Society policy as well as the impact of recent local governmental reform serving to test this hypothesis, and providing a platform for examination of the way in which this is exemplified in practice.

The parameters of this evaluation, however, have been intentionally narrow. Chapters 4 and 5 selected specific examples of recent reforms and local efforts to pursue sustainability so as to facilitate more detailed consideration of their workings and operation. The importance and relevance of the sustainability principle, however, is not merely limited to institutions and initiatives herein discussed, and nor is it restricted merely to localism in the UK. It is a principle that has ongoing significance and broad application, as already noted in Chapter 2. Consequently, this final chapter brings together and summarises the conclusions that have been reached in respect of sustainability and localism in the UK and seeks to cast the net a little wider. In doing this, it addresses issues relating to accountability and citizen participation highlighted in chapters 4 and 5, and considers how these might be overcome and how pursuits of local sustainability in the future might be enhanced as a result. It then discusses the recent *Local Sustainability 2012* report, published on the occasion of the 'Rio + 20' conference;[1] engaging with its discussions and examples, it considers the extent to which conclusions and evaluations from this book can be relevant and applicable across the wider world. Whilst not comprehensive in this last endeavour, the chapter serves at least to provide something of an insight into the manner in which accountability and citizen participation impact on local sustainability around the globe.

1 ICLEI, *Local Sustainability 2012: Taking Stock and Moving Forward. Global Review* (Bonn: ICLEI, 2012) ('*Local Sustainability 2012*').

Summary of conclusions

This first section of the chapter provides a summary of the book's discussions and conclusions, and highlights briefly the way in which each chapter has contributed to the book's thesis.

Chapter 2 sought to explore the principle of sustainability, extracting its definition from a range of international sources and tracing its development and growth in UK government policy through consideration of the Strategies for Sustainable Development. It justified the principle's application at the local level through noting that 'local decision-makers should "shape the place" because they "know best"',[2] also highlighting *Agenda 21*'s concession that 'many of the problems and solutions being addressed by *Agenda 21* have their roots in local activities'.[3] It culminated in the exposition of a 'model of local sustainability', which sought to reflect the accepted interpretations of the principle at the local level, breaking it down to explain its constituent elements and putting in place an understanding that could be easily considered in later chapters.

Following this, it was the purpose of Chapter 3 to explore the relationship between local sustainability, accountability and citizen participation. It defined the principle of accountability and explained the way in which it operates in respect of relationships established between decision-makers and those affected by their decisions, giving the latter the mechanisms through which they can not only scrutinise and question the process but also seek to control, to a degree, the course of decision-making and ensure responsive results.

Though arguing that a representative system of democracy is perhaps insufficient to providing adequate opportunities to enforce accountability, Chapter 3 suggested that 'where there is a strong culture of participation, then accountability will occur naturally . . . in that those most affected by the decision have been a part of making it, and will be immediately aware of its implementation'.[4] On the basis of this analysis and drawing from a range of authorities, the chapter then explored the manner in which accountability and citizen participation can be said to be conducive to the achievement of local sustainability. It demonstrated, first, that, on the basis of affording citizens the opportunity to question and scrutinise decisions and to ensure representatives understand and take account of local needs, accountability is a crucial element of achieving local sustainability. It then showed that, through participation, local objectives can be better achieved as citizens' local knowledge and expertise can directly inform decision-making and ensure that those who know best have the opportunity to influence the development of local areas.[5] Chapter 3 concluded that accountability and citizen participation are crucial

2 A Layard, 'Law and Localism: The Case of Multiple Occupancy Housing' (2012) 32(4) *Legal Studies* 551 at 552.

3 UN, *Agenda 21*, 1992, A/CONF.151/26, Vol. III, New York: UN, para. 28.3. Made available by the UN Division for Sustainable Development at <http://sustainabledevelopment.un.org/content/documents/Agenda21.pdf> accessed 7 November 2013.

4 J Onyx and B Dalton, 'Accountability and Advocacy' (2006) 12(1) *Third Sector Review* 7 at 15.

5 See Layard (n 2) 552.

to the achievement of local sustainability and can be said, as a consequence, to enhance its achievement.

It was the purpose of Chapters 2 and 3, therefore, to provide the conceptual foundations for the book and to explain the hypothesis that it set out to test, namely that accountability and citizen participation enhance the achievement of local sustainability. In order that this might be tested, however, Chapters 4 and 5 then sought to explore the achievement of sustainability at both the local governmental and community levels.

Chapter 4 set out, in the first instance, to explain the turbulent developments in local governmental power and democracy over the years. It explained the manner in which reforms enacted from the mid-1960s through to the mid-1990s effected drastic centralisation and stripped local authorities of many of the powers that they had previously enjoyed. The chapter then discussed in detail the manner in which the 1997–2010 Labour government and the subsequent Conservative–Liberal Democrat Coalition government sought to empower local authorities and local people, decentralise autonomy and reinvigorate local democracy. In doing this, it considered recent local governmental reform in respect of strengthening local leadership, decentralising power and empowering local citizens, and it analysed the extent to which this facilitated the achievement of accountability and encouraged citizen participation. Though it highlighted a number of issues that are discussed later in this chapter, it noted that the reforms at least demonstrate the potential for accountability and citizen participation. Consequently, following application of the 'model of local sustainability', Chapter 4 concluded that local authorities were well placed to lead the achievement of local sustainability through democratic means, and that local governmental reform, on paper, demonstrates the extent to which local sustainability can be enhanced by the potential for accountability and citizen participation. It noted, however, that challenges as regards the full realisation of that potential need to be addressed in order that that potential can be fully realised and that local government can consequently lead the achievement of local sustainability on the basis of such means.

Whilst Chapter 4 explored the extent to which UK local government tested the book's hypothesis, Chapter 5 considered local community sustainability, analysing the effectiveness of community-led initiatives and programmes under both the Labour and Coalition governments. It outlined the establishment and development of the NDC programme and both the nature of its operation and the extent to which it sought to achieve local sustainability. Using the EC1 NDC as an example of the manner in which the programme worked on the ground in local communities, it examined the degree to which its decision-making processes and community-led approach accorded with the principle of accountability and the encouragement of citizen participation. Though it identified a range of mechanisms for accountability and opportunities for citizen involvement, it noted that, across the NDC programme as a whole, the community-led nature was generally reliant on a core group of empowered citizens and that there were some issues as regards more widespread citizen participation. In addition to this, the chapter also demonstrated that, as with local government in Chapter 4, there is reluctance on the part of central government to 'let go' of local powers and to afford communities the appropriate freedom to shape local development, in locally relevant ways, free from centralised objectives and requirements. Despite these issues, however, which are discussed in greater depth below, there was undoubtedly a strong element of local participation embedded within the NDC programme and, where citizens did participate, they did so to good effect and input their local knowledge and experience for the benefit of their communities' development.

Following the General Election of 2010 and the expiration of the NDC programme, the new Coalition government brought with it its flagship policy of the Big Society. This included the Localism Act and set out a broad range of policies that, like Labour's, were aimed at the decentralisation of power and empowerment of local people. Though it is perhaps too early to embark on any substantial or meaningful analysis of the Coalition's policies and reforms, Chapter 5 offered consideration of the potential for the community rights and neighbourhood development provisions set out in the Localism Act to promote accountability and encourage citizen participation in the process of local regeneration. In this regard, it suggested that the reforms encourage greater local innovation and freedom in determining the direction of local development and give local communities the power to instigate change themselves through a process of local referenda, rather than through centralised direction. Despite this, the chapter noted that there are already concerns that the new provisions do little to overcome problems previously identified relating to citizens' reluctance to get involved, and that it will perhaps be the 'usual suspects' who make best use of them at the end of the day. Regardless, the Coalition's reforms and policies display a clear potential to afford local communities valuable freedom and innovation in the process of local regeneration which, if fully embraced, could lead to real community-led change in local areas.

At first glance, therefore, the Labour and Coalition governments' policies and reforms set out a range of mechanisms through which local people can hold decision-makers accountable in respect of decisions and actions in pursuit of local sustainability, and a plethora of opportunities for citizen participation through which individuals can play an active role in the process and input their local knowledge and expertise to ensure democratic, relevant and responsive development in local areas. Consequently, in terms of what successive governments have set out, local governmental reform and community-led initiatives and programmes demonstrate the extent to which accountability and citizen participation can enhance the achievement of local sustainability. In practice, however, research reveals that there are a number of issues as regards the effectiveness of local accountability and the sufficiency of citizen participation. In terms of recent local governmental reform, Chapters 4 and 5 highlighted the fact that a lack of local choice has led to compromised strength of local leadership, and that central government has, over the years, been reluctant to 'let go' of local powers and is consequently over-prescriptive in its supervision of local authorities and community bodies. They also noted that concerns relating to the willingness of citizens to participate, combined with constant shifts in centralised policies and reforms, have led to issues regarding widespread citizen empowerment. With this in mind, it is the purpose of this next section to consider these issues in greater detail and to explore how lessons might be learned from them to improve approaches to local sustainability in the future.

Lessons for the future

The issues that were identified throughout Chapters 4 and 5 can be broken down into three subheadings: the strength of local leadership, reluctance at the centre to 'let go' and issues underlying citizen participation. This section is structured to explore each of these in turn, outlining the issues and considering ways through which they might be overcome in the future.

Strong local leadership

As Chapter 4 explained, the structural arrangements of local government, outside London and exclusive of metropolitan boroughs, consist of either the two tiers of county and district councils or the single, unitary councils. Within these, councils have the option to have executive leaders or directly elected mayors as their executive arrangements, with a mixture of both being currently in operation across the country.

It is here, however, that we find the first issue, relating as it does to the hybrid models of local government that are seemingly adopted around the country. With unitary authorities in some places and two-tier arrangements in others, there is no uniformity to the system. Though a blanket 'one size fits all' approach should generally be discouraged in respect of local issues, the manner in which local governmental structures have been altered over the years has been somewhat untidy. The widespread introduction of the two-tier approach in the early 1970s was unpopular from the outset,[6] whilst attempts to implement unitary authorities, starting in the early 1990s and gathering momentum during Labour's terms in government, were driven largely from the centre[7] and reluctantly welcomed by citizens.[8] The result is a system that is made up of unpopular, centrally driven and unwelcome models of local government, and one that is in need of reform. Local authorities should be arranged in a manner that is clear, transparent and easy to hold to account, as well as in a way that satisfies the broader public.

6 Chapter 4 noted (n 23) that Michael Heseltine felt that the two-tier approach could 'lead to excessive bureaucracy and duplication of effort' (HC Deb 23 April 1991, vol 189, col 901, cited in K Parry and J Roll, House of Commons Library, *Local Government and Public Involvement in Health Bill*, 10 January 2007, Research Paper 07/01 at 14).

7 Under LGPIHA, s 2, for example, change to a unitary authority was by invitation from the Secretary of State.

8 King notes the extent to which the public were content with the status quo of two-tier authorities (A King, *The British Constitution* (Oxford: OUP, 2007) 158), whilst Wilson and Game note that the public were not convinced about the prospect of unitary authorities, with many opposing the Commission's proposals for adoption (D Wilson and C Game, *Local Government in the United Kingdom* (5th edn, Basingstoke: Palgrave Macmillan, 2011) 69).

In terms of future development here, the case for more widespread unitary authorities is potentially a strong one, with the two-tier approach being regarded by some as unsustainable.[9] If this is the case, then central government needs to find the most suitable way in which to introduce them and to gauge the extent to which the public desire them. Concerns relating to their cost were noted in the Localism Act's second reading,[10] but if they are to be the future of local government, then it is an investment that is well worth making. Local government has long needed the kind of overhaul that would come with a total shift to a unitary system.

If unitary authorities are the future, however, then it is important also to ensure that wherever they are introduced, the geographical area which they cover should not be too large.[11] Chapter 4 noted the extent to which unitary authorities differ in size compared with their two-tier predecessors, and it undoubtedly brings into question the strength of local leadership if councillors have to serve too large a constituency. If unitary authorities can be introduced to serve smaller areas, and consequently fewer local people, then they could ensure stronger local leadership with clearer accountability. This could, in line with arguments made throughout the book, give rise to a better coordinated approach to local sustainability with increased accountability and, consequently, enhanced achievement of its objectives.

The second issue with the strength of local leadership relates to the seemingly limited choice that local authorities have with regard to executive arrangements. Chapter 4 noted that, on the foundation of recent legislation, local authorities have the option of operating within a structure overseen either by an executive leader and cabinet executive or a directly elected mayor and cabinet executive.[12] Whilst directly elected mayors bring an obvious democratic advantage,[13] referenda for their introduction in cities across England were widely rejected. As a consequence, there are only 15 such mayors throughout the country. Some argue that the reasons underlying this rejection are linked to the lack of a strong case being made for

9 As Chapter 4 noted (n 101), Wilson and Game cite a headline from 2009 stating that civil servants told 'a private meeting of council leaders that, on efficiency grounds, "two-tier local government is unsustainable" and further unitary reorganisation is likely to prove necessary' (Wilson and Game (n 8) 69).

10 Eric Pickles emphasises the cost of transforming existing two-tier areas into ones governed by unitary authorities (HC Deb 21 October 2010, vol 516, col 1155–6).

11 See Chapter 4 (n 106 and n 107) and also Wilson and Game (n 8) 74 and 76. Also see C Copus, 'British Local Government: A Case for a New Constitutional Settlement' (2006) 21(4) *Public Policy and Administration* 4 at 12 and 13.

12 As Chapter 4 noted, Part 3 of the LGPIHA, amending the Local Government Act 2000, provides that councils are required to adopt models made up of either an executive leader and cabinet executive or a directly elected mayor and cabinet executive.

13 Larsen notes that 'it seems . . . a reasonable assumption that a mayor elected directly by the citizens could enjoy and would make claims to a different and stronger legitimacy than one indirectly elected by the councillors' (HO Larsen, 'Directly Elected Mayors – Democratic Renewal or Constitutional Confusion?' in J Caulfield and HO Larsen (eds) *Local Government at the Millennium* (Wiesbaden: Springer Fachmedien Wiesbaden, 2002) 111 at 113).

directly elected mayors in the run-up to the referenda, with low turnouts supporting claims that the 'yes' campaigns were lacklustre and failed to make any real impression on local people.[14] More fundamentally, however, it is suggested that the issue relates to the persistence with which central government seeks to instruct and supervise the manner in which local authorities should be arranged. As Jones and Stewart note, 'central government thinks it knows better than the local authorities concerned and their citizens',[15] and these referenda provide an appropriate example. Before the Localism Act, local authorities themselves already had the power to hold referenda as regards the introduction of directly elected mayors, yet those cities that were targeted by the Act had never chosen to do so and those that had held such referenda had rejected the proposition of a directly elected mayor.[16] Central government seemed determined to push for their introduction despite clear opposition.

The crux of the issue, therefore, rests with the manner in which local executive arrangements are selected. As the rejection of directly elected mayors goes to demonstrate, local government benefits little from centralised supervision and direction of the manner in which it organises its local councillors. Local authorities need to be able to enjoy greater freedom, and this means being able to choose for themselves the executive arrangements most suitable for local people.

This section has considered two key issues which have, in recent years, affected the strength of local governmental leadership – namely, the current state and recent development of local governmental structural and executive arrangements. The system of both two-tier and unitary approaches has come to create something of a confusing hybrid system, whilst central government's persistence in instructing local authorities with regard to the most appropriate executive arrangements has meant that local authorities have had little freedom to choose the most suitable models of operation. If local sustainability is to benefit from the accountability that can come from strong local leadership, therefore, the structural organisation needs to be clearer and the possibilities for executive arrangements based on greater local freedom.

Reluctance at the centre to 'let go'

The second issue to consider here relates to central government's apparent reluctance to 'let go' of local powers. In Chapter 4 this was evident in respect of the over-prescriptive nature of reforms that are and have been intended to set out

14 S Wilks-Heeg, 'The Widespread Rejection of Elected City Mayors Is a Spanner in the Works for the Government's Localism Agenda', *British Politics and Policy Blog, LSE*, 5 May 2012 <http://eprints.lse.ac.uk/48293/1/blogs.lse.ac.uk-The_widespread_rejection_of_elected_city_mayors_is_a_spanner_in_the_works_for_the_governments_localis.pdf> accessed 10 November 2013.

15 G Jones and J Stewart, 'Local Government: The Past, the Present and the Future' (2012) 27(4) *Public Policy and Administration* 346 at 359.

16 Ibid. 358–9.

the decentralisation of power, whilst in Chapter 5 it was reflected in the heavily centralised supervision of the NDC programme.

Decentralisation is crucial to the accessibility of power both in terms of local accountability and in relation to the ease with which local people can adopt active roles in local processes, as well as to encouraging local innovation and freedom and locally relevant and responsive decision-making. This, in turn, affects the extent to which local sustainability can be achieved. Where power is heavily constrained by centralised authorities, it stifles that local innovation and freedom and means that decisions and policies are based more on centralised objectives and requirements rather than on local needs and interests.

In respect of recent local governmental reform, for example, the Localism Act's 'general power of competence' is drafted in such a way as to ensure that central government can 'stop local authorities using the power to do things the Government dislikes',[17] thus limiting the extent to which they can truly be said to have 'the power to do anything that individuals may generally do'.[18] Furthermore, with respect to the NDC, Chapter 5 has already noted the manner in which the programme was heavily supervised in terms of both local spending and the broad framework within which it operated, and it came to devote much of its time to striving to meet centralised targets rather than seeking to focus on the responsive development of local areas.[19] There was a real sense that communities did not 'have the freedom to determine their own priorities'.[20] This was counter-productive in terms of local sustainability and meant that local bodies had less freedom to pursue locally relevant and responsive objectives.

It is not that central government is unaware of this need to decentralise and 'let go' – successive governments have stated the intention and desire to push power down to the local level, to move away from a centralised 'one size fits all' approach, and to empower communities and citizens.[21] However, given the mixed success of this over the years, there is evidently an issue regarding the effectiveness of governments' decentralising provisions and policies and the manner in which they have sought to empower those at the local level. The issue, it is suggested, rests on the over-prescriptive nature of these provisions. Examples considered above, as well as those explored throughout Chapters 4 and 5, are

17 R Hambleton, 'A Jekyll and Hyde Localism Bill? (2011) 80(1) *Town and Country Planning* 15 at 16.

18 Localism Act 2011, s 1.

19 P Lawless, 'Can Area-Based Regeneration Programmes Ever Work? Evidence from England's New Deal for Communities' (2012) 33(4) *Policy Studies* 313 at 321.

20 DCLG, *The New Deal for Communities Programme: Achieving a Neighbourhood Focus for Regeneration* (London: HMSO, 2010) para. 8.17.

21 See DCLG, *Strong and Prosperous Communities: The Local Government White Paper* (White Paper, Cm 6939-I, 2006) 4, © Crown Copyright, contains public sector information licensed under the Open Government Licence v2.0 <http://www.nationalarchives.gov.uk/doc/open-government-licence/version/2/> and DCLG, *Communities in Control: Real People, Real Power* (White Paper, Cm 7427, 2008) para. 1.3, © Crown Copyright, contains public sector information licensed under the Open Government Licence v2.0 <http://www.nationalarchives.gov.uk/doc/open-government-licence/version/2/>.

indicative of this. They demonstrate a willingness and enthusiasm to empower local authorities and community bodies with the autonomy to make decisions and introduce policies relevant to local issues, but, at the same time, they set out in detail how that power is to be used and the requirements and criteria which must be fulfilled and prescribe clear limitations and restraints.

This is not a fresh concern. Perrons and Skyers note, for instance, that 'the formal devolution of responsibility to the local community often occurs in parallel with a centralization of effective control',[22] whilst Beatty *et al.* go so far as to note that NDC partnerships 'lived within a delivery mode laid down, funded, audited and controlled by the centre'.[23] The result of this, however, is local authorities and bodies that are unable to use the powers accorded them to full effect, which is reflective of a central government that is reluctant to 'let go' and to allow local decisions-makers the freedom to decide for themselves how local powers should be exercised in order to pursue objectives aligned with local sustainability.

In terms of future reform, therefore, if local democracy is to provide a foundation for the achievement of local sustainability – particularly in terms of accountability and the encouragement of citizen participation – then local authorities and community bodies need to enjoy greater freedom and scope to use the decentralised powers to better effect. Whilst the nature of the UK's predominantly unitary constitution is such as to require local authorities to be subordinate to centralised government, the demands of local democracy and the potential benefits of subsidiarity and localised decision-making provide ample justification for this. Local power should be capable of being put to the best possible use in order to respond to local issues and solve local problems, rather than being restrained by centralised limitation and having to spend time and effort fulfilling centrally set criteria and targets.

Issues underlying citizen participation

The third and final issue to consider stems, in part, from central government's reluctant decentralisation of power and relates to issues underlying citizens' participation in local affairs and decision-making. Chapters 4 and 5 highlighted two concerns here: first, that local governmental policy and reform has shifted rather frequently, giving rise to constantly changing opportunities for citizen participation; and second, that where there is citizen participation, it is generally not widespread but instead reliant on a core group of individuals.

In respect of the first of these, the argument is that if opportunities for citizen engagement are in a constant state of flux, then citizens could become potentially disenchanted with the process. As Stanton notes in respect of recent local governmental history, 'constantly shifting reforms and policy-bases have meant

22 D Perrons and S Skyers, 'Empowerment through Participation? Conceptual Explorations and a Case Study' (2003) 27(2) *International Journal of Urban and Regional Research* 265 at 265.

23 C Beatty, M Foden, P Lawless and I Wilson, 'Area-Based Regeneration Partnerships and the Role of Central Government: The New Deal for Communities Programme in England' (2010) 38(2) *Policy and Politics: Studies of Local Government and Its Services* 235 at 247.

that there has been no stability to local government development over the last few decades. As a result, any success there has been has not been long-lasting.'[24] Indeed, and in line with this, Chapter 4 outlined how reforms introduced by the LDEDCA setting out duties relating to involvement, petitions and the promotion of democracy were repealed after just two years. Whilst such reforms were justified on the grounds of minimising bureaucracy,[25] the constant shifts in policy and continuous reforms suggest an instability of governance that cannot be conducive to ongoing and beneficial engagement. The effects of constantly changing policies and reforms are exemplified by consideration of other fields of governmental activity. Writing in respect of the NHS, as an example of public sector reform in the UK under New Labour, Pollitt cites Webster in noting that 'the time intervals between structural reforms . . . progressively diminished to the point that the NHS risk[ed] becoming caught up in a vortex of permanent upheaval'.[26] Crucially adding that such issues affect other aspects of public sector reform – including local government, which Bovaird and Downe note 'consisted of several generations of reform'[27] – Pollitt stresses the extent to which this constant organisational change makes it harder to work out which systems work best, brings increased costs and creates a general loss of faith in stability.[28] This, it is argued, can also be said of constant local governmental reform, where stability of process is necessary to ensure citizens can enjoy consistent opportunities to engage.

The second concern, about issues relating to widespread citizen participation and the 'usual suspects' getting involved, is by no means new.[29] Chapter 4 noted how it is generally the same sort of people who engage with participatory opportunities at the local level, whilst Chapter 5 demonstrated the way in which, in respect of the NDC, less than a quarter of citizens came to involve themselves in the programme's decisions and activities, with the partnerships generally relying on a small number of core community participants.[30] The heart of the issue,

24 J Stanton, 'Localism in Action?', *UK Constitutional Law Group*, 14 March 2013 <http://ukconstitutionallaw.org/2013/03/14/john-stanton-localism-in-action/> accessed 10 November 2013.

25 As Chapter 4 noted, for instance, s 45 of the Localism Act 2011 repealed the duty to promote democracy as part of a wider effort to reduce 'radically the burden of regulation on local government' (HC Deb 17 January 2011, vol 521, col 520).

26 C Webster, *The National Health Service Re-organization: Learning from History* (1998) OHE Lecture, London: Office of Health Economics, as cited in C Pollitt, 'New Labour's Re-disorganization: Hyper-modernism and the Costs of Reform – A Cautionary Tale' (2007) 9(4) *Public Management Review* 529 at 530.

27 T Bovaird and J Downe, 'N Generations of Reform in UK Local Government: Compliance and Resistance to Institutional Pressures' (2006) 9(4) *International Public Management Journal* 429 at 452, as cited in Pollitt (n 26) 532.

28 Pollitt (n 26) 539.

29 M Lee and C Abbot, 'The Usual Suspects? Public Participation under the Aarhus Convention' (2003) 66(1) *Modern Law Review* 80.

30 Chapter 5 showed that 22 per cent of those who were aware of their local NDC partnership were involved in some way – DCLG, *Involving Local People in Regeneration* (London: HMSO, 2010) para. 2.26. Also see P Lawless, M Foden, I Wilson and C Beatty, 'Understanding Area-Based Regeneration: The New Deal for Communities Programme in England' (2009) 47(2) *Urban Studies* 257 at 269.

then, is the need to empower a much wider circle of local people to get involved in local decision-making and activities, whether that is in respect of community regeneration initiatives or local governmental affairs. Indeed, this need is particularly important in respect of local sustainability, relating as that does to the introduction of changes and developments with an impact across local areas. As Holder and Lee state, environmental decisions, such as those relating to the achievement of sustainability, 'rest on values as well as expertise, taking those decisions without democratic involvement is untenable in terms of either a good decision or a good process';[31] 'public values inherent in an environmental decision . . . mean that "experts" have no monopoly on judgment'.[32]

If a substantial proportion of local citizens are not minded to involve themselves in local processes relating to sustainability, however, then the resultant decisions and policies will not have benefited from the full and representative range of expertise and knowledge that could potentially be drawn from across a local area. More needs to be done, therefore, to encourage wider participation and motivate a broad range of citizens to engage with local decisions and actions that seek to improve their local areas. Whilst the prevalence of the issue demonstrates the difficulty in finding an appropriate solution, it is argued that efforts to increase local choice and freedom, coupled with a less centrally driven, politically prescribed process, would perhaps go some way to encouraging more widespread citizen participation.

This section has considered in detail some of the issues that have impacted on the extent to which local accountability and citizen participation can enhance local sustainability. In Chapters 4 and 5, whilst the potential for the local pursuit of sustainability to be enhanced was clearly evident, concerns relating to the strength of local leadership, the appropriate decentralisation of power and citizen participation meant that the full local democratic potential was perhaps not being realised, which in turn impacted on the effectiveness of local sustainability. In exploring these issues here, however, this section has sought to consider how some of these concerns might be addressed, demonstrating potential ways in which local sustainability might be enhanced further in the future.

Local sustainability in the wider world: the *Local Sustainability 2012* report and 'Rio + 20'

The arguments and evaluations that this book has set out have focused chiefly on sustainability in the context of UK localism. Placing the microscope over reforms affecting local authorities, as well as examining policies and initiatives aimed at community invigoration and the encouragement of locally led drives to regenerate, it has provided something of a platform on which to test the hypothesis suggesting that accountability and citizen participation enhance the achievement of local

31 J Holder and M Lee, *Environmental Protection, Law and Policy* (Cambridge: CUP, 2007) 87.
32 Ibid. 85.

sustainability. As Chapter 2 sought to demonstrate, however, sustainability is a global principle, affecting the lives of millions across the world and relevant at all levels of governance. Indeed, as the *Local Sustainability 2012* report, published on the occasion of the 'Rio + 20' conference, notes: 'local initiatives for sustainability are taking place all over the planet under many titles and labels'.[33] It is important now to consider, therefore, the extent to which the conclusions and evaluations in respect of accountability and citizen participation drawn from this book can be said to apply to local sustainability throughout the wider world.

In doing this, this section explores aspects of the *Local Sustainability 2012* report. Indeed, this report provides a conveniently timed consideration of local sustainability across the world and enables examination of how far the themes in this book are consistent with key objectives explored at 'Rio + 20' and in the context of the principle's international importance. Whilst global 'local sustainability processes can be characterized neither by a common name nor a common methodology',[34] this section, structured around mutually important themes, considers the extent to which conclusions reached here on the basis of the UK system and approach are relevant throughout the wider world, laying the potential foundations also for further study in this area.

Strong local leadership

The first theme to consider relates to the strength of local leadership. This was discussed in Chapter 4 in respect of recent local governmental reform and was also identified in the 'Rio + 20' report on local sustainability as being important to the achievement of local objectives. The strength of local leadership is crucial to ensuring effective accountability as it provides the transparency of process necessary to enable citizens to scrutinise and question decisions and actions. In addition, it is vital to ensuring the appropriate exercise of powers decentralised to the local level. In terms of the UK system, this is evident in respect of reforms setting out, *inter alia*, the possible introduction of directly elected mayors and the implementation of unitary authorities. In terms of sustainability, this could provide a stronger platform for its achievement and serve to enhance local decision-making, meaning that the needs of local people can be met more effectively.

The emphasis on strong, local leadership in the pursuit of sustainability is also recognised by the *Local Sustainability 2012* report. This notes the importance of the dependence on strong, individual leadership that has the courage to innovate and the ability to encourage members of a wider community to engage with the process of development.[35] It also serves to minimise the risk of local sustainability processes being abandoned in the event of changing political situations.[36] On this

33 *Local Sustainability 2012* (n 1) 22.
34 Ibid. 25.
35 Ibid. 26.
36 Ibid. 26.

last point, in particular, the report uses by way of an example the city of Curitiba, in Brazil. 'One of the pioneers in bringing sustainable development to the local level, Curitiba has been long recognized internationally as a "sustainable city".'[37] Crucial to its development and the implementation of its plans was 'the leadership of Jaime Lerner, an architect, experienced urban planner and a three-time Mayor of Curitiba'.[38] The approach in Curitiba 'ensured . . . continuity in implementing the city's strategy', which linked the environmental, social and economic aspects of development in a way that was 'worth much more than a series of expensive one-off projects'.[39] Though focused on particular objectives aligned with the improvement of quality of life in the context of land use and transportation, this example of Curitiba serves to underline the importance of strong local leadership in achieving local sustainability.

Community-led approach

The second theme here considered relates to the importance of a community-led approach to local sustainability. Exemplified throughout this book by the NDC programme, as well as policies adopted as part of the Big Society, a community-led approach to sustainability is noted in the 2012 report as being based on 'civil society'.[40] Indeed, the report states that 'local networks for sustainable development emerge in communities where the local civil society has a strong commitment to and awareness of sustainable development issues'.[41]

This notion of civil society, however, is – according to the report – also responsible for the wider pursuit of sustainability by other non-governmental bodies, religious organisations, as well as science and research institutions, supported by the education sector.[42] This is due, it considers, to the commitment and expertise that can come from such an approach. The reason underlying the importance of the community-led approach and its connection with the notion of civil society, therefore, comes back to the significance of the local knowledge and expertise that citizens can bring to a process pursuing the development of their community. This was discussed at length in Chapter 3 and was illustrated later by the opportunities for citizen participation provided by the NDC programme, as explored in Chapter 5. In essence, it relies on the aforementioned view that decisions relating to sustainability 'rest on values as well as expertise, taking those decisions without democratic involvement is untenable in terms of either a good decision or a good process'.[43] '[P]ublic values inherent in an environmental decision . . . mean that "experts" have no monopoly on judgment.'[44] Participating

37 Ibid. 30.
38 Ibid. 30.
39 Ibid. 30.
40 Ibid. 31.
41 Ibid. 31.
42 Ibid. 31.
43 Holder and Lee (n 31) 87.
44 Ibid. 85.

citizens in the EC1 NDC area exemplify this, with developments at Spa Fields and on Old Street, for instance, serving to demonstrate the extent to which community input and citizen involvement can ensure that changes are relevant to local needs and desires. Furthermore, illustrating the importance and relevance of a community-led approach to sustainability across the wider world, the report cites the example of Freiburg, in Germany.[45] Development here was characterised by a range 'of activities and projects carried out by a multitude of civil society initiatives and organizations',[46] demonstrating the prevalence of the citizen-led pursuit of sustainability.

Despite the clear benefits of local participation, however, and the extent to which this has provided a platform for local development, the report also echoes the concerns discussed in Chapters 4 and 5 that participative opportunities are often taken up by the 'usual suspects'. Whilst it links the willingness of local people to engage with local projects and community-led pursuits of sustainability to this notion of civil society, it also notes that – in respect of the developments at Freiburg – many of those who participated in the civil society initiatives went on to become 'local councillors, officials or decision-makers in local companies'.[47] Nonetheless, the report's discussion here, and the example of Freiburg, underline the importance and benefit of a community-led approach to local sustainability, thus echoing conclusions that are at the very heart of this book.

National policy and local sustainability

The third theme to consider relates, more broadly, to the manner in which the UK's local governmental and community-led pursuit of sustainability originated. Though the focus throughout this book has been on the benefit of local approaches to local sustainability, it is undeniable that they have predominantly been rooted in national policy. This is evident in terms of the UK's approach, with legislation setting out both the form and scope of local governmental duties and responsibilities as regards local sustainability[48] and centralised policy outlining the nature and operation of the NDC programme and the Big Society. Whilst this has, on occasion, brought to issue problems regarding the appropriate decentralisation of power and the willingness of those at the centre to 'let go', the *Local Sustainability 2012* report notes that 'supporting local governments in initiating and conducting local sustainability processes' has become a key feature of national policy agendas.[49] Indeed, across the world,

> national governments have a whole variety of instruments to initiate and support local sustainability processes and strategies, as well as to create

45 *Local Sustainability 2012* (n 1) 32.
46 Ibid. 32.
47 Ibid. 32.
48 See Local Government Act 2000, s 4, and Sustainable Communities Act 2007, s 1.
49 *Local Sustainability 2012* (n 1) 38.

> favourable conditions for local action. These range from a clear legal obligation for local governments through provisions such as the adoption of sustainability criteria in sectoral legislations or funding programmes, to the establishment of national campaigns for local sustainability.[50]

Whilst UK legislation and policy, identified above, provide examples of such instruments, the report notes their prevalence across the wider world. In France, for instance, active local sustainability campaigns comprised legislation supporting and encouraging local *Agenda 21*s.[51] These set out requirements in respect of the integration of sustainability-related concerns into local strategic documents, focusing on 'broad stakeholder participation in the set-up and development of the campaign'.[52] This demonstrates, therefore, broader and more global examples that illustrate the extent to which the pursuit of local sustainability by local government and other local bodies and initiatives can derive from centralised policy.

Accountability, participation and sustainability across the wider world

The final theme to consider here relates not so much to a particular aspect of local sustainability in the UK but rather to the theoretical foundation on which this book's evaluation has been based – namely, the importance of accountability and citizen participation in its achievement.

The benefits of accountability and citizen participation in terms of pursuing local sustainability have been lauded throughout this book, with evaluations of recent local governmental reform and community-led drives for regeneration demonstrating the extent to which they can be said to enhance the achievement of sustainability-related objectives at the local level. As this chapter has already summarised, accountability, as a dialectical activity, enables citizens to question and scrutinise decision-making processes, ensuring that representatives understand local needs and interests and are responsive to them. In addition, citizen participation ensures that local knowledge and expertise can influence decision-making, providing an avenue through which local needs and interests input into the process. As Lee and Abbot note, 'a commitment to participation is embedded in the rhetoric of sustainable development itself'.[53]

Thus far, as illustrated by the *Local Sustainability 2012* report, this section has already demonstrated the way in which many of the considerations that have been identified in this book as being crucial to accountability and citizen participation in the achievement of local sustainability are evident throughout the wider world as well – strong local leadership, a community-led approach to regeneration, as well as the importance of national policies supporting local bodies and people in

50 Ibid. 38.
51 Ibid. 41.
52 Ibid. 41.
53 Lee and Abbot (n 29) 83.

meeting objectives aligned with sustainability. In addition to this, however, the *Local Sustainability 2012* report also independently emphasises the importance of both accountability and citizen participation. In respect of the former, it states that 'the success of local sustainability depends . . . on . . . a trust-based dialogue between various groups that make up the local community',[54] thus echoing notable aspects of the principle discussed in Chapter 3. Also, with regard to citizen participation, the report notes that 'the enhanced culture of public participation is often quoted as one of the most remarkable achievements of local sustainability processes worldwide. For many decision makers and citizens alike, this shift in governance is itself regarded as a major step towards more sustainable cities and towns.'[55] This is true, as the report stresses, not only in respect of participation in decision-making but also through wider engagement with local activities aimed at achieving sustainability,[56] as analysis of the NDC programme, for example, has already served to demonstrate.

The importance and benefit of citizen participation across the wider world are exemplified, in the report, by experiences in Kampala, Uganda. Here, whilst issues were identified as regards citizens' input,[57] their participation provided 'much-needed, reliable information' and made the 'implementation much easier', ensuring that it was 'in line with local priorities'.[58] This echoes many of the benefits that have been identified throughout the book in respect of the achievement of local sustainability in the UK and serves to demonstrate the extent to which its conclusions are relevant and applicable throughout the wider world.

This section, therefore, has played a key role in broadening the scope of this book's evaluations and conclusions. Whilst it has by no means sought to analyse and explore in any detail the nature of local sustainability across the world, it has provided a brief insight into the relevance and applicability of the discussions relating to accountability and citizen participation in local sustainability, and has laid the foundations for potential further research in this area.

Concluding remarks

This final chapter has provided a suitable conclusion to the book's evaluations of accountability and citizen participation in local sustainability. It has summarised the findings on how lessons might be learned for the future, and it has discussed the *Local Sustainability 2012* report, from the 'Rio + 20' conference, and the pursuit of local sustainability throughout the wider world. The effect of this has been to demonstrate the wider relevance of the book's conclusions, emphasising the way in which accountability and citizen participation can be said to influence

54 *Local Sustainability 2012* (n 1) 65.
55 Ibid. 65.
56 Ibid. 66.
57 Such issues include: sustaining community interest, lack of immediate results and low levels of participation (see ibid. 68).
58 Ibid. 68.

and enhance the achievement of local sustainability across the globe. As has been noted, there is scope for more research in this area, particularly in respect of wider and further efforts to achieve local sustainability, and the hope is that this book will have provided something of a platform for this.

For now, however, the book has sought to provide an evaluation of the way in which accountability and citizen participation enhance local sustainability, seeking to demonstrate this on both a conceptual and a practical level. There is evidently a natural role for both these democratic principles in the achievement of local regeneration, and whilst there are inevitably practical issues to overcome, their value in respect of local sustainability and the achievement of its objectives is self-evident. They serve very well to complement and enhance processes aimed at tackling local deprivation.

Bibliography

Beatty, C, Foden, M, Lawless, P and Wilson, I, 'Area-Based Regeneration Partnerships and the Role of Central Government: The New Deal for Communities Programme in England' (2010) 38(2) *Policy and Politics: Studies of Local Government and Its Services* 235.

Bovaird, T and Downe, J, 'N Generations of Reform in UK Local Government: Compliance and Resistance to Institutional Pressures' (2006) 9(4) *International Public Management Journal* 429.

Copus, C, 'British Local Government: A Case for a New Constitutional Settlement' (2006) 21(4) *Public Policy and Administration* 4.

DCLG, *Strong and Prosperous Communities: The Local Government White Paper* (White Paper, Cm 6939-I, 2006), © Crown Copyright, contains public sector information licensed under the Open Government Licence v2.0 <http://www.nationalarchives.gov.uk/doc/open-government-licence/version/2/>.

DCLG, *Communities in Control: Real People, Real Power* (White Paper, Cm 7427, 2008), © Crown Copyright, contains public sector information licensed under the Open Government Licence v2.0 <http://www.nationalarchives.gov.uk/doc/open-government-licence/version/2/>.

DCLG, *Involving Local People in Regeneration* (London: HMSO, 2010).

DCLG, *The New Deal for Communities Programme: Achieving a Neighbourhood Focus for Regeneration* (London: HMSO, 2010).

Hambleton, R, 'A Jekyll and Hyde Localism Bill? (2011) 80(1) *Town and Country Planning* 15.

HC Deb 23 April 1991, vol 189, col 901.

HC Deb 21 October 2010, vol 516, col 1155–6.

HC Deb 17 January 2011, vol 521, col 520.

Holder, J and Lee, M, *Environmental Protection, Law and Policy* (Cambridge: CUP, 2007).

ICLEI, *Local Sustainability 2012: Taking Stock and Moving Forward. Global Review* (Bonn: ICLEI, 2012).

Jones, G and Stewart, J, 'Local Government: The Past, the Present and the Future' (2012) 27(4) *Public Policy and Administration* 346.

King, A, *The British Constitution* (Oxford: OUP, 2007).

Larsen, HO, 'Directly Elected Mayors – Democratic Renewal or Constitutional Confusion?' in Caulfield, J and Larsen, HO (eds) *Local Government at the Millennium* (Wiesbaden: Springer Fachmedien Wiesbaden, 2002) 111.

Lawless, P, 'Can Area-Based Regeneration Programmes Ever Work? Evidence from England's New Deal for Communities' (2012) 33(4) *Policy Studies* 313.

Lawless, P, Foden, M, Wilson, I and Beatty, C, 'Understanding Area-Based Regeneration: The New Deal for Communities Programme in England' (2009) 47(2) *Urban Studies* 257.

Layard, A, 'Law and Localism: The Case of Multiple Occupancy Housing' (2012) 32(4) *Legal Studies* 551.

Lee, M and Abbot, C, 'The Usual Suspects? Public Participation under the Aarhus Convention' (2003) 66(1) *Modern Law Review* 80.

Onyx, J and Dalton, B, 'Accountability and Advocacy' (2006) 12(1) *Third Sector Review* 7.

Parry, K and Roll, J, House of Commons Library, *Local Government and Public Involvement in Health Bill*, 10 January 2007, Research Paper 07/01.

Perrons, D and Skyers, S, 'Empowerment through Participation? Conceptual Explorations and a Case Study' (2003) 27(2) *International Journal of Urban and Regional Research* 265.

Pollitt, C, 'New Labour's Re-disorganization: Hyper-modernism and the Costs of Reform – A Cautionary Tale' (2007) 9(4) *Public Management Review* 529.

Stanton, J, 'Localism in Action?' *UK Constitutional Law Group*, 14 March 2013 <http://ukconstitutionallaw.org/2013/03/14/john-stanton-localism-in-action/> accessed 10 November 2013.

UN, *Agenda 21*, 1992, A/CONF.151/26, Vol. III, New York: UN. Made available by the UN Division for Sustainable Development at <http://sustainabledevelopment.un.org/content/documents/Agenda21.pdf> accessed 7 November 2013.

Webster, C, *The National Health Service Re-organization: Learning from History* (1998) OHE Lecture, London: Office of Health Economics.

Wilks-Heeg, S, 'The Widespread Rejection of Elected City Mayors Is a Spanner in the Works for the Government's Localism Agenda' *British Politics and Policy Blog, LSE*, 5 May 2012 <http://eprints.lse.ac.uk/48293/1/blogs.lse.ac.uk-The_widespread_rejection_of_elected_city_mayors_is_a_spanner_in_the_works_for_the_governments_localis.pdf> accessed 10 November 2013.

Wilson, D and Game, C, *Local Government in the United Kingdom* (5th edn, Basingstoke: Palgrave Macmillan, 2011).

Index